Japanese Popula

CW01654671

Japanese popular culture has been steadily increasing in visibility both in Asia and beyond in recent years. This book examines Japanese popular music, exploring its historical development, technology, business and production aspects, audiences, and language and culture. Based both on extensive textual and aural analysis and on anthropological fieldwork, it provides a wealth of detail, finding differences as well as similarities between the Japanese and Western pop music scenes. It shows how Japanese popular music has responded over time to Japan's relationship to the West in the postwar era, gradually growing in independence from the political and cultural hegemonic presence of America. Similarly, it explores the ways in which the Japanese artist has grown in independence, vis-à-vis his/her role in the production process, and examines in detail the increasingly important role of the *jimusho*, or the entertainment management agency, where many individual artists and music industry professionals make decisions about how the product is delivered to the public. It also discusses the connections to Japanese television, film, print, and Internet, thereby providing, through pop music, a key to understanding much of Japanese popular culture more widely.

Carolyn S. Stevens is Senior Lecturer in Japanese Studies at the University of Melbourne and Deputy Director of the Asia Institute. She worked for several years in the 1990s as a consultant to a Japanese entertainment management agency, and this experience in the industry led to publications on Japanese rock fans, rock video analysis, and concert souvenir consumption. She is also editor of Contemporary Culture for the journal *Japanese Studies*.

Routledge Media, Culture and Social Change in Asia

Series Editor
Stephanie Hemelryk Donald,
Institute for International Studies, University of Technology, Sydney

Editorial Board
Devleena Ghosh, *University of Technology, Sydney*
Yingjie Guo, *University of Technology, Sydney*
K. P. Jayasankar, *Unit for Media and Communications, Tata Institute of Social Sciences, Bombay*
Vera Mackie, *University of Melbourne*
Anjali Monterio, *Unit for Media and Communications, Tata Institute of Social Sciences, Bombay*
Gary Rawnsley, *University of Nottingham*
Ming-yeh Rawnsley, *University of Notingham*
Jing Wang *(MIT)*

The aim of the series is to publish original, high-quality work by both new and established scholars in the West and the East, on all aspects of media, culture, and social change in Asia.

1 **Television Across Asia**
Television industries, programme formats and globalisation
Edited by Albert Moran and Michael Keane

2 **Journalism and Democracy in Asia**
Edited by Angela Romano and Michael Bromley

3 **Cultural Control and Globalization in Asia**
Copyright, piracy and cinema
Laikwan Pang

4 **Conflict, Terrorism and the Media in Asia**
Edited by Benjamin Cole

5 **Media and the Chinese Diaspora**
Community, communications and commerce
Edited by Wanning Sun

6 **Hong Kong Film, Hollywood and the New Global Cinema**
No film is an island
Edited by Gina Marchetti and Tan See Kam

7 **Media in Hong Kong**
Press freedom and political change 1967–2005
Carol P. Lai

8 **Chinese Documentaries**
From dogma to polyphony
Yingchi Chu

9 **Japanese Popular Music**
Culture, authenticity and power
Carolyn S. Stevens

Japanese Popular Music

Culture, authenticity, and power

Carolyn S. Stevens

Routledge
Taylor & Francis Group
LONDON AND NEW YORK

First published 2008
by Routledge
2 Park Square, Milton Park, Abingdon, Oxon OX14 4RN

Simultaneously published in the USA and Canada
by Routledge
270 Madison Ave, New York, NY 10016

Routledge is an imprint of the Taylor & Francis Group,
an informa business

Transferred to Digital Printing 2009

© 2008 Carolyn S. Stevens

Typeset in Times by
Integra Software Services Pvt. Ltd, Pondicherry, India.

All rights reserved. No part of this book may be reprinted or
reproduced or utilized in any form or by any electronic, mechanical,
or other means, now known or hereafter invented, including
photocopying and recording, or in any information storage or
retrieval system, without permission in writing from the publishers.

British Library Cataloguing in Publication Data
A catalogue record for this book is available from the British Library

Library of Congress Cataloging in Publication Data
Stevens, Carolyn S., 1963–
Japanese popular music : culture, authenticity and power / Carolyn S. Stevens.
p. cm. -- (Media, Culture and Social Change in Asia series ; 9)
Includes bibliographical references (p.) and index.
ISBN 978-0-415-38057-7 (hardback : alk. paper) 1. Popular music--Social
aspects--Japan. 2. Popular music--Japan--History and criticism. 3. Popular culture--
Japan. I. Title
ML3917.J3S74 2007
781.630952--dc22
2007004361

ISBN10: 0–415–38057–X (hbk)
ISBN10: 0–415–49221–1 (pbk)
ISBN10: 0–203–94501–8 (ebk)

ISBN13: 978–0–415–38057–7 (hbk)
ISBN13: 978–0–415–49221–8 (pbk)
ISBN13: 978–0–203–94501–8 (ebk)

To Tomo, Sora, and Zen
for insisting on quality music in the car

Contents

Figure and table

Table

Figure

Acknowledgments

This book reflects a personal engagement with Japanese popular music for close to two decades, beginning with my first Japanese CD purchase in 1989 (which were, incidentally, two CD singles: Imai Miki's "Boogie Woogie Lonesome High Heel" and Saitô Yuki's remake of "*Yume no Naka E*" [Into a Dream]). These CD singles, frayed at the corners, sit generally untouched in a much larger collection but they symbolize the start of a journey that has resulted in this book.

No journey is truly solitary, and here I mark the important contributions of others that have accompanied me on this journey.

The writing process: Vera Mackie helped to streamline my ideas in a proposal that captured the imagination of Peter Sowden from Routledge and series editor Stephanie Donald, and gave me collegial support throughout the writing of the manuscript. Caroline P. Norma assisted with proofreading and translating. Michelle Hall (East Asian Collection, Baillieu Library, University of Melbourne) and Mayumi Shinozaki (National Library of Australia, Canberra) were both very helpful with identifying and accessing Japanese materials. Craig J. Norris taught me about *anime* and keeping my spirits up while slogging through the word count. I thank all of my colleagues in the Japanese and other programs at the Asia Institute but especially Nadine Blair, Robyn Borg, Mary Kidd, Linda Poskitt, Michael Ewing, Michael Leigh, Diane Manwaring, Jun Ohashi, and Abdullah Saeed.

Musically: Takamizawa Toshihiko started me on this journey; my encounter with Takamizawa and his album JOURNEY (1992, Pony Canyon Records) inspired me to explore this path he had chosen years before. Imawano Kiyoshirô responded to an unsolicited letter from me and graciously released copyright for one of his songs (thanks go as well to Aizawa Jiyûri of Babys Ltd, as facilitator). Hosokawa Shûhei has been a wonderful mentor and friend; he gave me the confidence to write about music as well as teaching me nearly everything I wanted to know (which was a great deal). I am extremely indebted to my good friend and colleague, Shibata Kaoru. A veteran in the radio and television industries, she was enormously helpful giving me her personal experiences and pointing me in the right directions, in terms both of subject matter and Japanese publications on relevant topics. I have benefited greatly over the years from the friendships with members of the now defunct Liberty Bell 21, especially Mineta Shôko. Christine R. Yano has been a welcoming peer and a kindred spirit in the field. I am also grateful to Marika Leininger-Ogawa for her collegiality teaching postwar Japanese pop music to undergraduates at the University of Melbourne. I also wish to thank senior colleagues Ted Bestor, Allen Chun and Ned Rossiter, Roger Goodman, Joy Hendry, Bill Kelly, Laura Miller, Brian Moeran, Ian Reader, and Judith Snodgrass for supporting my work on pop music, either informally at conferences or by publishing my work in their edited volumes.

In Melbourne: I am grateful to my family GP, Hubert van Doorn, who kept a working mother of small children sane throughout the fevers, snotty noses, and infected thumbs, and my friends Barb, Val, Vita, and Fiona, for giving me much-needed breaks. Finally, I am always grateful and indebted to my husband Tomo for his encyclopedic knowledge (he could have easily written this book instead of me), and I thank my children for cheerfully listening to J-pop in the car on the way to and from day care. I am very grateful to my parents, brother, and sister-in-law for the support they have lent over the years. Lastly, I thank my late mother-in-law, Matsuoka Hideko, who never knew of the book's existence but contributed in many ways.

Note on transliterations and translations

In this text, I have used the Hepburn system, except in cases where words have entered common use in English (Tokyo, for example). Japanese names are presented in the order of family name first, personal name second, as is Japanese linguistic custom. In some cases, the capitalization of some musicians' names will appear nonstandard (such as the artist "hide" and the band names "globe" or "GLAY") but this is because to preserve nuances in the original Japanese transliteration. Translations, except where noted otherwise, are by the author. Japanese works that have been released in English use the production studio's official translation (e.g., Miyazaki Hayao's *Majo no Takkyûbin* was released as "Kiki's Delivery Service").

Due to constant changes in the overseas currency market, I have kept monetary figures in the text in yen; in November 2006, the Japanese yen was trading at 117.81 yen to the US dollar.

1 Introduction

Popular music is the background noise of our everyday lives. "Popular music" has been defined as the "music that people value the most" (Blacking in Fujie 1989: 197) or music that is "accessible to a broader range of people," most often through the mass media (Wade 2005: 45). The English word "popular" arises from the concept of "people"; to be truly "popular," it cannot be exclusive; it stands for and comes from "an aggregation structured of multiple [types] of people" (Yamada 2003: 4). Popular music must be accessible, with no special training required to facilitate its appreciation and consumption. Economic class and social status will always have a part in defining audiences, but ideally popular music transcends many of these boundaries. Its existence is dependent on its integration with the mass media, which are explicitly aimed at a cross-class, multilayered public audience.

The meaning of popular music relies on a number of defining attributes including descriptive terms such as *popularity* (a term that includes sales figures, radio play, and critical versus general acclaim), a *recognizable structure* ("introduction," "alternation between verses and chorus," "verse progression," and "conclusion" [Hennion 1990: 189–191]), and a *sociohistorical context*. With this in mind, we are reminded that popular music is not merely about sound. A large social collective of creative musicians, executive producers, distribution intermediaries, and interpretive audiences – in other words, human beings themselves – contribute to the definition of any kind of music. This book is about the people, the popular, in Japanese postwar music. Therefore, this book is filled with a variety of characters: musicians, managers, recording studio producers, record label executives, retailers, critics, and fans.

This book's aim is to define and analyze developments in Japanese popular music since 1945. Japan is the world's second largest music market (Condry 2004a: 345) with overall sales in 2002 of almost 4.6 billion yen (Ugaya 2005b: 165), and Japan has held this position in the international market since the late 1980s (Kimura 1991: 328). With these figures, it is not surprising that the Japanese popular music industry has captured the interest of foreign audiences, even those who are not well versed in the language or culture. What are its main characteristics, its primary modes of production, and its musical messages? This volume contains five connected yet self-contained essays that address these questions regarding Japan's cultural, social, and economic practice in the field of twentieth-century popular music. Due to the vast parameters of this market and the similarly large number of analytic issues that arise from it, I have necessarily narrowed my focus to three salient concepts, intertwined and interdependent: culture, authenticity, and power. In these essays, I explore their definitions, how they interact with each other, and what they mean for the artist, the producer, and the audience of Japanese popular music.

In the discussion of popular music, we include, implicitly, in our definitions varied but specific notions about production processes, consumption patterns, audience, taste, and value. Negus writes that when we talk about music, we are really talking about genre, a term that combines both the music and the audience under one rubric (1999: 27–28); in other words, music does not exist in a social vacuum.

Despite this contextualization, genre is as subjective as personal preference, and these tastes die-hard. Genre classification has long been a source of contention between scholars, critics, and fans of any nationality: take "rock," for example. One of the gurus of Western rock and pop music analysis, Simon Frith, has argued that "rock is dead" since the 1980s: "[t]here are now just scattered 'taste markets' " (1994: 240). Critics do not agree on a unified definition of rock that includes aesthetic content, the audience, and its consumption styles. This is not dissimilar to what has occurred in late postwar Japan. Condry offers Miyadai's concept of "islands of taste" as a way to describe the current scene, where "increasing diversification" in Japan's popular music market has led to specialized modes of consumption (2004b: 20). Japanese popular music contains a wide variety of artistic expressions, but I have focused on *mainstream* (in other words, widely recognized and distributed) popular music. Perhaps because of a clearer sense of demarcation, other important Japanese pop music genres, such as idol music, *enka*, jazz, hip-hop, and underground music such as "noise," have been explored in depth by other scholars (e.g., Aoyagi 2005; Atkins 2001; Caspary and Manzenreiter 2003; Condry 2006; Yano 2002). Instead of specific genre, I look at music which has had a wide-ranging impact on Japanese audiences based on nonmusical criteria such as innovation, sales performances, media coverage, and longevity.

Methodology: writing about Japanese popular music

My interest in Japanese popular music stems from my experience in a number of roles: as an academic, trained in cultural anthropology and interested in music and its representations; as a consumer and a fan who lived in Japan for an extended period of time and enjoyed Japanese popular music; and lastly, as a participant and a somewhat unseasoned professional in the Japanese show business industry. Thus, my methodology is also multiple: textual analysis of written, visual, and aural materials; and participant/observer fieldwork – as a consumer, who integrated music into her daily life and interacted with other consumers in a social network, and as a producer, who applied her musical training and linguistic skills to a production process for financial gain. This book is a result of all these activities: reading, listening, experiencing, watching, participating, and writing.

The role of producer represents a rare opportunity for academic researchers; working directly in the music industry gave me insights into the way music was made and distributed in Japan. I started in 1992 as a casual contract employee of an entertainment agency in Tokyo where I contributed English language materials for promotion goods (such as concert tour posters and pamphlets); later I graduated to writing song lyrics. When I started working at the company in April 1992, I did not really know much about the Japanese world of entertainment; much of my exposure was limited to what I had seen on television (later, I learned, the most important disseminator of popular music to the Japanese public). By 1995, I had attended dozens of live concerts, was a voracious music magazine reader, had collected hundreds of Japanese CDs, and had two liner credits for songs in commercial release to my name, despite the fact that I was born, raised, and educated in the United States. Interestingly, about this time, I began to lose interest in US and UK popular music, which constituted the mainstay of my compact disc library, and began to listen to, almost exclusively, Japanese popular music.

What can an American-born "convert" add to our understanding of Japanese popular music? Witzleben's "Whose Ethnomusicology? Western Ethnomusicology and the Study of Asian Music" (1997) is useful in this discussion of popular music in a non-Western context. Many Western ethnomusicologists and anthropologists have framed non-Western cultural phenomena according to their own conceptual frameworks. There are, however, "extensive indigenous written traditions of talking about music: history, theory, aesthetics, and the relationship to musical traditions to cultural sensibilities and other art forms" (Witzleben 1997: 222), and this is equally true in the context of Japanese popular music. Many Japanese publications on popular music are authored by members of the Japanese Association for the Study of Popular Music (JASPM). JASPM was established in November 1990 in Tokyo. This academic organization is under the umbrella of the corresponding international association, and JASPM hosted the 9th Conference of the International Association for the Study of Popular Music (IASPM) in Kanazawa, Japan, in 1997, showcasing Japan's contributions to the global ethnomusicological academic community.[1]

It is also important, however, to acknowledge the vigorous nonacademic musical publishing industry in Japan, aimed at general readers, in paperback and magazine formats; I have benefited from reading these publications as well, despite their label as "sales-oriented products" in contrast to " 'serious' writing" about music (de Ferranti 2002: 199). Some of the writers in this field have academic qualifications; others do not, but I have included them for two reasons. First, because they are widely read by consumers, they have real influence; secondly, because the publication time lag is very short, the content is more up to date than academic books and journals.

Popular media writers are called *ongaku hyôronka* (or *ongaku hihyôka*) in Japanese, and accomplished music critics or commentators use a subtle blend of reporting, criticism, and social analysis. They are a small and elite group of freelance writers who often cross boundaries between print, visual, and audio media, serving as writers as well as experts who appear on television as radio shows.[2] Largely, these critics "introduce" music (e.g., new artists, or new work by established artists) to the public. *Hyôronka* tend to specialize by genre both within national boundaries and outside them – in Japanese rap or overseas reggae music, for example – creating a veneer of authority.

The status of *hyôronka* is often dictated by status of the publication with which they are associated. Some of the more respected music magazines in Japan include *Myujikku Magajin* (Music Magazine) and *Rockin' On*,[3] but these two tend to focus on rock rather than on pop, reflecting the association of "serious" writing with "serious" music; pop stars tend to be featured in fan publications and/or weekly gossip publications about public figures, including politicians and actors. Even in elite publications, content is generally uniform, revolving around interviews with musicians, photo layouts, concert information, and tour and album reviews.

In recent years, the Japanese terms *hyôronka* and *hihyôka* have been gradually replaced by the English inspired loan word *raitâ* ("writer"). More closely aligned with the "industry," these journalists work to promote contracted artists. Similarly, a new group with influence in the pop music media is the *baiyâ* ("buyer") for large record franchise shops (Tower Records and HMV, e.g., which both have a strong presence in the urban sales market). "Buyers" are interviewed by *raitâ*s as experts, and the larger and the more fashionable the location of the franchise, the more respected is the knowledge of the buyer. Their neutrality, however, is questionable due to their explicit relationship to the retailer (a Tower record buyer, in most cases, will recommend new artists with which their chain has retail contracts). At the same time, their affiliation with a multinational corporation also gives them a veneer of sophistication and credibility to the general public, and their ideas carry weight with journalists who interview them for pieces in magazines and newspapers.

There are always shadowy rumors of writers' relationships with record companies and *Oricon*, the Japanese equivalent to *Billboard* in the United States (established 1967 and incorporated in 1999). Not surprisingly, it is alleged that some writers receive kickbacks from these companies to portray the artist in a favorable light. Rigorous reviewing is usually eschewed for gentler "introductions" to the new work of established artists or to new artists breaking into the field. The extent of this corruption is unknown; despite these problems, the popular press cannot be completely ignored. Japanese pop music texts from *ongaku hyôronka*, *raitâ*, and *baiyâ* have influenced audiences' interpretations of trends, creating a mass "preferred reading" of pop music. These writers – more so than the academics – are the real "arbiters of taste," shaping the public response to the mass media. In sum, I have tried to absorb the "preferred readings" from these nonacademic publications, noting the potential for conflict of interest where appropriate, but also being mindful of their very real role in shaping public reactions, using them as a kind "primary source." Too few of the writings of Japanese lay writers as well as academic ethnomusicologists have been translated, and I hope this book accomplishes an introduction of their ideas to English-speaking readers.

"Every researcher is an insider in some respects and an outsider in others" (Witzleben 1997: 223). This quote brings to mind a fruitful collaboration with a Japanese ethnomusicologist in the 1990s when we undertook research on Japanese music television.[4] My colleague, as a "native," had decades of experience with the culture, and he joked often that I was the real "expert" in the field. He did not own a television, and thus had not watched music television since he left home as a university student. I, on the other hand, was a "nonnative amateur" but a ferocious TV addict, informing him of the latest developments with respect to SMAP and other high-profile J-pop acts on television. Together, we explored Japanese music television from both sides, past and present, inside and outside, an enlightening experience for both of us. Reprising Witzleben, we all benefit from the insights of both insiders and outsiders, Japanese and English sources and ideas, in the exploration of a field that is equally culturally diverse.

The interaction between culture, authenticity, and power

The field of postwar Japanese popular music has a rich and colorful landscape; to make sense of the dizzying array of artists, songs, and trends, I identify three key concepts – cultural identity, authenticity, and positional power – which interact with each other to explain how certain trends are created and promoted to the public.

Cultural identity in any context is evolving in the current age of globalization. Cultural identity in Japanese popular music can be perceived from a variety of standpoints – the French *anime* fan's perspective, for example, will differ from that of the Tokyo resident. Japanese cultural identity in popular music is defined as a created concept in response to external scrutiny. It is more often defined negatively rather than affirmatively (e.g., it is easier to say what it is *not* rather than what it *is*) and responds to changes in international relationships. Shared cultural preferences give rise to a framework of values, but this framework can, and does, change over time based on the changes in the power relations between those positions. I call an awareness of the relationships between these positions "positionality." The consequences that arise from these relationships are acclimatized to global trends; as diplomatic, cultural, and financial positions change, so does the awareness of the relationships between these positions, which can be held by individuals, groups, corporations, or nations. One example of the recent shifts in positionality in Japanese cultural identity is what has been frequently termed *kokusaika*, or internationalization, resulting in new modes of cultural expression that encompass a variety of foreign symbols but are unmistakably "Japanese."

Positionality can take its point of reference from a variety of sites. The everyday business activities of the Japanese popular music industry are also affected by shifts in the positions of any of the players involved, and the audience is always conscious of these roles. Changes in the aesthetics of the market – what's hot, what's not – are related to positions in the field of production (*à la* Bourdieu). In the domestic arena, the postwar Japanese popular music scene saw great internal changes in the roles of composer, producer, and artist, and their related images of "professionalism" versus "musicality" and again, "authenticity." In the early postwar period, professionalism prevailed; the 1970s saw a conflation of these roles. As the market peaked in the mid-to-late 1990s, artists' needs and audience tastes were diversified enough to support a number of models: the old "professionalism," the "amateur" who was self-produced, and the latest hybrid form, the "retired musician/new generation professional." Each mode of production (which is constructed of social roles with various power relations) is associated with its own style and values, and projected image.

Audiences value cultural identity – whether Japanese or non-Japanese – for its authenticity. Japanese identity is "authentic" when it is distanced from the globalized culture of the industrialized urban centers. Perhaps precisely because of this, non-Japanese identity is "authentic" when it is associated with these urban centers and is often best expressed through the use of foreign languages. Once "authentic" expressions are established, to be accepted in a competitive market, an "authentic connection" between artist and audience must be established. This relationship is mediated by media technology, which has evolved over the past fifty years to include digital technology and satellite transmissions – all methods of producing and consuming that musicians in the early 1950s would have never dreamed of. While technology is thought to distance people from art in most contexts, in the Japanese pop music industry, it works to enhance notions of authenticity in the artist/audience relationship. Authenticity is a crucial concept to the construction of the definition of Japanese popular music; yet its meaning is hotly contested. According to Baudrillard, our postmodern world is so multilayered that there is no "authentic reality" anymore: everything is a reflected construction. Yet, even in the most postmodern society, we continue to use the word "authentic" to describe a positive aesthetic experience. Style, technology, and language all work to create an "authentic" musical experience, highly valued by the Japanese listener.

Chapter outline

An understanding of the mechanics of culture, authenticity, and power helps to make sense of many of the trends in Japanese popular music. Specifically, these themes are addressed in five content-based chapters summarized here.

Definitions

This chapter explores concepts of cultural identity or cultural awareness, in Japanese popular music, both on the part of native and nonnative listeners. This cultural awareness is dependent on a constructed "tradition" as a response to Westernization (or Americanization). Musical concepts particular to Japan are introduced, allowing a demarcation of the traditional spheres of "Japanese" music (and musicology) and "European" musicology, so that postwar Japanese popular music, often described as a fusion of the two, is more readily understood. This is not to say that the development of Japanese popular music follows a neat, linear progression of incorporating "European" or "Western" musical forms to create new styles. Uneven and sporadic development marks much of this process, and the end result is often so intertwined and hybridized that it is difficult to discern its origins. Yet "authentic" Japanese cultural expression does exist, and I argue that it relies on regional identity to maintain this "tradition."

The particulars of history

Because popular music mirrors the political, cultural, and economic developments in wider society, power and positionality are key concepts in this chapter. Japanese popular music has responded over time to Japan's relationship to the West (and primarily the United States) in the postwar era, gradually growing in independence from the political and cultural hegemonic presence of America. Concomitantly, the artist too grows in independence vis-à-vis his/her role in the production process as well. Another important outcome of this historical analysis is that it demonstrates new ways to define musical genre, which are more contextual: for example, "New Music" (1970s to present) is just as recognizable through its consumption practices as its sound, and idol music (1980s to present) can also be defined by the extent of its media penetration as its image.

The business side

Power and culture are also concerns of this chapter on the structure of the Japanese pop music industry. Despite the recorded successes of certain artists in Asia, the vast majority of J-pop sales are made in the domestic market; while US/UK music constitutes a truly "globalized culture," Japanese pop music is still "localized" (Ugaya 2005b: 164–165). Still, Japanese record companies – both solely owned and in partnership with international corporations – dominate the world pop market. Japan is thus a critical site for the understanding of the entertainment industry as a local business operating in a global community.

Business practices in the Japanese music industry are just as diverse as its genre, and a variety of relationships exist to address a set of a diverse business requirements. Chapter 4 looks at the process of production as a social one, but avoids cultural determinism as a prime business motivator; most actors in this arena work in ways that best suit their abilities and maximize their outcomes. Special focus is given to the *jimusho*, or the entertainment management agency, where many individual artists and music industry professionals make real decisions about how the product is delivered to the public.

As a foreign resident in Japan, one of the ways I most frequently consumed music – or was coerced into consuming it, perhaps – was through television. Television, a mature, complex, and far-reaching media industry in Japan, has had a long and fruitful association with the music industry since the early 1960s. Many other developed nations have used this medium to promote and disseminate popular music, but the Japanese case is distinguished by certain mutually beneficial practices which have cemented relationships between television stations, record companies, commercial products, and artists (or their management agencies). "Tie up" or "image" songs (songs targeted for release through television and associated with a commercial or other media product) are discussed to show how television visibility is one of the most important factors in controlling the hit charts since the early days of postwar Japanese popular music. This kind of hit, however, has a different kind of "shelf-life" than other sorts of releases, and thus television profoundly affects the pace and the content of the Japanese charts.

Technology, consumption, and authenticity

No other era has seen greater shifts in the technological means to produce and consume music than the half-century after World War II. From the vinyl record to the cassette tape to the compact and mini disc and mp3, the production and consumption of popular music have been revolutionized by advancements in musical technology, and no other market demonstrates this more dramatically than Japan. This chapter analyzes changes in music technology, utilizing the metaphor of simulacra to the production and consumption of music technology in Japan. Karaoke as a social practice that combines music and technology with social relations and personal identity is presented as a case study. Technology is so important to Japanese popular music that it even constitutes one aspect of its current definition; Ugaya Hiromichi writes that one of J-pop's defining marks is that it is "digitized" and notes that the greatest growth period in the Japanese music business can be "synchronized" to the shift from analog to digital recording and playback (2005b: 6). Along with a detailed discussion of material objects of music technology, this chapter includes an examination of the consumption of live music as well, to demonstrate how the utilization of technology helps to create an "authentic" relationship between audience and performer. This chapter confronts the complicated interaction between technology and authenticity in Japanese popular music and argues that technology does not always interfere with the "authenticity" of the music, and instead enhances this important concept in the production and consumption processes.

Translations: "internationalizing" language and music

The final chapter blends culture, authenticity, and power in the symbolic language of music – lyrics. This is a particular interest of mine due to my work as a translator. I was fascinated (and astonished, at times) at the rate English lyrics were woven into Japanese text, resulting in a variety of meanings. I also became interested in the translation of musical styles as well as words. Lyrics are an important part of the symbolic communicative power that popular music holds, and in this chapter, I explore the ability of language to impart meaning to a song. I include an ethnographic section that describes the songwriting and recording process from the perspective of "translation" (in this case, Japanese to English). The chapter also explores the meanings behind other translations and transformations, including those from English to Japanese, to discover the various artistic and consumer aesthetics associated with any use of foreign language and/or music, replete with notions of cross-cultural meanings – or even completely new meanings. English to Japanese translations (or "covers," defined as a Western "standard" re-recorded in Japanese) constitute another kind of cultural and musical transformation. I argue that due to its acceptance as a Western hit, a Japanese cover song can be manipulated by the artist to convey multiple, and sometimes subversive, meanings. Language is about power, and Japanese songwriters are exercising their cultural power in taking and transforming language into new cultural expressions, and this has occurred in the context of Japan's rising presence in international business and politic spheres since the 1980s.

Concessions – conclusion

A full exploration of postwar Japanese popular music would constitute a multivolume publication; to keep to the limits of this book, I kept a tight focus on mainstream popular music, relying on the mainstream chart *Oricon* to define the boundaries. Oricon is considered the main database for sales figures in the industry; it maintains many different kinds of rankings, but its longest running charts are those for Japanese pop music, Western pop music, and *enka* (see Chapter 2). My interest is in the first chart, *hôgaku* (Japanese pop music), which can include a variety of pop, rock, dance, R&B, hip-hop, and mainstream rap styles. Though Western rock and pop are still considered a source of Japanese *kayôkyoku*, we must be able to distinguish between its past and current roles. As we will learn, today's Japanese pop artists do not necessarily view the West as their artistic roots; instead, they claim their music has been influenced by Japanese pop musicians who have created their own independent canon. Cultural adaptation has resulted in this Western tradition being viewed as Japanese. In the postmodern global music industry, the process of cultural diffusion is accelerated; the Internet and satellite broadcasting provide immediate information transfer. Keith Negus argues that technology is, to a certain extent, responsible for the concomitant rise of world markets in pop music, and a global "homogenisation of taste" (1992: 6). Despite this leveling of taste,

> a whole generation [of Japanese listeners] has now grown up in an affluent Japan, and these young people do not idolize the West in the same way . . . Japanese pop music is no longer dominated by cover versions or slavish imitations, and to accuse Japanese artists of only possessing the ability to copy others is to ignore the fact that all pop music is the product of the assimilation and adaptation of other forms of music.
>
> (De Launey 1995: 207)

Much of the music recounted in this book is of this generation; J-pop, for example, is not viewed as a copy but is received as fresh and innovative in its own market.

This volume can be read from cover to cover, but recognizing the subjectivity of musical taste and the limitations of readers' time and energy, it was also written with the goal that each chapter could stand alone as a discrete essay. I fully expect that many readers will use the index and read selectively of this book. Whether read in consecutive order or in bits and pieces, it is my hope that this research will bring depth to the understanding of fans and scholars of Japanese popular music alike, and encourage individuals to seek out further information about, interpretations of, and artistic expressions of the wide-ranging genre I call Japanese Popular Music.

2 Definitions

"Japanese popular music" is a phrase that lends this book its title, yet what does the phrase mean? Some scholars define it by its differences to "Western" music (Cahoon 1993: 1284) while others are focused on departures (or lack thereof) between Japanese *popular* (implying contemporary) music and Japanese *traditional* music (de Ferranti 2002). This chapter explores cultural markers associated with Japanese popular music and reexamines some of the notions that inform our concepts of "Japanese-ness" and national identity as expressed through music.

Though Cahoon and de Ferranti have given us valid definitions above, this chapter problematicizes the process of classifying pop music by nationality. How is Japanese music different from the Western classical and popular traditions? What is Japanese popular music's cultural heritage, and how does it influence contemporary musical life in Japan? Of course, not all musical definitions that are considered "indigenous" to Japan are present in contemporary mainstream Japanese pop music; some are more distantly located in its prewar history. These elements do provide a foil against which Japanese popular music distinguishes itself from its past and at the same time is connected to its present. Not all of these elements are necessarily manifested in today's charts, but I include them here to provide a springboard by which today's music launched into its contemporary form. These elements offer us a vocabulary by which to understand to what extent contemporary songs rely on the traditional repertoire of sounds, rhythms, and modalities.

While the first part of this chapter identifies a number of ethnomusicological signposts as part of the identification process, the second section explores other kinds of conceptual markers in Japanese music, arguing that "Japanese-ness" is not necessarily limited to musical aspects such as modulation and instrumentation but also entails ideologies of cultural and even intercultural identity, positioned against a dominant Western viewpoint. Indeed, the "J" of J-pop refers not necessarily to Japan, "the nation," but to concepts that are associated with contemporary Japanese lifestyle and culture (Ugaya 2005b). This lifestyle (or, a longing for this lifestyle) is not limited to Japan's geographical boundaries. The prefix "J-" illustrates the construction of a new national and transnational Japanese identity, built on ideas of the interactions of human beings, people, and technology, people and space. It is this concept that is more fluently exported, as per Iwabuchi's concept of "odorless culture" (1998). Products without "cultural odor" do not specifically carry strong connotations of its country of origin, and instead "blend in" with local custom ("glocalization"); they are among the most successful transnational cultural commodities. This has been true for many years with respect to Japan's international trade, especially during the earlier periods when the marker "Made in Japan" did not inspire the same consumer confiden[illegible] overseas as it does today. Japan's cultural and business interactions with Asia [illegible] rest of the world have developed to the point where both "fragranced" [illegible] nfra-granced" products, including music, flow between national bord[illegible] latter section of this chapter focuses on how a variety of Japanese mu[illegible] aveled overseas, what paths have been successful for Japanese compo[illegible] artists, and why.

Traditions of Japanese popular music

Much of the following section summarizes what other Japanese and foreign ethnomusicologists have categorized as "Japanese" in popular music past and present.[1] Hugh de Ferranti's detailed introduction is helpful to a primarily Western trained audience who prefer to see a constructed image of "Japanese music" in a purer form, untouched by outside influence (2002). He borrows from Bourdieu's concept of *habitus* to describe the historical and social "habits" that explain the practice of perceiving and producing music (196), and this allows a more inclusive definition of Japanese popular music that puts "neo-classical" film soundtracks (referred to later in this chapter) as well as J-pop dance divas in the same category as part of a "present past that tends to perpetuate itself into the future by reactivation in similarly structured practices" (Bourdieu 1994b: 98). For example, de Ferranti finds continuity with the singing styles (or "vocal tone-color") of Hamazaki Ayumi and a genre of Edo Period shamisen songs called *kouta* (2002: 202) by tracing the development of this premodern style of female singing, through the war years and finally to the postwar era. This is useful as it allows the listener to see links between contemporary J-pop and classical Japanese music and thus supports the idea of conceptualizing Eastern and Western musical traditions in a continuum rather than relying on essentialist, binary oppositions to describe sound.

Tradition in terminology: the development of a popular music

Often Japanese as well as foreign scholars look to a Redfieldian "little tradition" of folk music to launch their understanding of indigenous musical culture. Japanese folk music (not as in 1960s "folk," but "folk" interpreted as in the German "*volksleid*") is defined in a variety of ways. Nakamura believes that *sôran-bushi* ("work songs") are the most "representative" of the Japanese folk tradition; this genre consisted of spontaneous melodies and lyrics sung by fishermen in northern regions while at work (1991: 275).[2] These songs were notable for their immense variety, showing how individual performers could interact with the oral tradition and create new traditions during their lifetime.[3] The most frequently used term to describe "folk" music in Japan, however, is *minyô* (Malm 1996: 221; Yano 2002: 32), but de Ferranti defines *minyô* as "regional songs" (2002: 197), emphasizing its peripheral origins. Most important to this discussion is the conflation of a Japanese "folk music tradition" with a cultural identity that is associated with a geographic periphery. The use of the term *minyô* is documented approximately from the 1890s and usually consisted of vocals with an instrumental accompaniment; *minyô* are "work songs, game songs, [and] love songs" (Fujie 1989: 202), the topics of everyday life. *Minyô* provided a categorical contrast to urban music in the premodern Edo period (1600–1867), called *zokuyô* (Kawabata 1991: 334). Nakamura states that urbanites were first exposed to Japanese folk music by traveling street singers who adapted them, and geisha who may have picked them up and rearranged them to their own performance styles (1991: 275). Later, to preserve the vanishing discourse, scholars transcribed *minyô* songs as an indigenous musical "tradition."

Minyô as a genre was created in response to Japanese musicians and music historians confronting Western music terms (Malm 1996: 221); thus the term was purposefully used in ambiguous ways to allow a variety of music to fall under its rubric (Nakamura 1991: 275). Encasing musical traditions under one acceptable genre was important because it allowed popular music to gain some social status in the public sphere. Music from premodern urban centers battled with its image of "vulgarity" and borrowed from countryside *minyô* the image of tradition and legitimacy (276). Urban music struggled in the wider artistic community in part because of its association with a

> hedonistic class of nouveau-riches who had no social standing but enormous means. . . . The painful difference of the level between the earlier Japanese music and the popular town music of the Tokugawa era is a consequence of this particular social development.
>
> (Harich-Schneider 1973: 490)

The above quote is of interest particularly because it demonstrates the association of popular music in the premodern era with a negatively perceived social status, as opposed to the morally superior realm of classical Japanese music. This idea is also shared by certain ethnomusicologists who were often more concerned with elite traditions than common music, and this is expressed in the language they use to describe it. After the Meiji Restoration (1868) when bans on international travel were lifted, the government wished to legitimize the new urban culture for not only the Japanese but also the newly arrived foreign observers, and borrowing images from other regions helped to balance its negative urban image. An increasingly mass media literate society made it possible for musicians to borrow traditions from the periphery and make them part of their own musical tradition (Malm 1996: 221–222).

More inclusive, both historically and in terms of genre, is the phrase *nihon no ongaku* (Japanese music, or musical culture), and it is thought to have come into use before the end of the Meiji Period (1868–1912) (de Ferranti 2002: 197).[4] This definition is also used by Kitagawa (1991: 318) and includes both contemporary and traditional forms. This is contrasted with the somewhat more narrow term *hôgaku* that generally means "traditional Japanese music" (Wade 2005: 42). The Meiji Period represents a turning point in Japanese music history, because at this time Western music and instruments were being imported on a much larger scale and integrated into the public educational system and the military as a modernization project (Malm 1996: 245). The tightly controlled music guilds[5] of the Tokugawa Era (1600–1687) were breaking down and amateurs could choose to enter the field; this meant increased competition for musicians and, consequently, a flourishing of public participation in music both as profession and as hobby (246). Thus, prewar urban Japanese popular music formed a moving target, a "tradition" search of a label: it needed to define itself first in order to ensure its survival, both in terms of competition with imported Western music and in terms of maintaining quality and cultural value in the professional musical community.

The Meiji Period was also when Japanese scholars began publishing histories of Japanese popular music (de Ferranti 2002: 197), and they began using new terms to communicate these developments. *Taishû ongaku* was used to describe the music of the "masses," was particularly used during the 1920s, and was part of the general trend of attaching the prefix *taishû* to any cultural forms to describe the new concept of public or "mass" culture that was disseminated through a commercial media.[6] *Ryûkôka* is the sinic reading of *hayariuta*, which was used to describe commercially created music of the Tokugawa or Edo Period. *Ryûkôka* thus became the Meiji, "modern" translation of the term (Malm 1996: 246).[7]

> Popular music of the early modernization period was more creative than its military, educational and religious competitors because it had no firm dogma. Its major rule was (and probably will always be) that it had to sell.
> (ibid.)

In the 1930s, *ryûkôka* was used to describe a music that was industry-made, as opposed to tunes which were transmitted orally in the city streets or in the countryside (known as *enkashi*). This was a change in not only musical terminology but also consumption and was brought on by the inception of new technologies that facilitated new ways to make, buy, and listen to music: records, film, and radio. From this point on, institutions, such as record labels and film studios, rather than individuals, "made" the music to which people listened. *Ryûkôka* songs were Western in structure, in that the rhythm was taken from American and European jazz and pop tunes but the tonality was explicitly Japanese. *Ryûkôka* lyrics spoke of the loneliness of the soldier, as well as love, loss, bitter farewells, and happy reunions. This style of music and lyric composition in the 1920s–1930s is considered a predecessor of *enka* (see p. 45 for a definition of postwar *enka*).

During the 1930s, two government ministries (Information and Education) were closely involved in the production and dissemination of popular music as a larger project of wartime propaganda (Wade 2005: 132). *Gunka* originated in the late nineteenth century and continued to be popular until the end of Japan's imperial period. These songs incorporated both Japanese and Western music styles with Western instrumentation (mainly in the form of brass marches). Patriotic lyrics were common, as well as images of the loneliness of the soldier in the battlefield; Yano gives a poignant example of the *gunka* song "*Kudan no Haha*" (Kudan Mothers) referring to women visiting the Yasukuni Shrine in the Tokyo district of Kudan, which enshrines the Japanese war dead (2002: 38). Consequently, this kind of music was banned in the immediate postwar period by the Occupation forces as promoting prewar militaristic culture, but this tradition of prewar popular music persists in parts of contemporary Japanese society. For example, one of the most common occasions heard today is via right wing political groups, which campaign city streets with vans that blare *gunka* along with their political messages (usually regarding the role of the emperor or changes to the constitution). When I visited a Yokohama public nursing home for the elderly in 1993, I was somewhat surprised to hear *gunka* being played over the loudspeakers during the patients' leisure activities. Yet later I considered the possibility that for these patients, many suffering from dementia, *gunka* represented their present, and this association could be used therapeutically. *Gunka* does not surface in postwar Japanese pop discussions, but a careful listen to Nakajima Miyuki's 1995 "*Tabibito no Uta*" (The Traveler's Song) reveals some continuity between the postwar pop song and the military march. Though the song contains clear "Western" elements (e.g., distorted electric guitars, and gospel-type backing vocals in the chorus), the main verses' marching rhythm and minor scales recall a prewar atmosphere. The lyrics, utilizing masculine pronouns, speak of wandering and rootlessness; but in this postmodern version, the social disruption is not war, but generalized *anomie*.

From the mid-1920s, *ryûkôka* faded from use and the term *kayôkyoku* became interchangeable with "mainstream pop." Fujie defines *kayôkyoku* as popular music with "a known composer" (1989: 202), implying that previous popular musical traditions did not always have clear origins. The term was used by NHK (*Nippon Hôsô Kyokai*, the national broadcasting company) over *ryûkôka* at the end of the 1920s (203). It was also used in the immediate postwar era and is still used today to describe what one mostly hears on the television, on the radio, and on the *Oricon* charts.

Kayôkyoku thus became the general term that was used to describe postwar Japanese popular music, but there are still other terms used today to distinguish Japanese popular music from its foreign counterparts. *Hôgaku*, as defined by Wade, is used in some contexts to describe traditional or "classical" Japanese music, but it also used more widely to describe *any* music produced and distributed in Japan. Record shops divide their offerings between *hôgaku* (domestic music) and *yôgaku* (Western music), with Japanese artists occupying the former shelves and North American and European artists filling the latter. Kawabata is not confident, however, that the content of two categories are significantly different. He notes that it is not uncommon for a European retailer to separate "domestic music" from "international music" but these can be said to be the left and right profiles of Western music – though the languages of the lyrics may be different, the rules of the musical grammar are the same (1991: 334).

In other words, the overwhelmingly global influence of Western popular music has made non-Western music less distinctive, so differentiation (either on record store shelves or in the minds of critics and audiences) becomes less meaningful. In this context, contemporary *hôgaku* is merely "imitated Western sounds with little conversion" (335). What really distinguishes *hôgaku* and *yôgaku* is "first, the nationality of the original record; second, the singer's nationality and third, the language of the song's lyrics" (ibid.). Context, rather than musical content, is the defining issue when mapping of genre in the contemporary pop music scene.

Although *hôgaku* is still widely used in the commercial sense, a more recent surge in popularity of Japanese popular music has given rise to yet another term: *J-poppu* (hereafter, J-pop). As previously mentioned, the prefix "J-" is combined with other words to create a hybrid sign that signifies "a Japanese version of something trendy" through melding the Anglo signifier of Japaneseness (the Roman letter "J") with another noun, usually a borrowed term from English. By utilizing English, Japanese promoters have taken advantage of this self-consciousness that arises from Japan's global position, an international gaze domestically created and applied. J-WAVE, a radio station discussed later in the volume, is noted as the first organization to utilize this strategy in 1988; in 1993, the professional soccer league "J-League" was established (Ugaya 2005b: 6), demonstrating the allure of this linguistic hybridization. J-pop exploded in the late-to-early 1990s, when million-seller artists were no longer a rarity to the charts. J-pop as a genre also encompasses specific marketing strategies that utilize a variety of mass media, unavailable to many consumers before the mid-1990s: the Internet and the mobile phone, for example. Through these technologies, J-pop became a part of the global music scene, without its audiences ever having to travel overseas to listen or buy the music.

Wade writes that " 'J-pop' applies to the idol scene and encompasses boy groups and girl groups as well as individual stars" (2005: 151), but this definition, focusing on limited styles and types of performers, is not nearly as nuanced as others that incorporate J-pop's audience, its associated mass media, technology, and the wide variety of genre. J-pop in reality is constructed of many styles, from more mellow, folk-based pop to funkier dance music and rap-influenced techno-pop. Another important attribute of J-pop is that its market is "fast-paced," its audiences are "fickle," as demonstrated by the Anglocized prefix, and there is a conscious global identity, especially with regard to its audience.[8] J-pop, as used in the mass media, seems to be used most often to distinguish its artists from other kinds of genre in *hôgaku*, such as *enka*. Recently, this usage has diversified to include *J-rokku* (J-rock), which describes bands whose style is categorized as rock rather than pop or techno, but their use of technology, promotional campaigns, and demographics are not unlike their J-pop counterparts. "J-pop" is widely used by East Asian audiences to describe music from Japan overseas and has become so integrated in a wider East Asian consumer market that this terminology has recently been transformed to describe other Asian pop cultures: "K-*poppu*" (Korean popular music and culture) is another trend seen in both Japan and other international markets.

Musical foundations

In the following section the reader is asked to imagine the sounds described below. Cook notes that there is "always a disparity between the experience of music and the way in which we imagine or think of it" (1990: 135). In other words, talking about music is not the same thing as listening to it. But words do help to describe structural aspects, for example. Popular music generally follows the format of "introduction," "alternation between verses and chorus," "verse progression," and "conclusion" (Hennion 1990: 190–191); in addition to the occasional bridge and/or change of key, this framework generally describes much of postwar pop music in Japan. Length is generally three to five minutes (Fujie 1989: 199). Verses and choruses are easily recognized and reproduced; rhythm is up-tempo (70–150 beats per minute) for pop, rock, or dance songs but slower for love or sorrowful ballads. Yet, it is only through listening that one truly "feels" the music, and readers are encouraged to seek out examples from the discography to form their own interpretations.

Mode (scales)

One of the most basic ways to analyze and categorize music is by its construction. Arguably, melody has been considered the most important aspect of the pop song because of its immediately identifiable quality; however, the melody is of secondary importance to the overall impression that the pop song creates psychologically when first heard by the listener. The importance of melody lies in its ability to act as a marker that identifies the memory of the moment for the audience (Hennion 1990: 191–192).

Even if melody merely provides the backdrop to an emotive moment in time, in order to evoke that memory at playback, musicologists have analyzed the construction of music for centuries finding structure and meaning. Melodies consist of tones that fall into a pattern called scales (or *onkai* in Japanese). These scales have pitches, and those that remain steady (neither rising nor falling in duration) are called definite. An indefinite pitch slides around a note, yet in Japanese artistry and musicianship, individual skill is judged on the artist's creation of the bending, or sliding sound. Unpitched sounds are a part of the Japanese musical repertoire: the sound of air rushing through a *shakuhachi* (Japanese flute) is an example of an unpitched sound, making for one of the more basic departures between "Western" musical definitions (which is almost always pitched) and other traditions that incorporate a variety of sounds (Cook 1990: 10). Scales, however, consist of definite pitches and constitute the melody of any song. The melody is, in turn, contrasted with the other basic elements of popular song: its rhythm and lyrics.

Music categorized as "traditionally" Japanese is constructed of scales that differ from classical Western music.[9] Pentatonic scales (those which contain five "core" notes – plus two additional notes) are identified as part of Japanese folk music and are often used in the folk music traditions of other Asian countries including China. Western ethnomusicologists studying Japan construct five- to six-note pentatonic scales that mirror their own tradition, while Japanese musicologists "often deal with three note units [tetrachords] . . . this reduction of the research data is meaningful in Japanese music . . . [because it demonstrates how] it is aharmonic and linear" (Malm 1996: 223).[10]

Western scales often display the harmonic relations between notes; Japanese tetrachords demonstrate a general lack of Western harmonic concern in its musical theory. Furthermore, Fujie notes that there is diversity in the Japanese indigenous systemization of tones, that musicians may not share the same set of pitches when they play (1992: 321), and that different sets of scales are associated with different instruments, and thus genre (1989: 201).

There are several pentatonic scales associated with Japanese music, and Malm identifies several scales as the basis of "Japanese tonal theory": the *in* and *yô* are the two basic scales, with their variants the *ryo*, *ritsu*, *ryûkyû*, *minyo*, and *miyako* (1996: 223). The most interesting feature of these modes is not their construction (as pentatonic minor scales exist in other musical cultures) but their aesthetic and psychological interpretations. As noted by Hennion earlier in this section, one function of pop music melodies – which are constructed of scales in certain keys – is to help the listener reproduce memories and emotions associated with the experience of consuming that song. This aural connection to emotion is also important in the Japanese case, as their scales are frequently attributed with psychological qualities. Even the terms for the two basic scales have strong emotive connotations: the *in* (translated as dark, or shadowy) and *yô* (positive, or light).

Different figurations of the *in* and *yô* scales create new structures, each with its own psychological tag. These two basic scales are the basis for a number of variations: the *minyô* ("folk") scale; the *miyako* or *miyakobushi* (referring to the Kyoto area) scale, the *ritsu* (associated with music of the Chinese court) scale, and the *ryûkyû* scale, the last found in Japan's most southwestern island chain (Malm 1996: 223). Whether "dark" or "bright," further emotional qualities are projected on these *in* and *yô* variants. The *miyakobushi* refers to songs from the city (*miyako* means "capital") and is in the *in* mode ("sophisticated or sad") as opposed to the *minyô* which is "naïve and healthy" (*genki*) (Koizumi 1977: 76–77). *Miyako* songs invoke "the music of the pleasure quarters and theatres since the 17th century" (Malm 1996: 223). Though this music was often criticized for low morals, at the same time it was also considered more sophisticated than the "naïve" tunes from the countryside. Okada describes another commonly used pentatonic scale, the *yonanuki* (*yo* = four; *na* = seven; *nuki* = omission), and says that its major scale contains the "bright, free feeling of the Japanese folk song" (*minyô*) while minor *yonanuki* "may therefore bring to mind some of the traditional sentiment associated with the corresponding traditional tetrachord" (1991: 286).

But what is a scale to musicians and audiences, anyway? In the case of Japanese folk music, scales merely represent choices composers have made after an oral tradition has already been composed, and musicologists are merely recording it for posterity. As previously noted, Japanese scales differ from Western ones; Koizumi says that the Japanese pentatonic scales arise from "disjuncted tetrachords" (a pattern consisting of three tones) (1977: 76). Yet these tetrachords were merely analytic units created by theorists. Just as most modern composers write melodies without the need for a new set of scales, Japanese traditional music was created without the help of pentatonic scales and tetrachords. As these modulations were formed only after Japan's interaction with the West, the creation of Japanese scales is a reaction to the Western construct (Okada 1991: 285). Yano writes that the *yonanuki* scale was "deliberately created" by one of the first Japanese prewar composers who had been educated in Western-style music and represents a "synthesis of Western diatonicism with the melodic structure of nineteenth century Japanese songs" (1998: 248), illustrating the self-conscious marking of Japanese music using Western musical vocabulary. Fujie concurs that the *yonanuki* is merely a Western major and minor scale with the two corresponding steps eliminated (1989: 201). Thus, we can see that Japanese modality, as the construction of melody, is really a "cultural marker," rather than a conceptual building block for the composer.

Today, we occasionally hear – or, at least critics tell us we do – pentatonic scales in Japanese popular music, and the ones most commonly employed in the postwar era are the *minyô* and the *yonanuki*. The *minyô*, as a tetrachord, can be translated into Western notation as (C – E flat – F). In its full pentatonic representation, it can be written as A–C–D–E–G–A (la – do re mi – so la) (Fujie 1989: 201). The *yonanuki* major is C–D–E–G–A–C (or do re mi sol la do), while the minor *yonanuki* is A–B–C–E–F–A (la si do mi fa la) (ibid.).[11] The *yonanuki* is not only said to be Japanese but can be found in the music of "China, Java, India, Mongolia, Annam and Kampuchea" as well as some folk songs in Scotland and Ireland (Mita 1992: 56). In the modern era, the *yonanuki* minor in Japanese popular music has been called the "Japanese 'blues' style" (Fujie 1989: 204) for its ability to combine Japan's ethnomusical tradition with emotion using a Western musical vocabulary.

Modalities also express other differences between Japanese and Western traditions. Okada points out that the reliance on pentatonic scales means that harmonies (as in the harmonics of thirds and fourths above the base tone) are not as easily integrated and thus are not a prominent characteristic of Japanese music. She writes "[b]ecause traditionally the Japanese people have no feeling for harmony," *enka* and other genre that rely on Japanese modes favor "stepwise motions" rather than "leaps" which are common in Western harmonic-based music (1991: 288). The establishment of harmony vocals as a common feature of the late 1960s' vocal pop music in Japan demonstrates a shift away from the Japanese modes, and toward harmonic, Western-based scales.

Although Japanese scales are more prevalent in prewar music, there are instances when pentatonic, minor scales appear in postwar music. Though they are most commonly associated with *enka* rather than J-pop or rock, there are cases when pentatonic scales are heard across a wider range of genre. For example, Sakamoto Kyû's groundbreaking 1963 hit "*Ue o muite arukô*" uses a pentatonic scale (Kitagawa 1991: 306). Nakajima Miyuki's 1976 single "*Konbanwa*" (Good Evening), with its minor themes accented by violins, could be considered an *enka* piece. Sakamoto Ryûichi's award-winning film soundtracks have frequently utilized pentatonic scales, yet he buries the "Japanese-ness" of these musical traditions in favor of a more pan-Asian flavor: one example is the inclusion of Chinese stringed instruments as well as his trademark piano in the theme of the film *The Last Emperor* (1987). Despite this flexibility, if the modulation of Japanese pop music appears "Japanese," then this becomes an enduring marker pinpointing cultural identity in music. For example, take Mita's description of early postwar pop: "If the scale is played on a piano or harmonica, the peculiarly Japanese feel is immediately apparent . . . and it is one of the secrets behind the distinctive 'Japaneseness' [that makes songs popular]" (1992: 56).

The key here is the combination of the *yonanuki* scale and a Western instrument (piano or harmonica) – it is the mix of musical vocabulary that strikes the critic as particularly "Japanese," suggesting that cultural identity is not as much representative of "tradition" as it is a "hybrid" mix of two seemingly opposed traditions.

The discussion of "Japanese" modalities as a part of contemporary Japanese pop music creates opportunities to explore cultural identity in music; yet, we should not over emphasize the connection between modality and culture. Cultural identity can be just as strongly felt in music composed using Western modalities. When asked if he considered Japanese versus Western scales when composing music such as the *yonanuki*, leader of the long-running band the Alfee Takamizawa Toshihiko replied: "*Yonanuki onkai* [scales]? I'm afraid I don't know [what you are talking about]!" (Personal Communication 2005). This composer's lack of awareness of modality in his music probably arises from his generation's focus on Western music in public education, but it also signals the ambiguous and ambivalent role that modalities play in both traditional and contemporary Japanese popular music.

Structure, rhythm, and tempo

Prewar Japanese popular music was usually set to a regular beat, but that could be altered for dramatic or other effects. Music prior to the mid-nineteenth century using traditional instruments had either a steady beat or a "flexible" one, meaning the beat was irregular. Meter in traditional Japanese music tends to be double, dominantly 4/4, and there is a uniform emphasis on each beat rather than weak and strong beats alternating (as is common in Western pop). If beat is flexible, it often leaves a "space" between moments in the performance. This space, considered especially "Japanese" by Westerners and Japanese audiences alike, is known as *ma*, defined as "a perception of space and time, a 'between' " (Wade 2005: 168).

Another characteristic of "traditional" Japanese music that combines structure with tempo is the musical form *jo-ha-kyû*. *Jo* means preface, or beginning; it is slow. *Ha* means to break – even to destroy – and constitutes the middle section; it is also considered as a "development" phase. Here the tempo quickens over a long phrase. *Kyû* means hurrying, or suddenness, where the tempo peaks and then fades to an end. Wade calls *jo-ha-kyû* an "aesthetic shape" which gives the musical piece its acceleration, climax, and deceleration (2005: 38–39). Familiar in the *nô* theater musical tradition, these terms can be used to describe the progressive quality of plays (Harich-Schneider 1973: 425) or sections that "imitate" court music (436).

The *jo-ha-kyû* structure is normally associated with classical Japanese music and illustrates the use of tempo to mark structural place in a piece, but tempo changes for dramatic emotional emphasis can be heard in more recent works. Many of the songs on the Alfee's album *Arcadia* (1990), such as the title track "Arcadia," "Masquerade Love," and "Countdown 1999" start with slow introductions and then suddenly thrust forward with markedly faster beats. These songs use Asian tonal themes over frenzied rock rhythms to express the conflict of contemporary Japanese national and personal identity; the underlying concern of this album is the Japanese quest for cultural self-affirmation within an Asian as well as a Western context. "Eurasian Rhapsody," from the same album, calls for listeners to "Get back to the Asian Spirit [sung in English]/in their hearts"; "Countdown 1999" goes from a classical acoustic introduction to a hard rock middle section with pronounced *ma* (where the music abruptly stops for two seconds just over one minute into the track). The *ma* pattern repeats during the second half of the song, but this time making room for a harp-like acoustic guitar flourish, a fusion of East and West musical traditions. Later, the vocalist screams, rather than sings, "for what purpose were you born / Yellow Child" [sung in English]. "Countdown 1999" represents a tense, postmodern definition of *ma*, a technique that "describes neither space nor time, but the tension in the silence and in the space surrounding sounds and objects" (Galliano cited in Wade 2005: 160). The entire album is a pastiche of "oriental" visual imagery (Persian rugs, classical sculpture, and Arabic writing as cover design[12]) with Western pop/rock mixed with Asian themes, sitar introductions, English and Japanese lyrics. Japanese-ness is Asianized with other "Oriental" elements, defined vis-à-vis its cultural and musical counterpart, the West.

Vocal techniques and instrumentation

Certain vocal production techniques (*hasseihô*) are associated with "traditional" Japanese music, and though they are most frequently utilized today in genre such as *enka*, at times mainstream Japanese pop singers perform in ways that pay homage to their musical vocal traditions. de Ferranti notes that the study of "traditional" vocalization is important to the historicizing of popular music because of its strong association with the Japanese language (2002: 201). This idea carries into the postwar era of pop music stardom, where the pop song is closely associated with the person who sings it, making vocals the premiere music role in the production process. Vocals consist of a fluid tradition of language that changes over time, but certain "predilections" for creating sound linger in contemporary releases, creating an aesthetic "habitus" that surround practices of producing and appreciating music.

In contrast with the *bel canto* style of Western classical music, traditional Japanese vocal production generally values a nasal vibrato rather than a chest or purely head tone. Some of this quality is discernable in J-pop recordings: for example, ethnomusicologist Wade notes that J-pop female vocalists have a "youthful, sometimes even 'little girl' voice with a relatively nasal quality" (2005: 152). *Jigoe* – "ground" or "basic voice" (de Ferranti 2002: 202) or "natural voice" (Fujie 1989: 200) – is produced using tightened vocal cords and results in a clear tone. Whether "traditional" or "pop," most Japanese music utilizes this technique. hide's 1996 "Misery [remix version]" from the album *PSYENCE* demonstrates the *jigoe* style of singing in a rock style. *Uragoe* (falsetto) utilizes less restriction and is "softer" (Fujie 1989: 200). Mita, in his discussion of the 1960s' singer Ueki Hitoshi of the Crazy Cats, writes that this style of singing with its lack of restriction "liberates the life impulse" and suits the "carefree attitude" of postwar Japanese popular culture (1992: 93–94).

Whether natural or falsetto, one of the most distinctive attributes of Japanese vocal production techniques is vibrato. *Yuri* is a wide vibrato; another vibrato, *kobushi*, is defined as a "melismatic motion" (de Ferranti 2002: 204) between tones, used as embellishment. Often used in *enka*, *kobushi* is also called "a voice-trembling technique . . . closely related to traditional Japanese music" (Kitagawa 1991: 305). Okada too notes that Japanese *enka* singers' techniques are characterized by melismatic vocalizations (1991: 288). Melisma is a decorative or ornamental style of singing where single syllables, especially vowels, are drawn out over several syllables to showcase the singer's vocal ability; this is not limited to Japanese traditional singing but is heard in a variety of European styles such as Gregorian chanting, Baroque singing, and contemporary Gospel. Wade notes that Hajime Chitose's "distinctive vocal ornamentation . . . identifies it as Okinawan pop" (2005: 152);[13] in this case, Hajime's vibrato is combined with melisma. Another ornamental technique is *nori*, or "riding," which refers to vocalized text lines, spoken over music. *Nori* is originally associated with *nô* drama, but we also hear vestiges of this style in postwar classics such as Misora Hibari's "*Ringo no Oiwake*" (Apple Melody, 1952) where the vocalist speaks dramatically over an instrumental section between verses; furthermore, Fujie terms her performance in this track as having a "free rhythm, in folk song style" (1989: 206).

Miyamoto Kazufumi, lead singer for The Boom, uses vibrato in their biggest hit "*Shimauta*" (Island Song, in two versions, 1992 and 1993; re-released in 2002; and again for the I-pod in 2005), a song that relies on cultural borrowing of language, musical styles, and instruments of the Ryûkyû region. Importantly, Miyamoto does not use the vibrato in The Boom's other pop-, rock-, or ska-inspired work but employs it during a "traditional" song, one that uses pentatonic scales and the *sanshin*[14] along side the electric bass and guitar.

But to what extent does "traditional" vocalization affect contemporary music that does not consciously borrow from an ethnomusical tradition? Take, for example, the vocal style of Imawano Kiyoshirô, whose career spans thirty-five years from his 1970 debut single with RC Succession "*Boku no Suki na Sensei*" to his most recent solo album *KING* (2005). Imawano is a charismatic performer, and in the same way that dramatic actors are often divided between "romantic" and "character," Imawano's musical image veers to the latter. His lyrics range from witty to serious, and his vocal style varies from gritty to clear depending on the mood of the song and the content of his lyrics. Not infrequently his vocals are shaky in their delivery, which begs the question: is his technique grounded in "traditional" musical practice? Or does his wavering voice pay homage to the amateur Japanese folk/rock musician movement of the late 1960s and early 1970s, which allows the audience to relate to his sincere message? The answer is a bit of both. In fact, de Ferranti notes that for most Japanese male vocalists in the contemporary pop scene, vocal stylings are more inspired by Elvis Presley, Mick Jagger, and Bob Dylan than any classical models from premodern indigenous traditions (2002: 203). But a discussion of traditional musical practice when analyzing contemporary pop is important, de Ferranti argues, to move toward a sense of continuity in practice between traditional and contemporary musical forms, moving away from the binary opposition between old and new, Japanese and Westernized. We cannot say that Imawano is *not* influenced by his musical past any more than we can say he has not been part of a living culture that has continuous ties to its own history. Even if he is striving for a Presley sneer in some of his songs, we cannot overlook the fact he is an active member of a continuous musical history. More interesting to me in discussions of Japanese copying of Western vocalizations (de Ferranti 2002; Hosokawa 1999b) is the relative absence of Japanese female vocalists who copy other styles, suggesting that women are somehow seen as the keepers of an abstract cultural tradition, and may be expected to conform to these expectations more often than male vocalists are. Although men make up the majority of powerful national and cultural icons in other cultural fields such as tea ceremony, flower arranging, and calligraphy, it is Japanese women who keep these artistic traditions alive by contributing large numbers to the professional, semiprofessional, and amateur spheres.

Contemporary cultural identity in Japanese popular music

Not all aspects of cultural identity in music can be classified by musicology; language is an obviously important marker of cultural identity and is discussed in detail in the Chapter 6 of this book. But there are other markers recognized by musicians and audiences that determine Japanese-ness in popular music; the following section introduces a key concept regarding the content of cultural markers in Japanese popular music, that of "place." Here are I argue that culture is powerfully expressed through its association with a location, a place defined through its relation to the geographic location of the nation "Japan." Place in Japanese popular culture, as explained in Chapter 1, is often associated with regionalism – that which is not Tokyo or Osaka. This section continues this association by adding another layer of meaning: that place, or regionalism, is a powerful symbol of culture when it is accentuated by the notion of authenticity.

Japanese popular music today is made up of many "places," including non-Japanese sites. In the prewar era, public schools pushed the mainstreaming of Western musical education as a part of a modernization mission, to "catch up" with North America and Europe economically as well as culturally. After 1868, Japanese public education did not focus on *hôgaku*, including the teaching of indigenous musical traditions and instruments, and it is only since the 1980s that *hôgaku* has been introduced (de Ferranti 2000: 20–21). This means that many musical elements discussed in this chapter's earlier sections may seem "foreign," or at least "exotic" to the postwar generation schooled in Western musical traditions. Pop composer Takamizawa's inability to recognize the term *yonanuki* is a good example of this generation educated in a dominantly Western musical environment. Furthermore, many popular musicians are self-taught, with some or little classical training, or with study at the many musical schools throughout Japan that teach vocals, guitar, bass, keyboard, and drums in the popular style. To them, *hôgaku* can be truly considered a foreign tradition.

Location and self-identification

Japan, as an archipelago, has a long tradition of cultural diversity based on regional identity. This exists in tension with a centralized national ideology of homogeneity that has been used politically to unite the islands for centuries. One of the most interesting developments in the study of Japanese cultural identity – in both English and Japanese language scholarship – is the focus on "authentic" Japanese culture as associated with the periphery. The argument is large urban areas such as Tokyo and Osaka have been so inundated by Western culture since the late nineteenth century, true "Japanese" culture remains only in isolated parts of the countryside. As in the case of the prewar *sôran-bushi* (work songs associated with Japan's northern region) becoming the *minyô* or folk tradition of all of Japan, Japanese national culture is at times conflated with various regional identities because of this notion of untouched "Japanese-ness."

Today's Japanese pop and rock industries are, for the most part, firmly rooted in the cultural capitals of Tokyo, and then Osaka; yet musicians come from all over Japan. Sometimes a star's association with a regional area becomes part of the performer's overall image. This happens when the region contributes somehow to either the musical expression or the celebrity image. This section analyzes regional artists in the post-bubble Japanese economy consciously marketed as "Japanese," in terms of their association with an idealized version of both Japanese culture and authentic pop music.

Any discussion of national identity in the Japanese case must first consider the difficulties in pinpointing the differences between national identity and nationalism. The latter is usually seen in a negative light, both by Japanese and by foreigners, influenced by the concept of "the bad old days of the Japanese attempt to dominate the world militarily" (Mathews 2003: 168). New definitions of nationalism – or at least, definitions of what it means to be Japanese – must be devised to create a "bright Japanese present" (ibid.). In his examination of Japanese tourism, Mathews is looking at construction of a new national identity based on globalized commerce (which is not always neutral). I suggest transferring this to the domestic sphere, where an alternative domestic national identity, separate from Japan's wartime history, is created through association with peripheral culture (i.e., areas safely distanced from Tokyo's symbolic place as center of military and political power). Not only is peripheral Japanese culture seen as less contaminated but its geographic distance – and, especially in the case of Okinawa, the suffering experienced there during the war – allows the periphery to be conceptually removed from the dark history of wartime responsibility.

Striking is the number of successful Japanese pop artists who are associated with the Okinawan and Ryûkyû regions.[15] These areas have certain characteristics in common as seen from the mainland perspective: they are geographically isolated from urban political and financial centers; they have distinct histories and cultures; and they share a tropical climate that supports a thriving tourist industry from the mainland. Both areas express their musical culture through the term *shimauta*, or island song (the same term borrowed by the Boom, previously mentioned, as the title for their 1992 hit single), and this reflects a close association between their culture and their environment.[16] *Shimauta* tend to use pentatonic scales (specifically the *ryûkyû onkai*, which takes its name from this region), specific vocal ornamentation styles, and traditional instruments such as the *sanshin*.

Although other regional communities with distinctive linguistic and cultural markers exist throughout the archipelago, since the 1990s, this area has been unusually successful in launching stars both in Japan and overseas. Through this connection to popular culture, one can argue that this region has become an alternate identity for mainland, mainstream Japan. These island chains constitute a multilayered symbol that draws strength from its peripheral status (which includes notions of an untouched culture and a history of military suffering rather than military aggression). Ironically, through its proximity to US military bases, the area has also become a conduit of the most up-to-date and authentic American pop culture.

Okinawa, the largest island in this chain, features prominently in postwar Japanese popular music. Though the Boom crashed through the mainstream barriers with their version of *shimauta*, Okinawan musicians such as the Rinken Band and Kina Shôkichi and the Champloose have established themselves commercially in the postwar era; Kina scored his first national hit in 1972. Many of these artists are considered affiliated with the concurrent trend of "World Music" in the early 1990s (Roberson 2001: 211–212). The double meaning of this "global" link arises from the fact that mainland Japanese audiences, while consuming reggae and samba from overseas, saw Okinawan music as equally "ethnic" but, at the same time, were comfortable promoting this "ethnic" product as symbolic of Japanese identity to overseas markets. Okinawan (or Ryûkyûan) musical identity was internally foreign but externally domestic; the constantly blurred boundaries between these two simultaneous perceptions of cultural identity (Japanese, yet not-Japanese) can be explored through a number of J-pop artists, such as dance music vocalist Amuro Namie, rock band Orange Range, and *minyô* pop queen Hajime Chitose.

The Okinawa Actors School, located in Naha and established in 1983, is an important nexus of Okinawan cultural identity as defined by Western pop. Graduates of this school have conquered the Japanese charts with mainstream dance and R&B music in the mid-1990s and their CDs have also sold relatively well overseas in Asian markets. Amuro Namie is perhaps the school's best-known graduate, with the girl groups SPEED and MAX close behind in popularity. These groups, as well as R&B "boy band" Da Pump, borrow from the African American music scene associated with military bases, ubiquitous on the main island. Moving from the periphery to the center, these acts bring an "authentic" representation of American-inspired pop music with the regional image of a sun-kissed, leisurely resort-dominated lifestyle that is appealing to mainland Japanese audiences. The Okinawan Actors School has been successful exporting a holiday atmosphere through its graduates, presenting a "vacation in a CD" for mainstream audiences.[17]

Okinawan entertainment, in the extended Occupation (1945–1972), was "one of the most important sectors in the local economy" (Ogura 2003: 467) but tended to be uncritical of American culture and represented white mainstream interests due to its unequal and dependent relationship on the military bases (467–468). After the reversion to Japanese sovereignty, a second cultural colonializing process took place when mainland Japanese audiences began to consume Okinawan rock out of its cultural context, praising its authenticity because "Okinawan rock bands had played before 'American audiences' who . . . underst[oo]d 'real rock'n'roll' " (468). This early association with "authentic" rock in the late 1970s and early 1980s was carried over to the R&B music trends in the 1990s. The music from Okinawan Actors School artists represent interpretations of major trends in American music, reiterating the idea that proximity creates authenticity in Japanese popular music.

Orange Range is one of the more recent figures in the Okinawan music scene to break through to nationwide stardom. They stand separate from the Actors' School, and a look at how they use their regional identity (without being pigeonholed as "ethnic") illustrates the region's multilayered symbolic meaning to mainland audiences. For example, they do not use specific *shimauta* styles, yet their mainstream audience is fully aware of their Okinawan roots. This is in part due to their marketing technique (an Okinawan band) and partly due their interpretation of their Okinawan identity as one that straddles the East–West cultural divide. Roberson argues that hybridization is an important aspect of the region's cultural identity, locally known as *champuru* (a word of Indonesian origin that refers to the mix of cultures) (2006: 206). Orange Range has taken the Okinawan notion of *champuru*, mixed their Asian/Okinawan aesthetics with some American hip-hop and rock and roll, and have successfully sold it to the rest of the nation. For example, they use Okinawan instruments in the song "*Rakuyô*" (Setting Sun), underlaying the electric guitars in a repeating hook that is firmly rooted in the Western pop tradition with the *sanshin*. The band uses Ryûkyûan dialect in the song "*Onegai* [Please] Senorita" and have used Okinawan dance in their concert performances, but no critic I have read has used the term *shimauta* to describe their music. But this is not to say that Okinawa does not figure prominently in their commodified public image. Industry observers comment explicitly on their regional affiliation as expressed through music: "One can feel their love for Okinawa" (*Nikkei Entertainment* 2005b: 42). Their peripheral point of origin, though, gives them cultural "street cred" in terms of their Japanese-ness, but their cultural tradition of *champuru* also allows them to bend the rules. Orange Range's cultural expressions are not limited to references to Okinawa and/or Japan from a traditionally determined cultural view. Orange Range's album *1st Contact* (2003) contains many playful references to mainstream Japanese identity using stereotypes of the Self through the Other (in English) in tracks such as "*Samurai Mania*" and "*Japaniizu Piipuru*," the latter reminiscent of attempts at communication with GI. These songs act as parodies, emphasizing Orange Range's own peripheral position by assuming the outsider's gaze. In the title of the first song, the Japanese word *samurai* is anglicized by its representation in *katakana* rather than the accepted Chinese character;[18] the lyrics revolve around the image of a postmodern "samurai" who crosses time and space effortlessly (no doubt due to advanced technology), with sound (*oto*) acting as the blade he brandishes – in other words, he is the rapper whose pen (or, more precisely, his voice) is mightier than the sword. Yet this rap also utilizes word play with somewhat archaic-sounding vocabulary, relying on Chinese character compounds rather than contemporary colloquialisms or English jargon to create the puns, juxtaposing a stiff historical "tradition" with a new playful definition of Japanese identity.

Orange Range also looks outside Japanese national boundaries to inspire their music. "Shanghai Honey" and "*Xièxie*" ("thank you") blend Asian rhetoric and dance beats without distinction regarding national boundaries. On their second album, *MusiQ* (2004), we hear the instrumental ambient dance track "*Jipangu2Jipangu*,"[19] which cleverly mixes the sounds of a traditional Japanese stringed instrument (a synthesized *koto*, perhaps?) plucking a pentatonic strand of sound against a synthesized backdrop of Western-textured rhythms. This stands in contrast to other "mainstream" hits; Orange Range's hybridization of sound is very different from the more orthodox borrowing as heard in The Boom's "*Shimauta*." Orange Range appears to have mastered the synthesis of Japan/Asian identity with a Western pop tradition, as their 2005 release "*Hana*" (Flower) was the only Japanese single that year to sell over million copies (RIAJ 2005: 15).

Orange Range is not the only regional act to achieve critical acclaim in the twenty-first century. The female solo vocalist Hajime Chitose is a different example of how regionalism is marketed as retro-regionalism in Japanese popular music. Hajime was born and raised on Amami Ôshima, an island considered to be part of Ryûkyû but belonging to Kagoshima rather than Okinawan Prefecture. The Amami Island chain has its own musical tradition, especially with regard to its vocal techniques, which adds further decoration to the ornamental melisma associated with *shimauta*. Hajime mastered this vocal style and the *shamisen* as a teenager, winning the Amami *Minyô* prize as a senior in high school. In 2002, the NHK, the national broadcasting company, chose her song "*Kono Machi*" (This Town) as a theme song for a drama series, giving her nationwide exposure. Not long after that, her debut album *Hainumikaze* (Southern Wind in Amami dialect) won the Japanese industry's "best album" award, and her single 2002 "*Wadatsumi no Ki*" (The Tree of Wadatsumi; Wadatsumi is the name of the sea god, or *kami*) was the third top selling CD that year. Embracing traditional imagery and musical styles, her debut was touted as a return of the Japanese "heart" (*kokoro*) into popular music; the mass media even reported that Hajime's *shimauta* or island music had a psychologically healing effect on Japanese audiences who identified with her ethnic roots. Later, Hajime herself confessed that she was not completely "rooted" in this ethnic image: her producer had chosen the title of her hit single "*Wadatsumi no Ki*" and its meaning was vague to her (Hiraga 2005). Her second album, *Nomado Souru* (Nomad Soul), features a composition collaborating with New Music icon Matsutôya Yumi. Hajime's music suggests that cleverly marketed "renovated forms" (de Ferranti 2000: 23) of *minyô* do appeal to new listeners. Regional, and thus "pure," Japanese musicality, when backed by an enthusiastic mass media, succeeds when combined with "structures derived from Euro-American precursors" (ibid.).

Japanese music abroad

Regionalism, to this point, has been treated with reference to Tokyo as the center, and the national boundaries of Japan marking the periphery. Japanese musical culture is also increasingly consumed overseas; in what contexts are Japanese artists carving a "J-pop" market for themselves? What kinds of Japanese music do overseas audiences accept? The following section explores the cultural identity of Japanese popular music (or the lack thereof) specifically with reference to its reception overseas, focusing on the prominent genre in this field: dance music, and *anime* and feature film soundtracks.

Musical styles aside, critic Ugaya expresses a more economically driven view of what constitutes "Japanese" music at home and, perhaps more importantly, overseas: Japanese music is defined as whenever royalties are paid (through record companies, television studios, or radio stations) to musicians and copyright holders (e.g., composers and lyricists) who are Japanese (2005b: 166–167).[20]

The definition of Japanese pop music cannot be limited to that which is produced in Japan, because much of it is recorded, mixed, and mastered in the United States and Britain. The practice of recording overseas began in the 1980s when successful Japanese artists gained prestige by working with top engineers in the English-speaking music industry. The strong yen allowed many artists to travel overseas and stay for weeks in hotels and pay recording studio fees; in some cases, it was more efficient to pay for the travel and accommodation of a band in London to cut an album. These albums are no less a part of the Japanese pop repertoire, so the focus returns to the performer: the Japanese identity of the singer/musician appears to be the most inclusive definition of Japanese-ness in this cultural field.

While the national identity of the producers constitutes an important aspect of this definition, the national identity of consumers of Japanese popular music has changed. It is still true that Japanese people form the largest sector by far of the Japanese pop music audience. Ugaya states, harshly at times, that Japanese artists must be content making a living from the domestic market (2005b: 176–177). Hong Kong, however, has been a relatively successful market for Japanese singers since the 1980s, yet the financial benefits of investment and promotion there are limited. In comparison, Hong Kong's music market is just one-fiftieth of the size of Japanese market, so performers and their production company who sell 20,000 albums in Hong Kong have achieved the same market share as a million-seller album in Japan, but with substantially fewer royalties. For many performers, it may not be worth the effort to carve out a sector of the Canto-pop market – better to focus one's energies on a million-seller at home.

Yet, there are some artists who "make it" in other markets. Japanese pop music became prominent in Hong Kong in the mid-1980s through the introduction of specialized radio programs that introduced original songs by original artists (Ogawa 2004: 147). This initial success was connected to its previous media exposure through imported Japanese television dramas (which were less expensive than American shows to broadcast). It created a familiar context for listeners; in other words, the audience knew the songs before they hit the market. Furthermore, the Hong Kong market was saturated, and the industry had become out of touch with consumer demands – all of which pointed toward marketing or structural reasons for J-pop's success, rather than "cultural identification" (146–147). The common argument that Japanese pentatonic scales are "familiar" to Asian audiences cannot entirely explain why audiences embraced Japanese pop. Instead, Ogawa offers a compromise, acknowledging the musical issues as well as the concomitant boredom of Hong Kong audiences at that time: "a Japanese melody line offered the right balance of newness and familiarity" (147). This music was associated with a yearning for a middle class lifestyle which was in line with Japanese popular cultural products: technological and leisure oriented rather than intrinsically "culturally fragrant," as Iwabuchi might say.

What was considered "Japanese" to Hong Kong consumers in the 1980s and 1990s? Japan represented an association with technological quality and higher level of leisure. Japanese stars were also more glamorous than Hong

Kong stars, and their music represented the "scent" of heady celebrity scandal. Ogawa notes that this hyper-image of Japanese pop stars was apparent in Hong Kong because their media coverage was limited to "second-hand" translations of glossy magazines, and not backed by other kinds of media and tempered by the star's own organizational PR (152–153), resulting in audience interest but also mismatches between the audiences' perceptions of stars and their current persona (and causing, at times, trouble for visiting Japanese performers) (153, 156). In sum, the rise of J-pop in Hong Kong is just as much about the specifics of the market at that time and consumer taste in nonmusical areas as it is about the music, and the shared Asian identity of the two nations involved.

Most of the royalties paid overseas – representing the consumption of Japanese popular music in the international context – arise from the success of anime in the global market. *Anime* seems to be the main vehicle for delivering J-pop to a worldwide audience, but not all animated films are consumed overseas with the explicit identification with Japanese cultural identity, let alone "traditional Japanese culture," following Ugaya's and Iwabuchi's theorization that the recent global consumption of Japanese popular culture arises from social and aesthetic values that are transnational. Indeed, many of the internationally successful futuristic anime themes do not borrow from an indigenous musical tradition and instead sound more similar to Western rock and pop. Wade refers to anime themes that are made "Japanese" for consumption overseas, citing primarily the work of soundtrack composer Hisaishi Jô[21] who has a long-standing partnership with the widely acclaimed anime creator Miyazaki Hayao. Although Hisaishi's compositions range in style including Western pop standards (*Kiki's Delivery Service*, 1989), leaning toward new age (*My Neighbor Totoro*, 1988), and neo-traditional (*Princess Mononoke*, 1997), Wade focuses the last type of his work in *Princess Mononoke* and *Spirited Away* (2001) but is unconvinced of the authenticity of Hisaishi's cultural expressions: "I leave it to you to decide whether or not you hear rhetorical suggestions of 'Japaneseness' in this widely distributed music" (2005: 153). Obviously, the extent to which classical Japanese musical elements are integrated into Hisaishi's work is debatable, but I would argue this is not due to the listener's inability to recognize them but because of the fluid interpretation of these traditions by the composer. Many of Miyazaki's *anime* listed here contain themes of cultural awareness, especially in the more recent *Princess Mononoke* and *Spirited Away*; the former is a postmodernist dream of pastiche images drawn over many centuries of Japanese history and mythology.

Despite the debatable success of *anime* music communicating a music culture to an international stage, film soundtracks have been successful in exposing the West to Japanese music, making what might not be considered "popular" at least "of interest" to overseas audiences. Sakamoto Ryûichi's soundtracks have been internationally acclaimed, earning him an Oscar in 1988. But Sakamoto is not the only film composer who has brought Japanese music to Western interest. The compositions of Takemitsu Tôru (1930–1996) would not normally be classified as "popular," but his numerous scores for internationally acclaimed films such as Kurosawa's *Ran* (1985) and Imamura's *Black Rain* (1989) gave

Western audiences an idea of what Japanese musical culture fused with the European classical tradition could sound like and created a lasting Western impression of "Japanese music." Takemitsu's work juxtaposes classical Western training with Japanese instruments and a refined sense of the asymmetrical and linear qualities that categorize *hôgaku* of the past and present. His concert works such as "Requiem for Strings," "A Flock Descends into the Pentagonal Garden," and "November Steps" were internationally lauded as the ultimate in East/West fusion, probably because of Takemitsu's "authentic" connection to both traditions; in the late 1950s, Igor Stravinsky heard his "Requiem for Strings" and praised it. This "authentic" European master's public acceptance of Takemitsu's work gave him the *caché* to represent "Japan" using "Western" music discourse (and visa versa). I met the composer in 1989 when I worked on an exhibition of his manuscripts in New York City's Columbia University. Comfortable in English as well as in Japanese, the composer gave a lecture entitled "Sound in the East, Sound in the West: The Way to 'November Steps'," addressing the concept of cultural difference in music.

> How do the sounds of East and West differ? Of course notions of "east" or "west" are irrelevant to sound itself, which is a physical wave phenomenon . . . In a sound, in itself, there are no differences. However, when sounds are charged with meanings that arise out of life-style and from emotion, then sounds indeed take on various differences, for ways of living and of feeling are a product of diverse customs, of differing regions inhabited by differing people.
>
> (1989)

Although he was a master of music theory and composition, in Takemitsu's later years, he stressed the human interpretation of sound waves. He believed that the audience could be informed of this difference in emotion through listening to different kinds of music. Perhaps this educational aspect of his work lent some appeal to non-Western audiences; they wanted to understand the "different ways of living and of feeling" music from Japan.

Interlude: diverse cultural artistic identity in J-pop

The above-mentioned artists – from the Alfee and Orange Range to Takemitsu and Hisaishi Jô – are all publicly identified as Japanese nationals, informing the domestic and international markets of their affiliation with Japanese popular music. Although this cultural hegemonic image has long been promoted by the mainstream, it certainly overlooks the contributions of other artists to the Japanese pop music scene.

Japan's mainstream cultural identity is based on a perceived ethnic continuity; Mackie's research (2002) defines mainstream identity on the basis of a number of separate attributes; the most salient here is the concept of "Japanese blood" where the individual, through a blood relationship to another Japanese citizen, claims

Japanese ethnicity. Fluency in the language and culture, as well as residency within national boundaries, contributes to the anchoring of an individual's identity firmly in socially acceptable notions of Japanese-ness. A third-generation Japanese living in the United States whose Japanese is rudimentary holds less claim to Japanese cultural identity than a Japanese national who has lived his/her entire life in Japan, but holds more claim to Japanese identity than a foreigner who was born and raised in Japan.

Throughout history, there have been groups of foreigners interacting with Japanese society and culture, but the prewar era is most notable for the large numbers of Asians from Korea, Taiwan, and mainland China who were brought to Japan as indentured laborers after their homelands were colonized by Japan. The largest of these groups are the Koreans, and there were approximately 2,300,000 Koreans in Japan immediately after Japan's surrender in 1945 (Komai 1995: 232). Many were repatriated by the Occupation's programs, but those who stayed became members of Japan's largest ethnic minority group: *zainichi kankokujin* (or *chôsenjin*) or Resident Koreans. The government's 2000 census claims that 529,408 men and women are living in Japan as Korean "foreigners" (Ministry of Internal Affairs and Communication 2006), but this does not include those who have naturalized or intermarried, meaning that there are many more residents of Japan with Korean heritage.

Yano's study of Korean female performers in the *enka* industry (2004) explores diverse (but unequal) cultural identity in the Japanese popular music scene. Notable is the subgenre of Resident Korean (*zainichi*) *enka*, which includes vocalists, such as Tendô Yoshimi, who sing in both Japanese and Korean. This is an extraordinary juxtaposition of musical and national identities as *enka* represents the Japanese "heart" of musical culture; meanwhile, Resident Koreans are allowed full representation and participation in public life only if they meet certain citizenship requirements and renounce their Korean identity legally. Many resident Koreans are active in the entertainment industry, but not all of them advertise their status; their liminal status makes their affiliation unclear and at times unsettling to audiences.

Meanwhile, Korean-born entertainers are in the J-pop spotlight. In 2000, Korean broadcasting companies began exporting television drama series to China and broke into the Japanese market in 2003. Increased interest in Korean music, food, and even the study of the language was soon to follow, forming a *kanryû* (Korean wave) of popular culture in Japan. After starting her career in Korea, female vocalist Kwon Boa debuted in 2001 with Avex Trax under the name "BoA." Moving from "K-pop" to "J-pop," BoA's dance music made her the first overseas-born performer to achieve a number one album in Japan in 2002. In 2003, the overwhelming success of the NHK import drama, *Fuyu no Sonata* (Winter Sonata), meant the series soundtrack made the hit charts, and in 2004, Korean vocalists from this series appeared on the New Year's Eve Red and White Singing Contest. Following this trend, Japanese record companies have signed further Korean and a number of Chinese and Thai acts (Ohkoshi 2005: 24).[22] Korean and Chinese stars had sporadic success in Japan since the 1970s, but they were foreigners groomed especially for the Japanese market. This "wave" was the first time that Korean popular culture was reproduced in Japan "as is" and its main consumers were middle-aged women who identified with its perceived values, such as family loyalty and a steady romantic love, represented in the Korean story lines. Interestingly, this massive increase in interest in Korean popular and traditional cultures has not publicly been accompanied by a reexamination of the legal and social problems posed by the Resident Korean issue in Japan. The public face of Japan embraces Korean-born Koreans as a diversion to the problems unresolved over the liminal status of Japanese-born Resident Koreans.

Whether born in Japan or overseas, other foreigners are slowly entering the J-pop market. Frequently pioneers in the industry have been those with familial connections; Kawamura Kaori, born in Moscow to a Russian mother and a Japanese father, was part of the "girl rock" trend with hits in the late 1980s and early 1990s. French-born and biracial, Marc Panther was a member of Komuro Tetsuya's 1990s group globe, but Panther's rapping abilities took secondary status to the charismatic leader of the band. Today's hip-hop group Def Tech represents another group in an industry that is gradually acclimatizing to a globalized identity. Def Tech consists of two members, "Shen" and "Micro": Shen, a *gaijin* or white foreigner, was born in China and brought up in Hawaii; he spent his summer vacations in Japan and moved to Japan at twenty-one. Micro is from Tokyo, but claims internationalism through his musical influence (reggae). Their "unit" combines Hawaiian and Japanese culture, using both English and Japanese; yet, in playful inversion, the Caucasian member uses a Chinese name while the Japanese member uses an English nickname. Their ethnic mix of East and West, plus the liminal association with Hawaii (not East, but not West either) sets a new standard for globalized identity in Japanese pop music.

Conclusion

This chapter outlines concepts in Japanese popular music from a musicological perspective to demarcate ideas about "traditional Japanese music" versus "contemporary Japanese pop music." Despite this separation of the past and the present, we have seen that elements of this indigenous musical heritage arise from time to time in the postwar era; they are frequently identified by Japanese and non-Japanese audiences as cultural markers in a genre that is otherwise thought to have roots in a Western musical tradition. Musical characteristics that are most frequently associated with indigenous genres in the prewar and postwar eras show us that today's Japanese popular music exists in an ethnomusical continuum.

The notion of place is a crucial concept when defining cultural identity through music, in terms of internal imaginings of Japanese-ness. The internal exotic of the Ryûkyûan region constitutes an alternate identity for mainstream Japanese indigenous culture, which is attractive to Japanese audiences for two seemingly contradictory, yet coexisting, reasons: its physical and ideological distance from a Westernized Japan (representing diluted culture) and its pop authenticity due to its proximity to the West via the large number of American military personnel stationed in the region. Demonstrating that these two attributes of cultural identity and musical expression are not incompatible, Orange Range offers an example of how a band can straddle these two images, one that is "hip" to Western trends, yet one that borrows and plays with its own cultural heritage.

The image of Japanese music overseas seems to be divided into two areas of reception: one connected to Japanese traditional cultural identity and one not. The latter, J-pop and *anime* themes, constitute most of the sales of Japanese music abroad, but cultural marking does not seem to make a strong case for the appeal of these products to foreign audiences. The Hong Kong example demonstrates how concepts of novelty and leisure associated with J-pop, rather than cultural identity, boosted J-pop sales in the 1980s and1990s. The success of *anime* themes is similarly associated with lifestyle trends rather than Japanese-ness as traditionally imagined by both Japanese and foreigners. Film soundtracks, on the other hand, seem to rely on "Japanese-ness," or at least "Asian-ness," in attracting foreign audiences, although their appeal is mainly critical than popular. Japanese music overseas presents a double-edged image: one side is associated with a middle class or upper middle class lifestyle that includes consumerism as leisure and a high level of technology; the other is a more elegant Japan that is either fused with other classical cultures (Asian or Western) to give it an identifying anchor.

In each of the cases presented in this chapter – the musical construction of Japanese music past and present, the construction of cultural identity through place, the image of Japan outside Japan – the definition of "Japanese culture" is constructed, marketed, and consumed in a continuum. Elements of that identity can be found in a variety of contemporary Japanese music, but its "Japanese-ness" is not always solely attributed to a linear ethnomusicology but to influences that include the West, Asia, and other nonmainstream Japanese cultures.

Though to what extent the "Japanese-ness" of Japanese popular music has been, and will be, appreciated by audiences in Japan and overseas is difficult to measure and will be debated by scholars and fans for years to come. This chapter may not have arrived at a neat, linear theory of the development of "authentic" Japanese cultural identity in popular music, but it has asked some important questions that force us to refine our observations of cultural identity in popular music. The argument for rejecting a theory of linear cultural identity is put most eloquently not by a scholar but by composer and performer Hosono Haruomi (fellow member of Sakamoto Ryûichi in the 1980s band, the Yellow Magic Orchestra). He contrasts "traditional" Japanese music like *gagaku* as something explicitly and linearly China-influenced, while Japanese pop music is defined in a more aptly postmodern manner:

> Japan is insular as well as continental. It is ambiguous . . . The prototypes of Japanese *kayokyoku* may have something to do with Korea as is shown by *enka* . . . The other strain comes from the western continent. As its route passes through China and the Silk Road, the music is given European melody,

> mixed up with French Chinoiserie. This music is carried to the America continent by Columbus, then finally to Japan.
>
> (cited and translated by Hosokawa 1999b: 121)

In other words, cultural identity in Japanese popular music has flowed in and out of history, filtered by both Asian and Western cultures; then, after European styles were transplanted in the United States, it was later delivered to the Japanese postwar mass culture as an American product. Music does not travel in a linear pattern from West to East; it travels from East to West, and back to East again, with further trips back to the West, a conscious hybridity that spans both categories.

Hosono continues:

> The flavour of the [Eurasian] continent which the Silk Road transverses, sophisticated Parisian elegance, Spanish passion, African energy, the marine flavor of the Caribbean, all of them are cooked up in a stew. Then this stew gets taken to America, the inclusive, all-embracing continent, where the final spices are added. Then, after, I wonder "What will happen if I add one more spice?"
>
> (cited and translated by Hosokawa 1999b: 123)

Hosono's "one more spice" can be seen as his own particular "Japanese" element, but it is an integrated part of a whole. I believe the extent to which that final touch is interpreted as the defining element depends on the perspective of the listener. One person may take for granted the finishing touches and focus on the "Parisian" or "African" bases. Another may find the European or African elements ordinary and focus on the "marine flavor." The cultural mix will be distorted and reinterpreted depending on the listener's perspective.

Defining musical culture is a difficult project complicated by gaps between etic and emic viewpoints. In a study of Japanese musicians (often the most discerning of audiences), Mathews found that their perception of "Japanese-ness" as a category was exclusive, but its aesthetic could be identified and appreciated by non-Japanese (Mathews 2004: 339, 341). At the same time, the concept of Japanese-ness itself is a "myth" (344) partly because the musicians he interviewed could not agree on whether or not it existed in Japanese jazz or rock, let alone what it meant (345). Due to individual interpretations of music, even within the same national category, culture in contemporary Japanese music (even if all agreed that it did exist) was not something that could be defined simply and absolutely. It is possible that the Japanese musicians, by virtue of being Japanese, had more difficulty in determining the boundaries of cultural identity. Due to the essentializing tendency of the foreign perspective, Japanese popular music is more easily identified and consumed by the members of an "out group." For example, Witzleben notes that Japanese musical traditions are frequently cited by authors of cross-cultural comparisons as some how especially representative of non-Western music (1997: 225). Even if musicians and scholars cannot agree on precisely what "Japanese-ness" is in music, they seem to agree that it is definitely *not* Western.

Where does that leave us in Hosono's "stew"? "Japanese popular music" is a concept that can include structural definitions of music, but it is also integrated with abstract and blurred notions of national character that are filtered through prewar and postwar constructions of identity. These aesthetic elements, historical records, and created mythologies – and the social values connected to them – are part of the process of setting boundaries of cultural identity in music.

3 The particulars of history

> [P]op songs open the door to dream, lend a voice to what is left unmentioned by ordinary discourse. But pop is not only a dream machine: perhaps, like witchcraft in another age, it is the unofficial chronicle of its times, a history of desires existing in the margins of official history, which, except at rare moments of rupture, do not speak but act.
>
> (Hennion 1990: 205)

Introduction

The overarching theme of positional power that informs in this chapter arises from Japan's primary postwar historical experience: its relationship to the United States, which is seen as the leader of the global construct, "the West." By analyzing Japan's cultural identity with respect to this relationship, we can see that the history of popular music strongly reflects Japan's cultural positioning vis-à-vis the "West." This shift in position of Japan's cultural identity can be explained as a shift from the identity as a "conquered" nation to that of "customer" in a competitive global market. This chapter accounts for some of the major developments in postwar Japanese popular music, but it is a selective history, as one chapter cannot capture all the achievements of Japanese musicians in the postwar era. Therefore, I focus specifically on the notion of positionality, both with reference to Japan's relationship to the US and the positions of power that rise within Japan's postwar popular music industry.

Beginnings: prewar popular music

There were many social transformations that shaped Japan's prewar and wartime culture, but the most salient was a high level of migration from the country to industrial urban centers (Yano 1998: 247). Prewar popular music projected a new "modernity," which was always associated with these cities. Modernity was alternately praised and disparaged in lyrics that appealed to both alienated migrants and disgruntled city natives. At this time, we see a shift in what is termed as "national" popular music. Regional songs (*minyô*) constituted a seemingly distant but idealized cultural identity, but urban songs came to be associated with a unified national identity concerned with contemporary issues of modernization.

The genre that flourished in the pre-war and wartime era were jazz and the blues, and popular songs in minor scales and "Japanese style melodies" (Take 1999: 20) – in other words, *hôgaku*-influenced *kayôkyoku* (see Chapter 2). Live performances and sheet music were the main pathways for consumption; it would be years before the hit would be associated with a single singer's face or musical style. Songs could be performed on stage by any person at any particular time; because of this, the song was the star rather than the performer. The shift from song to performer foreshadows further shifts later in the century, as the producer takes the spotlight. These changes were primarily instigated through the reach and the power of the media, which allowed postwar audiences to consume by larger groups of people: through recordings, and radio and television, which were more far-reaching than the concert stage.

The early years

The Allied Occupation of Japan (1945–1952): its occurrence is arguably the single most important military, political, financial, and cultural event in Japanese modern history. By transforming the constitution, economy, and social structures, the Allies intended to do away with militarism or "feudalism" of Imperial Japan and replace it with notions of "democracy." The Occupation controlled the mass media by which they disseminated ideas about "democracy," including concepts of "freedom" and individual rights. Prewar *hôgaku*, such as *gunka* (military songs) that harked back to Japan's military past, was censored. This is not the first time that Japanese audiences had their popular music regulated by the government. In the early 1940s, US pop and jazz was banned, as well as any Japanese songs that used Western-style instruments such as guitars (Yano 2002: 37–38). Even "sad" songs were repressed to prevent the public from becoming too melancholic (38). In the first few years of the Occupation, *yôgaku* (at this time, this meant music imported from the West, as well as Japanese music in the Western style) was predominant in the 1950s and 1960s (Kawabata 1991: 335; Wade 2005: 134) as it was thought to possess desirable qualities for the new era: it was bright, light, and "modern." This was not the first time Japanese society had accepted foreign popular culture; Meiji and Taishô cultures had also been influenced by North America and Europe, but Japan under the Occupation was on a new coerced and clear path to "democratic" consumer society as defined by the Occupation's policies.

The first major postwar hit was "*Ringo no Uta*" (Apple Song) by Namiki Michiko, a performer who had lost her home and her mother in the Tokyo Air Raids (Take 1999: 15–16). Released by Columbia Records in January 1946, it was the theme song for the first postwar film released by Shôchiku Studios. Tansman describes it as a "lighter, Western melod[y] of hope" (1996: 109), despite its minor mode. Hosokawa uses more graphic terms to describe the song as "tied to the vivid memories" of the "fire devastated black market" (*yakeato yamiichi*). (1997: 1) The song resembled prewar styles in its instrumentation (ibid.) but used American-style vocal production. Furthermore, its scale, though minor, was not pentatonic (Yano 2002: 39). Take hypothesizes that the record's relatively low sales figures were not related to low public demand but were due to the record company's inability to produce large quantities because of a dearth of raw materials (1999: 16). To demonstrate the relative costs involved, he lists the cost of "*Ringo no Uta*" as seventeen and a half yen; an apple cost between three and five yen, while an average salaried worker's monthly salary was 300 yen (16–17).

The US soldiers brought with them jazz, boogie-woogie, and country and western records; soon Japanese musicians were imitating these styles in nightclubs that bordered the military bases. Songs such as Kasagi Shizuka's "*Tôkyô Bugiugi*" (Tokyo Boogie Woogie) were characteristic of the initial postwar reaction to Western pop culture. This hit spawned numerous "boogie" copies – Hakata, Osaka, Hokkaido, Nagoya, Ôshima, and other regional areas in Japan soon had their own "boogies" on the radio (Take 1999: 23). "*Tôkyô Bugiugi*" (Tokyo Boogie Woogie), composed by Hattori Ryôichi with lyrics by Suzuki Katsu, was released in 1948. Hattori's success with this single launched a composing career which led him to be called one of "the fathers of Japanese pops."

The lyrics of "Tokyo Boogie Woogie", according to Tansman, were frenetically joyous (1996: 110), perhaps as a distraction to the hardships of immediate postwar life, which included struggles with food shortages and disease. In 1946, Japanese consumers spent 70.2 percent of their expendable income on food, an intensive investment in the most basic human need, showing the scarcity and value of nutrition during this period (Fujioka 1993: 266). In the winter of 1945–1946, 1000 people died of typhus (Seidensticker 1991: 156) and many other Tokyo citizens died of malnutrition, exposure, and other illnesses such as smallpox, cholera, and pneumonia (158). Yet the producers of popular culture at that time chose not to dwell on the realistic pains of real life. This was no time to sing the blues, wrote composer Hattori: "We must go forward with bright rhythms (*akarui rizumu de iku beki da*)" (Take 1999: 18). This is not to say that the Japanese nation suffered from mass amnesia and/or blind optimism regarding the hardships of war and the early reconstruction period; due to the political situation at the time, it seems as if they had little other choice but to charge ahead.

The 1950s: on the road to recovery

American jazz during the Occupation was considered a mainstream genre. American-style jazz had been popular in the prewar era, but it exploded in Japan directly after the war, spreading from the bases to the urban areas. Jazz was still a major genre in the 1960s and early 1970s. The jazz coffee shop (*jazzu kissaten* or *jazzu kissa*), still found today especially near university campuses, was established in this period. In these cafes, the customer may sit for hours over a single cup of coffee while the owner acts as DJ, playing usually American jazz from the 1950s and 1960s. Hosokawa claims that the *jazzu kissa* of the 1950s were the predecessors of today's "live houses" (small- to medium-size night clubs which feature rock, pop, hip-hop, and any other genre that has an audience) (1997: 2). Murakami Haruki, a best-selling author in Japan today, owned a *jazzu kissa* before settling into a writing career, and his work is frequently sprinkled with references to American jazz from the early postwar era.

In the 1950s, rockabilly replaced boogie-woogie as the newest genre. Country and western had also been also a popular music genre emanating from US military bases. Related to "hillbilly" music (or white American folk music), country and western often employed imagery such as the lone country boy disillusioned by city ways, and this was, despite the expected cultural distance between the two cultures, very appealing to Japanese urban migrant audiences.[1] Country and western came to Occupied Japan primarily via the film industry, through American westerns shown in cinemas across the country. Kosaka Kazuya was one of the first Japanese rockabilly stars. His 1956 cover of Elvis' "Heartbreak Hotel" was one of that year's biggest hits, bringing American rock and roll into the Japanese pop scene mainstream. He supported his record sales through appearing in Hollywood-esque "westerns" that featured other Japanese rockabilly groups as well. Rockabilly utilized electric guitars from the rock and roll tradition, as opposed to acoustic guitars that were associated with country and western. At that time, music production was focused on genre rather than individuals; for example, concerts were advertised as featuring "rockabilly singers" or "jazz performers" rather than under the individuals' names (Take 1999: 71). Still, performers such as Hirao Masaaki, Mickey Curtis (a pseudonym), and Yamashita Keijirô were successful enough to merit the nickname "The Three Rockabilly Men" (Hosokawa 1997: 2; Takahashi 1993: 9–10). The popularity of rockabilly and country and western-inspired Japanese pop fell off in early 1960s, falling away from the mainstream as Beatles' inspired rock and roll swept the nation.[2]

Jazz and rockabilly were not the only widespread genre: Hawaiian and Latin American music (in particular, bossa nova) were also popular in the 1960s, adding to the international flavor of the Japanese scene. The 1959 single "Tokyo Night Club," a duet from "Frank" Nagai (Kiyoto) and Matsuo Kazuko, displays a soft Latin beat beneath a minor melody familiar to *kayôkyoku* listeners. Nagai had sung for years in US military base nightclubs, singing mostly jazz with little success until he switched to *kayôkyoku* and recorded this hit with Victor Records.

No discussion of the 1950s Japanese popular music would be complete with out reference to Misora Hibari, known as the "queen of *kayôkyoku*" (Kitagawa 1991: 306). Her career spanned four decades, making it difficult to categorize her overall influence on popular music to only one postwar decade and genre. She debuted as an adolescent in 1949 imitating Kasugi's boogie style; she also sang country and western in the early days, to varied audience responses, but her portrayal of a sweet but tough orphan in the musical film *Tokyo Kid* (1950) endeared her to mass audiences. Later, she eschewed modern developments in Japanese popular music and became more closely associated with *enka*.

One of her trademarks was weeping at the end of songs (Yano 2002: 121), a practice that set a standard for sentimentalism in performance not only in early *kayôkyoku* and *enka* but also later on for idol singers in the1980s. After Misora, emotional expression in pop music was an important part of musicianship. Tears were proof of authentic emotion, considered equal or even superior to musical talent. One of her most emotive performances is the song "*Ringo Oiwake*" (Apple Melody, 1952, lyrics by Ozawa Fujio and music by Yoneyama Masao). Compared to the more American big band sound of "Tokyo Kid," "*Ringo Oiwake*" is firmly rooted in the Japanese modal and vocal tradition, while a Western flute provides an introductory flourish. Misora's spoken soliloquy in the middle of song is in the now-classic migrant mode, reminiscing about the peach and cherry blossoms of the northern Aomori Prefecture. At the end of the spoken section, an analogy between the fallen blossoms and family members who died during the Tokyo Air Raids certainly creates an emotional moment for the audience as well. Thought of as the "symbol of post-war Japan" (Yano 2002: 121), Misora's emotive style carved a permanent niche for her in *kayôkoku* and *enka* history, before succumbing to cancer in 1989.

Lastly, the 1950s saw the establishment of the *mochiuta* system, which closely tied songs to individual singers, signaling the beginning of the modern star system. Musical production companies expanded their influence over the creative process: they oversaw composition, recording, and promotion as well as managing the artists' careers (Yano 2002: 40). This centralization of control made it easy for songs (and songwriters) to be strongly associated with certain performers, record labels, and even media (like making appearances on certain television channels). When the main object of music consumption became the record (with a photograph of the singer on the sleeve) rather than sheet music (which featured the composer and lyricist above the performer's name), the connection between the song and the singer's image was solidified and reinforced by the later developments in music television programming.

The 1960s: "Made in Japan"

In the early 1960s, a more mature Japanese pop sound emerged: more than a cover, it was a sentimental yet playful genre of pop music that integrated American style with Japanese sensibility.[3] *Wasei* pop, or "Made-in-Japan pop," spread throughout Japan, thanks to the proliferation of the newest format for listening music: television.

The emblematic performer of this new era – and outstanding in Japanese postwar popular musical history as the only Japanese singer to achieve a number one record in the US charts – is Sakamoto Kyû (1941–1985). Born into a large family in Kawasaki city south of Tokyo (his first name means "nine"), Sakamoto was sent to his maternal country home in Ibaraki prefecture to escape the air raids. Gaining experience singing in local nightclubs, he scored his first record contract in 1959. Sakamoto's first public success was as the lead vocalist for the Paradise Kings, a rockabilly group, but he rose to worldwide stardom as a sentimental solo artist. After conquering the nation and the world with his music, he receded from the public eye in the late 1970s and early 1980s. Just before his rumored "comeback," in August 1985, Sakamoto was one of the hundreds tragically killed in the JAL Flight 123 crash.

Sakamoto had numerous hits, but he will be best remembered for "*Ue o Muite Arukô*" (literally, "I'll Walk On, Looking Up," but often referred to in English by its American release title, "Sukiyaki"). This, as were many of his hits, was composed by Sakamoto's songwriting team, Ei Rokusuke and Nakamura Hachidai, who penned numerous songs for him.[4] "*Ue o Muite Arukô*" was initially released in Japan in December 1961, and sold well. An American jazz musician heard it in Japan and recorded a cover of the song on a US label; after its moderate success, American audiences were then introduced to Sakamoto's original version. Sakamoto's single reached number one in the United States and number six in the United Kingdom in 1963 and achieved significant sales in Germany. Its global success is often attributed to its "*kayôkyoku*-like" melodic construction, sounding "Western" to the Japanese audience; yet, because it relied partially on pentatonic scales, it was exotic to Western listeners (Kitagawa 1993: 122–123). Yet "a borrowed chord in its bridge, ABAA form and rhythmic pulses, and moreover, [no] fixed verse form" sounded familiar to American fans (Kitagawa 1991: 306).

Sakamoto's success abroad was no less impressive than his domestic accomplishments. His impish face, twisting from comedy to tragedy in a flash, loved the television camera, and he appeared frequently on the music variety shows that were on the rise. He and performers such as the Peanuts (a female duo of identical twins), Ueki Hitoshi and the Crazy Cats, and Nakao Mie appeared regularly on shows such as *Shabondama Horidê* (Soap Bubble Holiday; NTV, 1961–1972) and *Yume de Aimashô* (Let's meet in a dream; NHK, 1961–1966). These shows featured not only music but also dance and comedy, giving the Japanese public a diversified image of musical talent.[5] In particular, the *wasei* pop artists appealed to a growing sector of the Japanese population: urban white-collar workers and their families, who were avid consumers of home electronics associated with music (Yoshimi 1999).

Another notable example of early 1960s' *wasei* pop, the 1961 song *Sûdarabushi* (translated loosely as "Gliding Melody") by Ueki and the Crazy Cats, utilizes self-mockery as a comic device. This song is a self-mocking tribute to a "typical" businessman trying in vain to keep up with the hectic pace of the postwar economic boom. If Sakamoto Kyû were the boy next door whom one could meet in a dream, the Crazy Cats were the harried office workers down the street. They appeared regularly on *Shabondama Horidê*; even the title of this show communicated a certain irony without any sharp anger that could alienate audiences. The harried salary man dreamed of a holiday, no matter how fragile it might be. One can, with the benefit of hindsight, comment on the aptness of this metaphor for the salaried male office worker, for when the Japanese economic machine slowed, it was popularly referred to as the "burst of the bubble economy."

Diversification of genre: between pop, rock, and folk

Before the 1960s, popular singers, like Sakamoto, generally performed with orchestra or jazz-style accompaniments. The electric guitar had been featured in rockabilly, but it was much more widely used after the Ventures' records were first imported to Japan in 1960 (Takahashi 1993: 28). The Ventures' 1965 Japanese concert tour set off the *ereki bûmu*, or the electric boom, and thereafter electric guitars in ensemble became the standard format by which pop music was produced (Hosokawa 1997: 3). The electric guitar's place in public imagination was solidified by the Beatles' 1966 concert at the Budôkan, then Tokyo's premiere venue. The Beatles highly publicized performance was important in shaping the Japanese perception of popular culture and perhaps, more significantly, their self-perception in the international community. Events such as the Tokyo Olympics and the opening of the *Shinkansen* high-speed "bullet" train in 1964 and the Beatles' Japan Tour 1966 demonstrated to the rest of the world that Japan had fully recovered from defeat and was prepared to host the world's best athletes and musicians with top-level technology and facilities.

Many Japanese groups began imitating the Ventures' and the Beatles' styles and creating the *ereki* (electric) sound. Groups such as the Terauchi Takeshi and the Blue Jeans, the Tigers, the Spiders, and the Blue Comets usually consisted of two or more electric guitars, an electric bass, an electric organ, and the drums. These bands primarily performed instrumentals, but they also accompanied solo singers on television. After its initial popularity, the wider Japanese public regarded music associated with the electric guitar with suspicion because of its wild and possibly delinquent symbolic meanings (Kitagawa 1991: 311). Hosokawa hypothesizes that one of the reasons for the demise of the 1960s "electric boom" was the tightening of restrictions for youth music events due to increasing fears concerning juvenile delinquency; another reason could have been related to the shift in taste from instrumental music to vocal-centered music (Personal communication 1998). Those who survived the electric boom went on to establish a new genre known as Group Sounds, sometimes abbreviated as "GS"; basically, this was an electric boom group "plus one" (a vocalist). The Blue Comets, the Tigers, and the Tempters were arguably the more successful of the GSs bands; they had started during the electric boom but graduated on to GS because they added singers to their lineups. The Tigers' vocalist, Sawada Kenji, was particularly charismatic and attracted a great deal of female fan attention. Though the Tempters wrote some of their own songs, most of the GS groups hired professional composers attached to record companies to write hits for them; this was, however, standard practice for nearly all popular artists and groups at that time. "*Emerarudo no Densetsu*" (The Emerald Legend, 1968) was the Tempters' biggest hit and combines a romantic vocal against crisp percussion and electric guitars backed with strings; its guitar displays a clean melodic line, making the overall impression of the song as being melodic rather than rhythmic, and thus more acceptable to mainstream audiences (and their parents).

Folk music in the 1960s in Japan mirrored developments in the United States, in the tradition of Joan Baez, Peter Paul and Mary, and Bob Dylan. Instead of the "wild" electric guitar, folk singers played acoustic guitars that were less expensive and thus more accessible to amateurs who could participate in the movement with a minimum investment. Takahashi writes that folk music represented a new defining era in popular music: it was music that people "did," rather than just listened to, and this had an enormous impact on the way audiences viewed their relationship to popular music in the coming decades (1993: 57).[6] In other words, popular music became a leisure activity that amateurs could take part in through production, rather than just consumption. Mike Maki, Moriyama Ryôko, and Broadside Four were some of the more memorable "*wasei fôku*" ("Made-in-Japan Folk") acts of the mid-to-late 1960s. The arrangement of Maki's 1966 single "*Bara ga Saita*" (A Rose Bloomed) sounds spare, but clear and clean with its acoustic guitar and bass, taking student-oriented folk into the mainstream spotlight (Takahashi 1993: 56). At first, folk had a "feminine" image, with its soft acoustics and gentle rhythms as in "*Bara ga Saita*," but in the latter part of the 1960s, Japanese folk branched into the male domain after the releases of Takaishi Tomoya and Takada Wataru who sang about young people's disillusionment with socioeconomic inequality (Hosokawa 1997: 4). Folk became more "protest" oriented, with artists signed to the record label "URC" ("Underground Record Club"), established in 1969 by Takaishi and others. URC, later acquired by Apex, can be considered one of Japan's first "independent," artist-run labels.

The folk boom in Japan culminated in the three-day Nakatsugawa Folk Jamboree in 1969. Three thousand fans attended, making it the largest musical gathering at that time. But in its success were seeds of its demise. Part of its public appeal was its authentic concern for social and political solutions to serious problems in contemporary Japan; yet with commercial success came a weakening of that "authentic" connection, and folk came to be perceived as merely another "style" for the consumer. Another issue was factionalism within the protest movement and its association with students and campus life; the protest music associated with a crumbling student movement then lost wider appeal.[7]

During the folk boom, a reorientation of the power relations in the popular music industry began; these were fully integrated into mainstream pop music in the 1970s. Some GS performers were writing their own music, and so too were the folk singers. As previously noted, in the 1940s, 1950s, and early 1960s, composers and performers occupied separate spheres in the music industry. Often the composer was more powerful because singers were more easily replaced. Partnerships between composers and singers were common – the *Hachi Roku Kyû* trio is one, for example – but the relationship was seldom equal. Folk singers were some of the first figures presented to the public as self-supported amateur performers, not carefully groomed "professionals." Changes in the quality of the relationships between performers and producers would continue to fruition in the 1970s with "New Music."

Interlude: the split between kayôkyoku *and* enka

Before the mid-1960s, all "popular" music was called *kayôkyoku* (see Chapter 2). The increasing diversification of this *kayôkyoku* (from American-style pop to rock and roll and folk), however, meant that the original term's meaning became diluted. Performers and audiences who did not feel at ease with the new cultural trends needed a new rubric to express their identity in the music scene, and thus created *enka*. "*Enka*" came into use in the latter half of the 1960s, although the actual word has roots in nineteenth-century political movements (Fujie 1989: 207; Hosokawa 1997: 9; Nakamura 1991: 270–272). In the early postwar era, *enkashi*, or *enka* performer, was used to describe street musicians accompanied by a guitar or accordion. *Enka* was not necessarily a "new" style; Yano calls the conscious creation of *enka* "genre-izing" and labels it an "invented tradition," an "industry-determined cultural product" (2002: 41). Music was created in order to sound "old," relying on prewar imaginings of *ryûkôka* to inspire its composition and performance.

Enka arose in reaction to Japanese pop, and perhaps also as a reaction to the wider Western presence in popular culture, as symbolized not only by the electric guitar but also by fashion such as long hair and miniskirts.

> By the early 1970s the word *enka* came to be used by the media to describe a genre of popular music that filled a musical void for people not young enough to feel comfortable with rock and folk derivatives in Japan and who demanded their own music.
>
> (Wade 2005: 149)

Yet *enka* relies in part on a Western musical background. Though it frequently utilizes Japanese scales (such as the *yonanuki*), *enka* instrumentation comprises mainly of electric guitars and bass, drums and strings. *Enka* is usually slow to medium tempo, in a minor key with a soft rhythm, and utilizes traditional Japanese vocal techniques such as *kobushi* (Hosokawa 1997: 9). Lyrically, *enka* speaks most directly to culturally specific ideals such as the *furusato* (or "home"), nationality, and morality. Sentimentality, lost love, and drink are popular themes. Frequently, regional centers figure into *enka* imagery, using the migrant to cities such as Tokyo or Osaka as a frequent trope. Yano has argued that *enka* represents a longing for *furusato*: a nostalgic yearning for the simple country life in the face of a dreary urban reality (2002: 19–22). Other *kayôkyoku* artists such as the Crazy Cats too poked jest at the new urban lifestyle, but returning to the countryside was never an option for them; in contrast, *enka* singers sang of an idealized Japanese rural life that was always waiting for them.

Well-known *enka* singers such as Miyako Harumi, Ishikawa Sayuri, Mori Shin'ichi, and Kitajima Saburô have enjoyed long and respected careers, partly due to stable fan bases and partly because they can claim a wide public acceptance as the vanguard of Japanese tradition, both culturally and psychologically. Despite the high visibility of female *enka* performers such as Miyako and Ishikawa, Hosokawa notes that *enka* is primarily a male production category, with a majority of male composers and lyricists (1997: 9). In other words, this cultural tradition is primarily produced by men, yet is performed by both men and women. Not surprisingly, female imagery in *enka* is conservative and traditional. This supports the idea from Chapter 2 that women represent the "gatekeepers of tradition" in Japanese popular as well as traditional music.

Enka's popularity, at least as measured by sales and karaoke requests, can be viewed as under pressure. The year 1997 was the first year that an *enka* song was not featured in a national top ten list of numbers requested at karaoke bars. Conversely, *enka* still features prominently in each year's New Year's Eve Singing Contest on the Japanese national network NHK and is enjoyed as symbolic of Japanese cultural identity during a traditional holiday. For the rest of the year, however, this genre is increasingly associated with a diminishing audience.

The 1970s: music "anew"

Bands that emerged in the 1970s were called the "new rock" movement (*nyû rokku*). If group sounds represented "commercialism," new rockers strived for "authenticity" (Hosokawa 1997: 5).[8] There were generally two types of new rockers: those who sang in English, striving for complete cultural authenticity, and those who sang in Japanese. *Happii Endo* (Happy End), a band who sang in Japanese, released their first album in 1970 and set a standard for the rest of the Japanese rock musicians to follow in the new decade. Happy End's members were Hosono Haruomi, Ohtaki Eichi, Matsumoto Takashi, and Suzuki Shigeru. Their self-titled debut album represents a sophisticated assimilation of Western rock with Japanese sentiment and cultural symbolism. "*Haru Yo Koi*" (Come, Spring!) (1970), the opening number of their debut album, melds the two cultural sources into a hybrid piece. The instrumentation is pure bluesy folk-rock, *à la* Crosby, Stills, Nash and Young. The title is a classic Japanese phrase, and the lyrics tell of a young man's loneliness at during the New Year holiday, the most important event in the Japanese ritual calendar. As he hears the temple bell ring (and we do as well, in the background), his thoughts stray to his family, celebrating without him. Though Happy End broke up in 1973, this band's work is regarded as classic in the new rock *oeuvre*, and its members went on to produce important work in the 1980s and 1990s.

Hosokawa writes that the breakup of Happy End marked the start of "new music," but this was not just about style but also made reference to the production process as well:

> After the break-up of Happii Endo each of the four musicians developed their own independent styles, thereby contributing to the creation of a sophisticated pop genre, *Nyû Myûjikku* (New Music) in the 1970s. This genre broke away from the traditional music industry separation of the duties of the composer, lyricist, arranger, sound engineer, and singer, since the musicians involved could take on all of these roles.
>
> (1999b: 120)

Thus we can see that New Music had more than just musical roots in the folk movement: in both genres, performers assumed some of the disparate roles in the production process. To others, however, they were merely folk singer/songwriters who went "commercial," popularizing their generally soft, acoustic sound for larger audiences. Yoshida Takurô and Minami Kôsetsu (of the group *Kaguyahime*) were two folk singers who attracted wider audiences. Their brand of pop/folk has been nominated as the foundation for New Music (Fujie 1989: 9). By 1975, *Nyû Myûjikku* was the term in use to describe songs that varied from folk to pop to rock; the only thing they shared was a new sensibility for the interaction between the music and the musician. They wrote their own songs and presented the music in an authentic, accessible manner. New Music, though sensitive and authentic, was still commercial: Inoue Yôsui became the first *hôgaku* million-selling artist with his 1974 album *The World of Ice* (Kawabata 1991: 338). Yoshida crossed further commercial audience boundaries, composing a folk – *enka* song entitled "*Erimo Misaki*" (*misaki* means "cape"; Erimo is a town on the southern coast of Hokkaido), which was a huge hit for the *enka* artist Mori Shin'ichi in 1974.

Fujie notes that there is no one musical style that encompasses the New Music movement, but its focus on melody and "introspective" lyrics (1989: 209) was the key to its success. Both male and female listeners could identify with new music stars and project their own readings of the singers' messages. In 1978, 40 percent of total album sales in Japan were classified as new music (ibid.). Others have focused on the feminine face of New Music, citing Matsutôya (*née* Arai) Yumi, Yoshida Minako, and Yano Akiko (married to Sakamoto Ryûichi) as "representative" of the genre (Anderson 2002: 349). I would include here Nakajima Miyuki, who debuted in 1975, as a singer-songwriter whose introspective and personal lyrics have earned her devoted fans over her thirty-year career, though her "darker," moodier lyrics set her apart from the lighter, sophisticated sound of Matsutôya. Anderson's focus on female figures such as Matsutôya, Yoshida, and Yano echoes Hosokawa's definition which explicitly links New Music to New Rock, in that he notes the backing band for these female artists (as well as New Music icon Yamashita Tatsurô), Caramel Mama/Tin Pan Alley, consisted of ex-Happy End members, suggesting that Happy End despite its short career had truly far-reaching effects on the postwar Japanese music industry.[9]

Whether folk or rock, male or female, "dark" or "light," these performers shared a crucial characteristic: they were songwriters in their own right, so they did not have to rely on the production team of talent agencies for compositions. Furthermore, they were able to produce themselves (or produce each other), allowing them artistic and some financial independence from the mainstream "show biz" industry, which tended to be organized vertically, or *iemoto* style. These artists were not "manufactured" stars, but authentic musicians, not dissimilar to the immediate attraction offered by 1960s and 1970s folk performers. They also utilized television and radio in new ways (e.g., the tie-up song) to achieve commercial success in ways others had not. Furthermore, performers in the new genre appeared to be not so vulnerable to consumer trends, giving them a veneer of artistic authenticity and honesty. This was due to a well-established fan base, a general independence from trends in the larger music scene, and their ability to be active in other areas of the industry (such as writing hits for or producing other singers). Some artists went on to create their own record labels, such as Yoshida's For Life Records, which he created with Inoue, Izumiya Shigeru, and other stars from the folk scene, consolidating their power in the business. One of their early releases, "*Yume Ichiya*" (All Night Dream) (1978), was a huge hit for Minami Kôsetsu as a CM tie-up song for the cosmetic company Shiseido. New Music musicians (and For Life executives) took advantage of television immediately (Ugaya 2005b: 69, 71), and the complementary relationship, discussed in detail in Chapter 4, between the music, television, and product advertising industries was born.

Despite vigorously promoting their music through product affiliation on television, Japanese pop, folk, and New Music artists often refrained from appearing on music television variety shows personally. In the early 1970s, there was a divide between artists who had previously been put together in one genre (when folk and New Music were not yet distinguishable). Yoshida, Inoue, and a few members of *Kaguyahime* refused invitations to appear on television while their peers Horiuchi Takao (of the folk group *Arisu*), Minami (of *Kaguyahime*), and Yazawa Eikichi did. In the 1970s, New Music presented on television took on the identifying mark of "commercial"; meanwhile, music consumed off-screen was considered "artistic and creative" (Ugaya 2005b: 70). These off-screen artists were called "*shingâ songuraitâ*" (singer-songwriter) rather than the generic Japanese term *kashu* (singer), creating a new, "cool" image for young audiences (71). This is not to say that singer-songwriters did not take advantage of the promotional profits that television offered; they merely chose to promote themselves using objects or products (through commercials) rather than their subjective bodies (through performances on music variety or other talk shows).

Television reticence has served some New Music artists well. Matsutôya Yumi, cited by Anderson as emblematic of the genre, uses television to promote her music without appearing herself, allowing her work to achieve commercial success while still maintaining artistic integrity. Yuming debuted in 1969 as a teenage songwriter for another performer; she was only 19 when her first album, *Hikôki Gumo* (Jetstream), was released in 1973. In 1975, she married her producer, Matsutôya Masataka, and has taken his name since. Though she almost never makes appearances on television, she writes many themes for television dramas and commercials, starting with the 1975 hit "*Ano Hi ni Kaeritai*" (I Want to Return to the Past). She also appears regularly on radio shows, a strategy similar to that of her female New Music colleague Nakajima Miyuki. Mark Anderson writes that her preference for nonpolitical themes and blurring the lines between her public and private lives by working with her husband has been criticized as perhaps a typically female "a move from the public to the private sphere" (2002: 305).

In any case, New Music stars show wide variety in the interpretation of their genre. With such loosely defined musical boundaries, consumption patterns may be a better indicator of New Music's definition as a genre. Many New Music stars maintain loyal fan bases, which rely on the loyalty mature fans supplemented by new recruits. The long careers of Yuming, the Southern All Stars, Oda Kazumasa (formerly of Off Course) and the Alfee, amongst others, owe much to ongoing, stable fan bases. These artists continued to score chart hits in the 1990s and beyond, illustrating the influence New Music has had on postwar Japanese popular music.

The 1980s: idols, rock, and techno-pop

The 1980s represented the fulfillment of the postwar Occupation; many people felt at this time that Japan had reached the final stage of reconstruction. There was no more "catching up" to do with the West. Because products were readily available and within most consumers' reach, consumer trends shifted away from *objectivity* (practical objects for daily use) to *subjectivity* (psychological concepts) (Ugaya 2005b: 154). Previously, struggling consumers strived for a lifestyle full of "things" (*mono*), but in the 1980s, "things" were abundant, so consumers looked to express their "heart" (*kokoro*) with their purchases (ibid.). The music industry too reflected this popular desire to find emotional expression (primarily through ideal concepts such as "beauty," and "authenticity" or "sincerity") in the public "*kokoro.*"

From the Western standpoint, *aidoru* or "idol" music from the 1980s remains one of the most widely recognized (and criticized) genre of postwar Japanese popular music. Perhaps this is because this was the time when the West started to pay attention to developments in Japanese popular culture, most likely related to Japan's increasing economic presence in the international stage and the fact there were a few isolated attempts to export early pop idols such as Pink Lady to the US market in the late 1970s. But the most commonly discussed aspect of Japanese popular music overseas was not how these acts were perceived in the American market. Rather, overseas critics were more interested in the way young female singers were presented in the Japanese market. Although there were many young women performers in the 1970s who permeated the Japanese mass media in unprecedented ways – Yamaguchi Momoe, Mori Masako, and Sakurada Junko as well as groups like Pink Lady and the Candies – the juxtaposition of personality, fashion image, music, and commercialism, however, became more firmly "genre-ized" in the 1980s, becoming a clear subcategory of *kayôkyoku* in this period. The definition of this role (as opposed to a vocalist, a guitarist, or a "singer-songwriter") is a complex one. Like New Music, idol styles were varied. Some categorized idols by the kind of music they performed ("forgettable bubblegum pop" [Clewley, 1994: 143]), their looks ("cute"), and their age (teenaged or at least appearing so). But a more inclusive and provocative method of categorization is the performer's level of media saturation. In the 1980s, Japanese idols began the practice of extreme media exposure in the domestic market, which both intensified and limited their success; this continues to define the idol today. In contrast to the self-sufficiency of New Music artists, idols were handpicked in their early teens and groomed by production companies. Idols were, in most cases, expendable and could be exchanged for new individuals without too much audience backlash. Idols did not only sing but also worked as actors, models, talk show hosts, and commercial spokespeople, suggesting that time spent in front of the television camera rather than in the recording studio or the concert hall is the definitive attribute of an idol.

Idols were young (in their early or mid-teens) but more often than not, they looked younger than they were, creating an air of image artificiality. The cute idol was manufactured perfection in many ways, but his or her singing was often less than perfect. This was one of the strategies employed by professionals to humanize this doll-like figure. As most idols' looks were as important as their talent, many were not trained musicians. Complex vocals were not required of the idol performance; a concurrent *karaoke* wave of popularity meant that there was a growing market for hit songs with easy-to-sing melody lines and lyrics. After the split between *kayôkyoku* and *enka*, vocal technique and musicianship came to be associated with the *enka* artists. The idol's method was uncomplicated and easier for the amateur to reproduce, and this helped boost the popularity of *karaoke*. There were both male and female idols, but for many consumers, it was the female idol that personified the 1980s idol craze. Above all, the female idol was cute, childlike, and innocent, or at least she projected such an image. Female fans emulated her; male fans were attracted to her. A set of social practices surrounding pop consumption, institutionalized in the fan club, gave the idol's fandom a palpable quality. In the 1980s, idols achieved new levels of mass media penetration due to the increasing integration of the television and music industries, making the "household name" status of the 1980s idol possible.

Idols were perfect but not out of reach. The dream of becoming a star idol was played out in the audience's living rooms, in shows such as *Yûyake Nyan Nyan* (Fuji TV, 1986–1988). This after-school show featured an all-girl group, *Onyanko* Club, whose members were winners of auditions held with ordinary junior high school students.[10] This show picked up the "girl-next-door-makes-good" theme from the earlier hit television show "Star *Tanjô*" ('A Star Is Born', NTV, 1971–1983, Hori Productions). This "girl-next-door" image was again part of the formula to humanize the idol, and recalls the appeal of the "amateur" gloss associated with a number of Japanese rock and pop movements, such as Japanese folk in the 1960s, and predicts the rock revival to come a few years later. Although most Japanese music critics tended to view folk and rock musicians more favorably when it came to levels of artistic expression, it is possible to consider that these idol singers too held claim to an authentic musical expression through their amateurish performances.

The 1980s was also known as the "bubble period," where the economy was propped up by artificially inflated real estate prices. Like the general economic mood, idol music too glossed over many social problems in the industry and the country in general. Although the Japanese economy was booming, increased competition in the wider educational and employment spheres meant that many young Japanese people were dealing with new pressures, resulting in alienation and delinquency. Delauney believes that the end of the idol period occurred when Okada Yukiko committed suicide in 1985, shattering the image of idol cute perfection (1995: 209). Other idols have had their share of personal scandal; for example, Nakamori Akina struggled as an actress and singer after her suicide attempts and alleged drug use were widely publicized. Matsuda Seiko, perhaps the greatest of all the 1980s idols, has made headlines time after time since her debut in early 1980: scandals included a failed engagement to fellow idol Go Hiromi in 1985, alleged plastic surgery to westernize her appearance, her extra marital affairs, two divorces, her penchant for Chanel, and a 1998 sexual harassment suit brought against her by a male dancer. Despite this publicity, Matsuda remains one of Japan's top-selling female recording artists.

New Music, whether folk or pop based, established itself as mainstream by the late 1970s; the early 1980s was the era of the idol. Against this "pop" backdrop, developments in rock were brewing in reaction to the superficiality of pop music. Artists such as Sano Motoharu, Rebecca, Hound Dog, the Blue Hearts, and Boøwy debuted in the 1980s; their songs were anything but cute. Rather, these songs appealed to the audience's sense of social reality with lyrics about disappointment and struggles in superficially successful and materialistic "bubble" Japan. Sano was noted for using merely the pronouns "she/her" and "he/him" (*kanojo* and *kare* in Japanese) in his lyrics, rather than personal names (e.g., the 1960s tradition of "Carol" and "Paula"), which gave his songs an intimate feel and wide appeal to young audiences. (Takahashi 1993: 140) Even more blunt were the punk rock band, the Blue Hearts. Their 1987 anthem "*Shônen no Shi*" (Poem for Youth) contained a heart-wrenching line that symbolized the angst of a generation: "I don't want to turn into an idiot [*baka*] praised by adults/And so I stood there holding a knife...I stood there holding a knife." The 1980s rock boom acknowledged Japan's social complexity and difficulties in ways that idol music did not, making for a return to "authentic" audience social experience in pop music absent since the early days of the folk movement.

Much like the Ventures-inspired electric boom in the 1960s, the late 1980s saw a rise in rock bands in the "anyone can be in a band" vein (Hosokawa 1997: 10). This band boom consisted of amateur rock-style groups who, with a minimum of investment, managed to receive mainstream attention, "bypassing" the conventional route to commercial exposure (ibid.). The main vehicle for this "bypass" was the television show *Ikasu Bando Tengoku* (loosely translated as Cool Band Heaven) or *Ikaten* (TBS, 1989–1991), as it was commonly called. *Ikaten* promoted many new rock bands that were seen as more authentic and "real" than idols. Each week ten amateur bands were featured; they competed in front of a panel of judges, and the winner was given the title "king." The winners of each show then competed for the position of "grand king," who was awarded a major label recording contract. Some of the bands that gained exposure through this vehicle were FLYING KIDS, Blankey Jet City, Jitterin' Jinn and Tama.

Along with this renewed interest in rock and its authentic expressions came a renewed interest in live performances, especially because of the direct connection it supplied to the audience. RC Succession, which had debuted in 1970 as a folk band, had fallen on tough times, but revived their career as a rock band through acclaimed small-scale live performances in the early 1980s, using make-up and a harder rock style to appeal to new audiences (Take 1999: 227–228). Some of these rockers were affiliated with major labels from the start, yet others began on contracts with minor labels, starting a trend in "independent" music that was to grow later.

Parallel to the developments in idol music and renewed interest in rock in the 1980s was the rise of techno-pop in Japan. The most influential band of the early 1980s was the Yellow Music Orchestra, commonly known as YMO. This band is one of the select elite in Japanese pop to achieve significant international exposure, possibly because of the band's explicit appeal to a Western taste for the Asian exotic. YMO was active from 1979 to 1984 (with a reunion tour in 1993), and its members were experienced musicians: Hosono Haruomi (formerly of Happy End), Sakamoto Ryûichi (no relation to Sakamoto Kyû, he had trained at the prestigious Tokyo National University of Fine Arts and Music), and Takahashi Yukihiro (formerly of the 1970s glam rock Sadistic Mika Band). Inspired by German band Kraftwerk, their techno-pop kitsch instrumentals, at times reminiscent of video game music, met with great commercial success; their second single "Rydeen" hit number one in 1980.

YMO's audience, like the guitar-buying folk fans of the previous generation, sought to identify with their stars by purchasing synthesizers to create their own YMO sound at home. YMO was one of the first Japanese artists to mainstream sampling in original composition, which was being integrated in international popular music scene from the mid-1980s onward. They also changed the way chart topping acts presented themselves; they broke away from the standard "three chord/blues/guitar/band/love song" stereotype that had dictated the structure and content of Japanese pop and rock music in the postwar era and paved the way for other nonconventional bands to find audiences (Hosokawa 1997: 8). Their instrumental techno-pop gave them a "cool" but intellectual image that was fresh to those uninterested in or tired of idol music. It also paved the way for more avant-garde pop music (in other words, the start of an "alternative" pop genre) to find substantial audiences as electronic instrumental music was increasingly accepted.

YMO disbanded in 1984, but Sakamoto Ryûichi, the band's charismatic leader, remains its most recognized member. He went on to find the international acclaim that had long eluded other Japanese artists mainly through his work in film soundtracks, as mentioned in Chapter 2. His first success was *Merry Christmas Mr. Lawrence* (1983), directed by Oshima Nagisa (the film also starred Sakamoto opposite David Bowie). Sakamoto composed scores for the films *The Last Emperor* (1987), *The Sheltering Sky* (1990), *The Little Buddha* (1993), all of which were directed by Bernardo Bertolucci. *The Last Emperor*, which contained works by Sakamoto and American musician David Byrne (of the Talking Heads), received an Oscar for best score. One explanation for Sakamoto's success where others have failed is that he consciously tries to fulfill Western expectations of "Japanese" music by incorporating Asian or "Oriental" influences in his work. The resulting product sounds exotic to foreign and domestic audiences. His affinity for instrumental music bypasses the necessity to confront the language and culture barrier that has hindered Japanese vocalists for many years.

The 1980s also saw a proliferation of "international" or world music such as funk and reggae, plus a renewed interest in jazz and Latin music. This international boom in music took place in tandem with a renewed interest in "ethnic" restaurants in Japan and an increase in international travel due to the yen's high exchange value. Japanese consumers became connoisseurs of world music, not only consuming CDs at home but also traveling to exotic destinations to hear music first hand, their adventures buoyed by a favorable exchange rate. Orquestra de la Luz, a salsa band formed entirely of Japanese members who sing only in Spanish, became successful both in Japan and in Latin America; their high profile in Japan partly attributed to this "international" boom.

The 1990s: boy bands, dance divas, and visual music

As the nation entered a period of recession in 1991, Japanese people began to question the relevance of old institutional and social values. Yet the 1990s gave Japan its largest number of "million-selling artists"; music producers reversed the trend of the rest of the economy and became rich by finding new audiences. The "cute" female idol faded from its premiere representation of music stardom after the band boom, but idol music was yet to become irrelevant in the music scene. In this decade, it would be the male idols who would become one of the most important genre in the music market, and acts produced by Johnny's *jimusho* (management agency) set a new standard – in both fame and in sales – in the 1990s.

Johnny's brand of male entertainment in the form of classic idol music had been around for some time, but in the 1990s, boy bands signed to this talent agency hit the mainstream markets in unprecedented ways, and no discussion of this aspect of the pop scene is complete without reference to SMAP. SMAP was formed in 1988; it is an acronym for the phrase "Sports Music Assemble People," giving them a clean, healthful, and friendly image. Their musical style, from the early days, was equally cheerful and upbeat. When the original members formed, their average age was just over 14 (the youngest at 11). The members are (according to Japanese custom, listed in descending order by age) the leader of the group, Nakai Masahiro, Kimura Takuya, Inagaki Gorô, Kusanagi Tsuyoshi, and Katori Shingo.[11] Each member has developed a persona distinct from each other, yet complementing their overall group dynamic. Nakai is the emcee of the group, frequently providing a voice for SMAP. Kimura Takuya, also known as *Kimutaku*, is renown for his smoldering good looks, acting ability, and the smoothest singing voice. Inagaki is a quiet romantic while Kusanagi is the "sensitive" member who is also known for his acting. Kusanagi has participated in the recent *kanryû* phenomena by publishing a book on Korean conversation (he is fluent in Korean) and appearing in drama speaking Korea. His humble appearance and good humor gives him understated appeal. Lastly is Katori, the "baby" of the group, who is known for his outspoken, youthful ways; he is sometimes chastised by Nakai, the leader, for his candor but is always forgiven because of his perceived "inexperience." Katori has appeared on television in drag as "Shingo-mama," playing a young mother giving advice on housekeeping and childrearing as well as writing books on dieting and English conversation.

SMAP started out as backup dancers to another Johnny's group, the roller-skating and singing ensemble *Hikaru Genji*. This was to become common practice for Johnny's contracted acts: they were gradually introduced to the public as background personnel (as the generic junior grade group "Johnny's Junior") and then they debuted as individual acts. SMAP had a few hits in the early 1990s, but their appeal was limited. To increase their audiences, they turned to nonmusical work: variety shows, dramas, and TV commercials. Their first television show "*Yume Ga Mori Mori*" was broadcast from 1992 to 1995 on Fuji Television, but their main television success was "SMAP × SMAP" (pronounced *suma suma*, Fuji, 1996 to present). "SMAP × SMAP" combines comedy skits and choreographed performances of the group's latest releases, with a cooking competition in its famed corner "Bistro SMAP" where teams of SMAP member battle "Iron Chef"-style to create a gourmet meal for a celebrity guest who chooses a theme.

SMAP in the 1990s demonstrate the deepening of the idol's media intertextuality that originated in the 1980s. Their features are commonplace in all parts of the Japanese mass media: television, radio, newspaper, and magazines, even countless billboards in public spaces carry their images. They appear regularly on television dramas, commercials, and variety, and talk shows; Nakai was seen five nights a week in 2001 (Darling-Wolf 2004: 358). Though some might see SMAP as merely an updated version of other disbanded Johnny's groups, unlike previous artists, the members of SMAP have gone on to establish distinct personalities, sometimes finding themselves in the headlines. Kimutaku has managed to combine his heartthrob image with marriage after he wed a fellow idol singer, Kudô Shizuka (who had debuted on the 1980s show *Yûyake Nyan Nyan*) in 2000. Kudô was pregnant at the time of their marriage, but increasingly these "*dekichatta kekkon*" (marriage due to unexpected pregnancy) are more common in the *geinôkai* and not as frowned upon as they would have been in the 1970s or 1980s. Inagaki Gorô faced public scrutiny for his poor judgement during a 2001 traffic violation when he was arrested for interfering with a police officer and assault, receiving four months of house arrest. His return to the group was marked by a televised tearful apology.

One of the reasons SMAP was able to cross over from fleeting to lasting stardom was that the members had matured and were able to attract the attention of a wider range of fans, ranging from school children to women in their mid-thirties, or even older. Their appeal is not just musical; their members' physical appearance and personalities play a great role in determining their position in the market. They are presented as people, as bodies as much as personalities and voices; their songs are almost always performed with choreographed dance moves, so their bodies are a part of their overall sound. Kimura and Katori have posed nude or seminude for women's magazines, frequently utilizing cross-dress and cosmetics. Kimura and Katori's highly sexual and feminized image may again allow SMAP fans to imagine romantic relationships moving beyond the boundaries of currently dominant constructions of gender roles based on compulsory heterosexuality (Darling-Wolf 2004: 361).

Most of SMAP's music is up-tempo, almost burlesque, and though it does not fit into the 1990s' genre neatly, the combination of this music with the group's image has been a success. Now and then SMAP have employed different composers to present a more sophisticated sound to the audience, with real commercial success: take, for example, two of their 3 million-selling singles, 1998's "*Yozora no Mukô ni*" (The Other Side of the Starry Sky; lyrics by Suga Shikao and music by Kawamura Yûka) and their 2003 hit "*Sekai ni Hitotsu Dake no Hana*" (Only One Flower in the World; composed by Makihara Noriyuki). Both songs are medium tempo, a change from their somewhat frenzied dance numbers. Television performances of "*Yozora*" featured Kimura playing the acoustic guitar, accenting his reputation for being the most musical in the group. "*Sekai ni Hitotsu Dake no Hana*" composer Makihara is a talented performer in his own right, but his own career took a downturn after he was arrested for drug possession in 1999. This hit, besides showing SMAP's musical versatility, demonstrated Makihara's ability to overcome career-ending obstacles. Most importantly, both of these songs' lyrics projected a more mature emotional image for the boy band. Instead of cheerfully calling to their audience to "SHAKE" (1996) or "Let's get together!" in "Peace!" (1997), "*Yozora*" looks back wistfully on the early optimistic days of a relationship and "*Sekai ni Hitotsu Dake no Hana*" demonstrates the post-bubble sensibility when the group sings "it's okay not to be number one."

While SMAP are Johnny's most diversified and successful act, they have opened the door for other Johnny's acts to find a place in the male idol market. Because of the institutionalized *senpai kôhai* (senior/junior hierarchical) relationships found in many Japanese organizations, Johnny's groups are introduced according to their age – the newer the groups, generally, the younger the age of its members. After SMAP, the *kôhai* groups TOKIO and V6 were introduced to an eager public; they were followed by the KinKi Kids, *Arashi*, and the male duo Takki and Tsubasa. In 2005, Johnny's newest "family members" were NEWS and KAT-TUN. The continuous promotion of Johnny's acts does not seem to result in market saturation; the audience is always ready for more, suggesting that some of Johnny's idols are temporary figures in the media landscape. KAT-TUN performed at a concert at the Yokohama Arena even before they had released their first music CD; normally unreleased artists cannot book such large-scale venues (*Nikkei Entertainment*, 2005a: 13). What made this possible was that the group had gained widespread attention through the participation of two members in a television drama in the winter of 2005; then, the group also began appearing on variety shows. By the time they released a music CD, KAT-TUN were already established television stars, demonstrating Johnny's shrewd marketing strategy.

In the mid-1990s, yet another production empire was maturing. Komuro Tetsuya, keyboardist for the 1980s techno-pop band TM Network, turned his attention from writing and performing music for his own group to creating careers for others. In the same way that Johnny's produced a "brand" product (young men), Komuro's "family"[12] also were branded with his artistic style, which was generally viewed as Eurobeat. They were idols in the sense that media exposure was intense and many of his singers began performing in their early-to-mid teens, but their aesthetic was totally different; Komuro repackaged the female idol as part of the worldwide trend in dance music.

Most of Komuro's acts were women (or bands fronted by female vocalists) and combined dance rhythms with "karaoke-friendly" melodies. Most famous of his troupe were Amuro Namie and Kahala Tomomi, and the groups trf and globe. Komuro appeared on stage as a member of globe, but his backstage presence was also strongly felt in all the other acts: he wrote and arranged the music, produced their recordings and generally oversaw their promotion primarily through Avex, a label that specialized in dance recordings. Komuro's success was staggering; he was probably the first celebrity producer who, after earning a moderate position of fame as a musician, went on to super-stardom (and income) as a producer. Take Hideki calls this period in musical history the " 'long live the producer!' era" (*purodyusaa no banzaijidai*) (1999: 310). Other star producers of the 1990s include Okuda Tamio (producer of Puffy) and Oda Tetsurô (producer of Aikawa Nanase in the mid-1990s, but also songwriter and producer for countless others). Komuro, Okuda and Oda took advantage of young women's rising interest in music at the time (following the 1980s *karaoke* boom) and provided this sector of the audience with artists who corresponded with their ideals and aspirations. Amuro, for example, was in many of the structural definitions of the term an "idol," yet her image was completely different from the "cute," frilly, and feminine icons of the mid-to-late 1980s. She was only 17 when she debuted as a solo artist, but Amuro wore heavy makeup and high platform shoes with sleekly tailored pant suits that projected a new image of confidence for young women. Born and raised in Okinawa, she debuted in a girls' group in 1994 but was reintroduced to the public by Komuro through Avex Trax as a solo artist in 1996. Her mid-to-late 1990s' releases broke many sales barriers; her third single sold 4 million copies. Her eighth single, "A Walk in the Park" (1996), demonstrates Amuro's style and image (she debuted the song on television in a tailored pantsuit which would have been almost corporate except for the platform shoes and corn rowed hair) before she moved away from Komuro's style of Eurobeat which first made her famous, and toward a more US-rooted hip-hop style which she currently embraces.

While new versions of male and female idol music were reaching new heights, rock had not been forgotten. In the late 1990s, "visual" rock swept the charts. This was not really a new trend, as rock music that made a strong visual impact through hair, makeup, and costume had been around for many years. Independent labels (known as *indîzu* in Japanese) had carried acts such as X-JAPAN ("indie" debut 1985; major debut 1989) and Buck-Tick ("indie" debut 1986; major debut the following year) who eventually crossed over to major label sales, presenting a generally hard rock sound and flamboyant image to throngs of devoted followers. Yet these acts still were categorized in "alternate" music categories, with a harder sound and an outrageous image that could not crack the more conservative mainstream market.

The late 1990s saw mainstream breakthroughs for "visual" bands through the "softening" of their sound and image, such as Shazna (with lead singer and cross-dresser IZAM), L'Arc En Ciel, LUNA SEA, and GLAY, all of which were active on independent labels before breaking the major scene. LUNA SEA and GLAY, two bands that went on to million-selling status in the late 1990s and 2000s, were two "visual" bands originally signed by EXTASY Records, the independent label founded by X-Japan leader YOSHIKI. In crossing over to major labels, LUNA SEA's and GLAY's sound and appearance were toned down, but some "glam" remained to set them apart from other acts. For example, LUNA SEA's lead singer Kawamura Ryûichi lost his dark makeup and extreme hair and transformed himself into a teenage heartthrob with a little eyebrow shaping and hair gel, acting as television spokesperson for the convenience store Family Mart in 1997 and the candy manufacturer Morinaga in 1998, both mainstream household names in the Japanese consumer landscape. GLAY, a rock unit from Hokkaido, also played down their visual impact as their singles climbed the charts: they still used hair dye, styling gel, and dark eyeliner, but by that time, mainstream Japanese men were more comfortable with the idea of grooming products (helped along by a strong beauty product industry campaign and the encouragement of young women). Visual bands went from being "weird" alternative to "cutting edge" fashionable. Their music was still "harder" than the average pop release (e.g., if one compares GLAY's work to their contemporaries Amuro and SMAP), but they were fully integrated with "idol" intertextual media (television drama, talk show, and ad campaigns) necessary to establish mainstream stardom in this decade. One eloquent example of GLAY's crossover to major exposure is the double single release in 1998 of "*Yûwaku*" (Temptation) and "SOUL LOVE." These two singles were released on the same day in April and represented the confidence of the band to put out two singles (four songs) in competition with themselves on the hit charts. Their driving rock beat was a hit: "*Yûwaku*" went to number one as a tie-up song to the audio manufacturer TDK and "SOUL LOVE" to number five, tied to the cosmetic company Kanebo. Both singles achieved over one million sales each, allowing GLAY to dominate the top ten in the late 1990s as a harbinger of rock at the turn of the twenty-first century. GLAY became a national icon when they accompanied a delegation to China to celebrate the thirty-year anniversary of the normalization between the two countries in 2002. GLAY met with the then Chinese President, Jiang Zemin, in a widely publicized press conference (who joked with them about their hairstyles [Ugaya 2005b: 216]), proving that visual – both its sound and its image – had truly become part of the mainstream.

This is not to say that all visual bands have "lost" their edge in terms of defining themselves outside the square. Malice Mizer, Dir en Grey, and La'cryma Christi have made impact on the music scene without mainstreaming their aesthetic values. Most of these bands started out on indie labels, but through their hardcore fan bases attracted the interest of more established labels. There are distinct connections to be made between some of the more vibrantly visual bands and the somewhat gothic aesthetic that is popular in Japanese comic book art (*manga*) as well as videogame artwork today. For example, Malice Mizer's flamboyant French style in the early 1990s was not unfamiliar to audiences who were well versed with the now classic 1970s *manga, The Rose of Versailles*. Malice Mizer's popularity dove when their lead singer, deep-voiced but androgynous-looking Gackt, announced his solo career in 1999, taking many fans with him, and morphing away from an extreme persona to a more acceptable but still dramatic image.

Television's role in music in the late 1990s focused on building personal images of stars through talk show-type formats that allowed the star to build a multilayered public image whatever the genre of music. This image included music, but physicality and personality were equally – and some times even more – important. Since the idol days of the 1980s, looks had been an important marking tool for singers, but in the 1990s, personality also became part of the definition of stardom. Being able to tell a good story (usually, on TV but also on the radio) was as important to musicians as keeping their guitars in tune. Television continues to support these stars, and competition for airtime is tight. Senior figures, who had formerly eschewed TV invitations, now appear to have reconsidered. Nakajima Miyuki recently appeared in the national post office's annual New Year's Greeting (*nengajo*) campaign, and Yoshida Takurô, who refused appearances in the 1970s, became a major television personality when Fuji Television paired him the with the Johnnie's unit, the KinKi Kids (brothers Dômoto Kôichi and Tsuyoshi), for the evening music and talk show "Love Love *Aishiteiru*" which ran from 1996 to 2001. Yoshida played the wily industry veteran to the Dômoto brothers' fresh and sometimes naïve personalities, and their "GO GO BAND KIDS!" lessons, where New Music veterans Yoshida, Sakazaki Kohnosuke (of the Alfee), and Matsutôya Masataka (Yuming's husband and Caramel Mama member) taught the younger members of the cast (the brothers and another young female costar) how to play pop classics on guitar, bass, and drums; this was truly the case of the senior members of the industry opening the eyes of a new generation to rock and pop classics.

Diversification in the twenty-first century

The important role of "indies" was first recognized in the 1980s with the *ikaten* and band boom and again in late 1990s with Kiroro's massive hit "*Nagai Aida*" (Awhile, 1998). Kiroro's single, just two years before the twenty-first century, is worth including at the start of this section because it demonstrates the diversity of sound affiliated with the emerging independent genre. Previously discussed independent artists, primarily from the harder rock and/or the visual camp, tended to look and sound extreme. Indie artists at the start of the 2000s represent many styles: rock, punk, pop, and folk. A number of artists in the charts today in the mainstream have an indie release to their name: Orange Range, Asian Kung Fu Generation, and Elle Garden (in the rock and pop field) all boast indies starts. Even the postmodern *minyô* star Hajime Chitose, discussed in the Chapter 2, has recorded with both indie and major labels. The proliferation of independent labels in the 2000s demonstrates the diversification of sound; in terms of genre, no longer did major label music sound "major" and independent music sound "extreme."

Independent music has entered the mainstream, but idols are still part of the playing field at the start of the twenty-first century. SMAP demonstrated that the idol formula could be refined and reinvigorated in the 1990s with boy-power, but this was not to say that the Japanese market was uninterested in female idols. Morning *Musume*, an all-girl vehicle for the producer ambitions of Tsunku (the stage name of the lead vocalist for the Osaka-based visual band Sharan-Q), officially debuted in 1998. The group drew its original members from an open audition series the previous year in the television show ASAYAN, which revisited practices and perceptions about industry-made female idols. Another notable aspect of the Morning *Musume* is their transience: producers supplemented the original five-person lineup with three additional members not long after their debut single. Rather than destabilizing the group, this change was seen as a shrewd marketing technique. Television audiences watched eagerly to see how the new members could fit into the already-established personal relationships within the group, in the same way that audiences enjoy the voyeuristic drama of reality shows.

After Tsunku realized the audience's interest in the changing of the ranks, he rotated his idols frequently, citing reasons such as "graduation" (to solo careers) or "retirement"[13] and bringing in new, younger recruits as replacements. Another example of personnel malleability is Tsunku's direction to break up Morning *Musume* into a variety of temporary sub-"units" which release one or two singles under different group names, before "graduation" or return to the original lineup. Today, the pace of the idol genre has quickened: the replaceable idol of the 1980s can and is exchanged for a new member with lightening speed. In Morning *Musume's* appearance on the nationally televised live 2005 *Kôhaku Utagassen* (Red and White Singing Contest), original members appeared on stage with the new members (now in its sixth incarnation) singing a medley of their hits since the late 1990s, taking the stage and leaving as their moment in the spotlight faded.

Hamazaki Ayumi took the mantle of premiere pop diva from Amuro Namie in the 2000s. Like Amuro, her cosmetic style, her bejewelled and stencilled manicures and fashion sense are as much famed as her music, and this makes the Hamazaki phenomenon a total sensory experience. Yet Hamazaki is no constructed idol. Since 1999, she has written her own lyrics, allowing her to have some creative control over her repertoire, in the same vein as senior idol Matsuda

Seiko, and she is rumored to insist on a say in all artistic and managerial decisions. She is frequently chosen as spokeswoman for major cosmetic companies and one of the nationwide mobile phone companies, allying her personal image with two commercial industries closely tied to youth markets in Japan. Although Hamazaki's image is certainly glossy and multimedia friendly, she is not a puppet and presents a strong businesslike image to her public.

Her dance-driven music debuted in single form in 1998, but her "breakout" was when her first album debuted at the *Oricon* number one spot in 1999. This album takes its name from the song "A Song for XX." The "XX" in the title suggests the listener insert any name, personalizing the audience's experience but also depersonalizing the singer, contributing to Ugaya's designation of Hamazaki's image as the "cyberborg female warrior" (2004a). He writes that her main appeal to teenage female audiences lies in her ability to connect with their struggle to reconcile their "animus" (male side to the feminine identity) to socially accepted expectations of their gender role (2004a: 184–185). Her tough emotional side is balanced by her feminine appearance, making her uncontroversial and wholly acceptable to heterosexual audiences. The tradition of a young fighting woman is not new; like Joan of Arc (who is also well known in Japan, where warriors, both male and female, are cultural heroes; even in J-pop, there is a visual band called *Jannudaruku* or "Janne Da Arc"), Hamazaki has connected to a collective imagination of young Japanese women who fight against the mainstream as represented by symbols of mature masculinity: the father, the teacher, and the boss.

If Hamazaki represents adolescent struggle in Japan, Orange Range represents its youthful exuberance. Discussed in detail in Chapter 2 with reference to their Okinawan origins, their story is worth another mention here to demonstrate contemporary flexibility of genre boundaries. In the first half of 2005, three singles from the rock/pop/techno act Orange Range reached number one, making them one of the few consistently well-performing bands to watch in this era (*Nikkei Entertainment* 2005b: 40). Their name was inspired by GLAY (which is, incidentally, a Japanese pronunciation of "gray"), arising from the youths' perception that band names based on colors are successful. Much like many of their rock and techno contemporaries, they began as an Okinawan indie band, releasing their first album and single on the *Dejikkusu* label in 2002 and promoting their work through live performances with other Okinawan-based bands such as Mongol 800. The original band lineup consisted of three vocalists backed by a drummer, a bassist, and a guitarist; the focus on vocals in their lineup demonstrates their rap roots.[14] Yet their musical style is a wide-ranging blend of rock and pop, with techno arrangements and hip-hop-style vocals. The bands' relative youth (its members were born between 1983 and 1985) makes them appealing to a fan base in their teens and early twenties. Sony Music Entertainment did not, however, market them as an "idol band," despite their young fan base and their own youth (ibid.). Instead, they were marketed at "artists," and one demonstration of their musicianship is their ability to tie their hit singles closely to their album releases, both of which have sold well. Since the days of New Music, musicianship in the Japanese industry is evidenced by strong supporting album sales, in contrast to one-off commercial singles.

Orange Range's success demonstrates the fruition of a growing trend in postwar Japanese popular music: the movement from the West (primarily the United States and United Kingdom) to Japan as the source of inspiration of J-pop and rock. While many New Music and 1980s musicians cite Western artists as their main inspiration, Orange Range's drummer Katchan says he became a drummer because he was impressed by YOSHIKI's performances with X-JAPAN, and his band mate Naoto cites *Denki* Groove (a Japanese techno group) as one of his major musical influences (*Nikkei Entertainment* 2005b: 42). This is in stark contrast with the 1970s, 1980s, and even 1990s acts, who often cite Western artists as referential points to discuss their musical influences. In the twenty-first century, Japanese popular music has now defined itself as self-referential, its own "source of tradition."

History through music: position, position, position!

A record of twentieth-century Japanese popular music offers us the opportunity to consider this period of history from a different perspective than the usual viewpoints of economic, social, or political analyses; many cultural histories of this time are based on literature (Seidensticker 1991, for example). Using popular music as a lens to examine postwar Japanese history allows a new perspective, demonstrating the specific interaction between cultural and social institutions ("art" versus "politics," for example) and how symbolic representations are connected to and arise from the historical landscape.

According to historian Andrew Gordon, Japan's postwar period until 1990 is characterized by an embeddedness in an international community dominated by the United States, conflict and change despite political conservativism, and the tension between the reality of difference and variation in Japan and the conception of a strong single identity of the Japanese (1993: ix–x). David Edgington, in a later work, includes the 1990s in this timeframe, and writes that during this last decade "there emerged a new nexus of forces that threatened to undermine the stability and predictability of the postwar years. Disasters struck, the economy tumbled, and the social fabric unravelled" (Edgington 2003: 4).

Here, Edgington is referring to events such as the Great Hanshin Earthquake of 1995, closely followed by the *Aum* Sarin Subway Attack; the massive reorganization of the banking system following its collapse due to bad loans; increasing problems with juvenile delinquency; and a widespread moral panic that arose following a perceived rise in teenage prostitution under the label of *enjo kôsai* (subsidized dating). The postwar era is thus framed by social, financial, and political crises: on the one side by the surrender and destruction of the major cities of greater Tokyo, Hiroshima, and Nagasaki and on the other by the destruction of the Kobe area, the withdrawal of public confidence in government and business and pessimism about the future of Japan. The intervening period is characterized by variable growth, faster in the 1960s slower in the 1970s (due to the Oil

Shocks), a heady economic optimism in the 1980s, and the "bubble" that was to "burst" in the 1990s.

As argued in Chapter 2, Japanese popular music arose from a process of cultural diffusion, connected to a variety of cultural traditions (both East and West). Yet, Japan's position vis-à-vis the United States is most salient, affecting the course of both history and popular music in the postwar era. Yoshimi demonstrates Japanese reactions to the effects of American popular culture by analysing a 1980s' multivolume encyclopedia entitled *American Culture*, which explored the effect of America on Japanese popular culture 1945–1970 in three distinct periods. These consisted of first a "love–hate" relationship with the United States; the second occurred in the 1960s, a period of integration when American products and ideas were not seen as antithetical to Japanese daily life; and the third in the 1970s where America was no longer a place and a culture to desire and emulate, but merely a "source of information" (2003: 434–444). Yoshimi's analysis of this work illustrates the gradual realignment of Japan and the United States, yet he describes this cultural history as depoliticized because of its representations of American culture as merely abstract goals of the people (e.g., "a symbol of wealth") rather than recognizing the United States as a powerful actor in the Pacific area (434). Yoshimi calls for scholars to re-politicize Japan's postwar popular cultural history. I would argue, much like the real estate agent's mantra that lends its title to this section, that one way to read the politics of Japanese popular music is through the changes in its economic and political positionings vis-à-vis the United States.

One cannot overlook the specific political conditions of the Occupation as having overwhelming influence on the development of all kinds of Japanese popular culture after the end of World War II. The Allied censorship of film, radio, newspapers, and other media made certain that popular culture developed in a certain fashion – to the liking of the Americans. "The controlling and the censorious American presence" (Ivy 1993: 245) was omnipresent; film, music, and radio programming were screened for any references to Japan's military past, either directly or indirectly. Tastes and values were also affected by demand; it is no wonder that Japanese popular music developed in the immediate postwar period in line with American tastes and in close proximity to the US bases: often the troops and accompanying base residents were the only communities at that time with the time and resources to spend on leisure (Yoshimi 2003: 438).

Japanese musicians who wished to work often had no choice but to conform to these cultural standards: "postwar musical culture developed through the employment of Japanese musicians on American bases, and was decisively influenced by contact with American military personnel" (434). This led to an unequal and complex relationship between the Occupational "patron" and the Japanese "artist." The foreign customer was to be pleased and courted; this led to both resentment of his presence *and* the emulation of his taste in an attempt to procure some of his position of power. These mixed feelings are clearly communicated by entertainment agency legend Watanabe Misa, when recalling the initial location of their management production office, situated near the occupying forces in the

Hibiya section of Tokyo. She wrote that the noise and the smells emanating from the soldiers' nearby camps probably devalued the value of the area, resulting in cheap rents. At the same time, this proximity was attractive and made her yearn for an American way of life, which was, or at least seemed, easier than the immediate postwar economy of rations and shortages (Take 1999: 70). Success in Western-inspired show business was her family's path to this ambiguously attractive, and yet at times, repulsive, lifestyle.

During this period of contradictory messages and emotions regarding Japan's relationship with the United States, Misora Hibari's 1950s street-smart kid image appealed to audiences because of the public identification with postwar hardship. Families had been separated, and food and shelter were scarce in urban areas; although good humor carried many hit tunes, a closer look at this *joie de vivre* reveals a psychological need for distance from the sociopolitical reality of the postwar condition. Composer Hattori's comment, noted earlier in this chapter, that "we must go *forward*" (Take 1999: 18, emphasis added) surely implies a dark reality. Yet we must not mistake this emotional distancing as a negation of the day-to-day experiences of individuals. Rather, we can interpret it as a realistic human response to the recent experience of war, both personal and political. Japanese popular music in the late 1940s and early 1950s represented a coping strategy for a group of people who had been pushed to the brink by war.

The "*Shôwa* 40s" (1965–1974) were characterized by Japan's emergence from the reconstruction period, high economic growth and the seamless "incorporation" of American musical styles into Japanese composition (Satô cited in de Ferranti, 2002: 200). The final "conversion" of Japanese musicians, to a level where they could compete with foreign artists, is "related to the rise of Japan's economic power" (Kawabata 1991: 336). Sakamoto Kyû's conquering of international charts in the early 1960s was a psychological boost for the music industry, as was the successful hosting of the summer Olympics for larger society. Yet this flourishing local industry did not mean that Japan stopped consuming English language pop music (and culture). Economic and political independence allowed Japan to consume Western products on its own terms, so we can interpret the post-Beatles, post-Ventures boom in *yôgaku* as not merely a return to the Occupational relationship of cultural inequality but a recognition of Japan's changed position from "conquered" to "customer." This new self-awareness of purchasing power allowed the Japanese consumer to appreciate *yôgaku* and *hôgaku* simultaneously, for different reasons and resulting in different effects, all in the same market. *Yôgaku* represented international sophistication and authenticity and imparted social status on the listener; *hôgaku* was culturally immediate and addressed the audience's emotional needs in ways that *yôgaku* could not.

After the Japanese media featured the American student movement in the late 1960s and early 1970s, Japanese students began to question their government's compliance with the US-led war in Indochina. Many Japanese protested against the US involvement in the Vietnam War and Japan's support of this war by its renewal of the Security Treaty that allowed US troops easy access to Asian battlefields. Japanese university campuses erupted with social and political unrest during the Vietnam War, and many Japanese folk singers put the students' feelings into words. This was the first direct and overt politicization of popular music; in this sense, Japanese folk singers changed the way Japanese people listened to music, and made music, as well.

The student demonstrations of the 1960s and 1970s lost public support after the movement, factionalized through individual member difference and its troubled relationship with the Communist Party, was portrayed as too radical and out of touch with mainstream Japan by the mass media. Interest in Japanese popular music moved away from collective political statements and focused on the individual and the desire for individuation. This shift is illustrated by the long-term success of New Music, which has been characterized as having "an introspective self-absorbed point of view" (Fujie 1989: 209). After the 1970s, Japanese audiences thus preferred to consume music as an individualized, and an individuating, activity rather than a collective one (this trend was further compounded by developments in technology, as discussed in detail in Chapter 5).

Pop music in Japan continued to speak to the individual on a number of levels in the 1980s: the individual "idol" singer presented a gender-specific model, and techno-pop provided a cool image for those who felt that idols were too saccharine for their taste. The band boom merely presented a different reference point for consumers to define themselves individually. To what extent is this definition of personal political? It might be difficult to argue that the content of 1980s Japanese pop music could truly be considered political on a collective level, but to interpret it without reference to the concomitant shifts in the relationship between Japan and the United States in the music industry, we run of risk of overlooking the influence of the global politics of neo-liberal individualism. In the late 1980s, Japanese music corporations bought out many of their American and British counterparts, and the previously unequal relationship was turned upside down in this particular arena. For example, after the 1989 Sony buyout, New York-based producers for Columbia and CBS were now taking orders from the head office in Tokyo. Japan's financial success in the 1980s also helped to "de-domesticate" the face of the domestic music industry. As mentioned in Chapter 2, the strong yen and a familiar culture of international travel allowed Japanese recording artists to roam the world hiring the best studio technicians for their recording sessions. From "conquered" to "customer" and even "distant manager" (as in the case of Sony and Toshiba–EMI), Japan's pop music industry leveraged itself into the global community while maintaining a domestic market that was confidently Japanese in taste but polished by international experience and interaction.

This supposedly "neutral" postwar popular culture that acknowledges its "source" and seeks an "international" gloss to make it relevant in a globalized cultural economy is often consumed in a political vacuum (thus Yoshimi's critique), but at certain intersections, this popular culture cannot be separated from its sociopolitical background. Case in point is the Alfee's failed attempt to perform an outdoor concert in 1992 on an active US Naval base in Atsugi, Kanagawa Prefecture. Although their professed goal was to perform in an atmosphere of international cooperation, and the novelty factor certainly loomed large in their minds (being the first Japanese band to perform on "American soil" in Japan), the actualization of the concert was prevented by public protest over the timing of the concerts (August 9, anniversary of the Nagasaki atomic bombing) (Stevens 1999). Caught off guard by the political protest, the Alfee production company quickly changed venues and dates, eventually realizing their ambition of performing in "America," not by using the many military bases on the Japanese archipelago but performing a smaller scale concert in Forest Hills, New York, in 1998. In 1999, they took their show to Berlin and planned a 2001 concert in the Royal Albert Hall. The London concert was cancelled when the international political climate intervened: the concert was cancelled in the immediate chaos in the global travel industry that followed 9/11, due to fears regarding the safety of the fans and of the musicians traveling later that month. Two failed and two successful "international" concerts: this story demonstrates that Japan's pop culture, no matter how individualized its content is, pop music's production, and delivery are firmly entrenched in a highly political arena.

The postwar history of J-pop demonstrates the delicate tension between the two interpretative spheres of "politicized" and "neutralized" with reference to the Japan–US relationship. Gordon's assertion that the postwar era is "embedded" in an international community dominated by the United States is central to the discussion of Japanese pop music, but to what extent do its participants vocalize their perception of this relationship? Generations of musicians differ in their responses. During my repeated queries to Takamizawa Toshihiko (b. 1954), he seemed to be unable to separate his own "art" as a Japanese pop/rock musician with the cultural heritage of the West:

> [The] fundamental [elements of pop music], like the tone quality of the instruments and the melodies, are common through out the world; that's why I have never experienced a gap. Well . . . that's because rock and pop's 'birthplace' is the West [*ôbei*, a term using the two characters for Europe and North America], and we Japanese musicians have come all this way influenced by the West.
>
> (Personal Communication 2006)

As is common for someone of his generation, Takamizawa's music influences are firmly rooted in the West: Led Zeppelin and Deep Purple. As noted above, the million-selling band Orange Range cited only Japanese groups as their musical influences, demonstrating that between these generations (Takamizawa, born in 1954; the eldest of Orange Range, HIROKI, born in 1983) an important change occurred. Clearly Japan's self-articulated position vis-à-vis the United States has come of age, with the senior tier of musicians feeling more comfortable with a Western definition of their music, while the upcoming generation of musicians operate within a Japanese definition of popular music.

If the 1990s are the "lost decade" in Japan (Edgington 2003: 4), what do the cultural critics mourn? The loss of public confidence in traditional institutions of community, education, the workplace, and the government took the greatest toll in this era, and is still an issue in the 2000s as Japan struggles to adjust to new social, political, and financial pressures. Yet amid this loss, there is continuity. The persistence of *enka* represents a vision of perceived tradition in a quickly changing music industry. Although the main foci of this chapter have been the developments away from musical traditions associated with prewar music, *enka's* inclusion here demonstrates a kind of cultural "brake," where a group of Japanese songwriters and performers (and their audience) consciously made the statement that their music was no longer moving along the same lines as the rest of Japanese postwar pop and they declared a new genre to preserve their social and aesthetic values in music. This twin desire for novelty and yearning for familiarity of the past (e.g., the phenomenon of artists performing new compositions in "old" styles) is one musical expression of the tension Gordon describes in the postwar era between inevitable change and persisting conservatism. The deaths of the Emperor Hirohito and the "Queen of *Kayôkyoku*," Misora Hibari, both occurring in the first half of 1989 seemed inseparable to many, serving as markers of the "end of an era." Japan's postwar recovery was no longer linked as it had been (both politically and musically) to the past. The passing of Hirohito and Hibari led to a period of "tumultous" challenges in the 1990s:

> When she died in the last year of Showa and the first of the new Heisei era she was transformed with Showa Japan into myth . . . Yet her death, which seemed to symbolize the passing of an old-fashioned temperament, paradoxically ensured the survival of that temperament by transforming it to myth.
>
> (Tansman 1996: 106–107)

Conclusion

With reference to twentieth-century American popular music, cultural theorist John Shepard believes

> music as a social constructed symbolic medium speaks immediately, concretely and globally to the experiential worlds of different individuals. There is in other words little or no disjunction between people and music . . . both are in an intense dialectical relationship with the same social structure.
>
> (1994: 235–236)

American pop music is usually analyzed as an expression of resistance against the mainstream political and social values. Japanese popular music, on the other hand, has its resistant moments (protest folk in the late 1960s, as the most obvious example), but political protest is not a consistently dominant theme. Rather, this history has focused on Japan's changing roles vis-à-vis a conceived "West" (dominated by the United States) from "conquered" to "consumer," and aspects of this shift in ideological relations are important in later discussions in the final chapter on "Translations: 'Internationalizing' Language and Music." This shift, though not characterized by rebellion, is still a political statement, one that has occurred through slow incremental transformations in attitudes and ideas rather than through radical change. Its results – Japan's changed relations with the global community – are just as important and wide reaching as if they had been achieved through revolution rather than quiet change.

This history has also included descriptions of other important changes in the popular music scene: the strengthening of the position of the artist in the industry (to be further developed in Chapter 4 on the music business) and concerns about authenticity in pop music (to be further discussed in the chapter on technology). In this postwar history of Japanese popular music, we see a consistent tension between audiences' perceptions of the artists as an independent entity representing authentic emotion, and the attraction of slick and efficient professionalism that permeates larger scale institutions in the industry. Since the mid-1960s, this tension has been illustrated through pendulum-like movements: away from the professional *wasei* ("Made-in-Japan") pop to folk, and then New Music, back to the industry created idol, and away again through the 1980s rock boom. The next trend of professionally constructed dance music idols (this time driven by celebrity producers rather than invisible executives) makes sales history in the 1990s, but there are spaces in the market that allow diversification: indie labels provide contrast and choice to the consumer, yet at the same time serve as a spring board for artists to "make it" in the hit charts. This movement demonstrates public interest and how markets need to change to capture this interest. On the other hand, artists with songwriting and management skills want to maximize their influence (and profits) by becoming independent; even record companies and television studio executives will try to take advantage of new movements in music to find new audiences (the expanding indie record industry, for example, with its many crossover artists, can no longer be called an "underground" scene). The Japanese pop market has grown large enough in this postwar era to contain many sub-audiences with different aesthetic values and tastes.

The postwar history of Japanese pop music provides an insight into aesthetic values. New sounds such as New Rock and New Music in the 1970s, the techno-cool YMO in the 1980s, Amuro and Hamazaki as women of confidence, and the visual impact of GLAY are only some of the images that have found wide scale appeal in this era; there are many others. As the world's third largest music market, the size of the Japanese market allows for the development of significant diversity. Although Japan is often classified by the West as an Asian "corporate society" where collective identity is valued over individualism, in its postwar popular culture, the vast bifurcation of contemporary Japanese music collectives (dance, hip-hop, indie rock, teenage idol pop, techno, and so on) has made it impossible to state that mainstream popular music follows a single, collective pattern.

4 The business side: connections, culture, and contexts

> No matter if you think "This song is the best", if all the listeners say "This song is the worst", then the song *is* the worst. If you don't sell CDs, there's nothing to say . . . Even if it's only one person, and even if it's the composer himself, says "This song's no good", then there's nothing to say.
>
> (Takamizawa 2004: 148)

If music can, in some essence, contain an artistic "truth" that appeals to the public's sense of aesthetics, then it follows that talented producers will seek out talented musicians and make them stars. Yet it is certainly equally possible that the popularization of music is not merely based on musical merit but is significantly affected by the careful application of business processes, such as marketing, PR, and "spin." This chapter examines the interpersonal relationships that constitute the "business side" to the Japanese pop music industry and argues that the connections between business institutions are equally important as musical creativity in determining whether or not a song becomes a hit.

The media who provide the "spin" – promoters, advertisers, journalists, and critics – tend to focus on the end product of a recording session; similarly, this book too has, in many places, concentrated on music as a final product to be interpreted. Here, however, I discuss the *process* of recording as social and economic practices. These practices are constituted of linked actions that take place between individuals. This chapter first outlines the structure of the music industry and then focuses on the salient links in the process of making music: between the artist management agencies, the record labels, and television studios.

This multi-linked process chain is forced at every level to respond to the pressure of meeting deadlines and profit margins, for Japan's music industry is firmly entrenched in a late-capitalistic system, not unlike its Western counterparts. This chapter does not profess to uncover some mystical "Japanese-ness" to this industry to explain its successes or failures; I have no such essentialist ambitions. As Keith Negus writes,

> [A]n industry produces culture and culture produces an industry . . . By using the term *industry produces culture* I am referring to how entertainment

> corporations set up structures of organization and institute distinct working practices to produce identifiable products, commodities and 'intellectual properties.' [C]ulture produces an industry . . . in relation to broader culture formations and practices that are within neither the control nor the understanding of the company.
>
> (1999: 14, 20, italics in the original)

Negus admits that "culture" exists and has some influence over industry, but does not attribute culture with the ability to determine the quality and quantity of the output of the organization. Business people are not "slaves to culture," yet they work within it as the background setting for their activities. Note how Negus' version of culture here is not defined as having a vague atmospheric quality framed by ethnicity, language, or religious background. It is a concrete result of historical developments of organizational structure and of how agents operate within those structures in mutually meaningful ways – sometimes to the financial benefit to the parties involved, sometimes not – in the case of Japan, resulting in market competition.

What defines *this* industry culture is influenced by an immense variety of economic, political, and societal pressures; it is impossible to describe them all. Therefore, I have gleaned what I thought to be the most salient features. Personal connectivity is the key to linking the institutions. We discern connections between individuals (artists and managers manipulating their opportunities through organizations such as the *jimusho*), connections between corporations (record companies), and connections between media (the recording industry allying itself with the television industry for mutual gain. The main argument of this chapter is that the successful application of these connections – perhaps more so that musical talent – is what creates a hit.

This is not necessarily a new idea in sociological studies of popular music. The concept of an ongoing production process recalls Antoine Hennion's 1990 work on the French music industry. He was one of the first to break away from the notion of a mystical, hyper-creative mode as a formula for pop music stardom, stating that success was attained by singers whose producers could skillfully "draw out" their talent first in the recording studio and then to an audience, based on what the producers conceive as public demand. Hennion argued against the evaluation of musical structure as a mark of success and instead argued for social connections adroitly applied (1990: 186–187). This chapter applies Hennion's ideas to a non-Western context, focusing on popular music as a lengthy social process rather than merely an artistic end product.

As noted in the introduction, the Japanese music market is one of the largest in the world, and some of this expansion is quite recent: the industry output doubled from 1988 to 1995 (from 3000 *oku en* to 6000 *oku en*) (Ugaya 2005b: 6).[1] This chapter traces how this expansion occurred and how it has contracted after peaking in 1998. First analyzed is the *jimusho* (management company) which represents the "ground level" work in the music industry. An investigation of Japanese record companies follows, with special attention to how this aspect of the industry has globalized since the late 1980s. The record producer and the recording studio are next highlighted because of its increased visibility since the mid-1990s, as discussed in Chapter 3. Radio and television are the two communication industries most commonly associated with music promotion, but for reasons of space in this chapter, I will focus on TV (while radio will be discussed in the Chapter 5 on technology). The Japanese music industry has a close relationship to the commercial, free-to-air television industry, and so the latter part of this chapter focuses on television. Television creates a perception of public recognition and financial success with regard to Japanese popular music, as well as having a tangible effect on music sales, dictating the charts and the ebb and flow of individual artists' success.

Instead of one "star-maker" in the process, each organization in the chain has input into the making or breaking of a career. Some of these links are predetermined; for example, if an entertainment agency has established links with a record label, the signing of an artist to the agency means a particular record contract; otherwise, the agency must court contracts for their musicians. This chapter charts the process link by link, taking a variety of situations into account to illustrate the way CDs are made and sold, and stars rise in the field of Japanese popular music. This chapter does not, however, argue that the industry determines art, or that art determines industry: "[T]here is no point-to-point correlation between controlling the market place economically and controlling the form, content and meaning of music" (Garofalo in Negus 1999: 16). Therefore, this chapter does not aim to define Japanese music industry culture per se (and vis-à-vis other industry cultures) but to look at how the industry structures have been formed over time and how the agents work within them.

The structure of the industry

Jimusho: *management companies*

Jimusho is simply translated as "office," but in this context, it holds a special meaning: the entertainment management company. If successful and on a large scale, the jimusho represents the institutionalization of networking. In some situations, the decisions of businesspeople on this level can make or break careers for musicians; in others, the musicians have taken control of these roles. The following section explores the different settings of *jimusho* and how they work to meet specific needs of specific artists.

What exactly do these companies do?

> Traditionally, management company functions have ranged from finding new artists and promotion, roping in work for artists, negotiation of fees, even overseeing the personal lives of the artists to overall production work for music, videos, and film.
>
> (Haw 2005c)

On what scale do these offices operate? Johnny's *Jimusho*, discussed at length below, reported earnings of 6.3 billion yen (63 *oku en*) in 2000, compared to its 1992 declaration on 2 billion yen (20 *oku en*). Rising Production, which manages Amuro Namie and SPEED, reported less than 100 million yen earned in 1995, but in 2000 they declared 3.5 billion yen (35 *oku en*). (Ugaya 2005b: 95) Obviously, in the late 1990s, *jimusho* have expanded their activities and consequently, their profits. Mostly, these are on the part of "large-scale management" offices (Haw 2005c), which have diversified into several branches extending beyond personal artist management; they also handle music production, copyright, and sales promotion. *Hori Puro*, for example, manages not just musicians and actors but also artists, comedians, and sports professionals as well as moving into stage production, commercial advertising, and television programming (Takahashi 2005: 16). Reading the ranks of the *Hori Puro* stable over the years is like traveling through Japanese postwar pop history: Funaki Kazuo, The Spiders, Wada Akiko, Inoue Yôsui, RC Succession, Mori Shôko, Ishikawa Sayuri, Yamaguchi Momoe, Sakakibara Ikue, Suzuki Honami, and more recently Fukuda Kyôko (actress and singer). Yet, except for Wada and Sakakibara, the early *Hori Puro* stars have left the company (or retired), moved to other companies, or created their own offices. This is a constantly evolving industry, where individuals make professional decisions based on maximizing their own outcomes, rather than relying on an essentialized idea of group identity so common in the Western understanding of Japanese business culture.

When discussing the activities of an entertainment management agency, one must first unpack the term "management." In Japanese, "manager" has a variety of meanings: first, the "road manager" (Takahashi 2005: 66) is a kind of personal assistant to the artist so that the musician can perform at peak levels. Secondly, the "artist manager," is someone who acts in on a business level as well as having input on the artistic side. The "artist manager" performs a myriad of activities, including "uncovering new artists; [making] record company decisions and recording preparations, including arranging for back up musicians; and so on" (ibid.).[2] On the other hand, the star's road manager takes personal and professional mobile phone calls, drives the company car, keeps the daily schedule, and even holds his/her wallet. The personal interaction between stars and managers is crucial for success. The president of a subsidiary of *Hori Puro* is quoted as saying "The greatest work achievement [in management is hearing a star say] 'I want to work with that manager because s/he's fun' " (Takahashi *et al.* 2005: 18). Amiable personal qualities are just as important as task efficiency. An engaging personality, balanced with talent (for both music and business) and the ability to get along with others, is key for success: "Let go of guys who can't communicate" is the motto for one large *jimusho* ("*Shaberenai yatsu wa zenbu otose*") (Takahashi 2005: 18).

The manager physically spends more time with the artist than any other business colleague and is seen to be someone who "cares for" and is "trusted" by the star (66). In the case of the *jimusho* where I was employed, the two road managers were men approximately ten years younger than the band members. The managers were the favorites of the office, with endearing nicknames, and they definitely showed deference to their artists. On the other hand, I once met the road manager of Takizaki Hideaki, signed to Johnny's *Jimusho*, and there was a very different dynamic to this business relationship. The manager was at least fifteen years senior to his star assignment, and rather than endearing and humble service, there was quiet but confident paternalism in this manager's interaction with the star; he was obviously looking out as an elder brother for his young charge. In fact, I was asked to meet with the young star briefly, not because of my research in the industry but because I was college professor, and the manager thought that "Takki" (who had left school to join the *jimusho* at age thirteen) needed exposure, however briefly, to intellectual life and people outside his close-knit circle.

The following sections discuss in more detail two major yet distinct *jimusho*: *Nabe Puro* and *Johnny's Jimusho*, identified as two of the more prominent large-scale management offices in Japan today. Finally, smaller scale or artist-focused (or artist-run) *jimusho* are featured as industry alternatives which demonstrate diversity in this particular "field of production."

Nabe Puro

The management company *Nabe Puro* (an abbreviation of *Watanabe Purodakushon*) pioneered the field of commercialized music and entertainment management. Established in January 1955 (Take 1999: 70),[3] *Nabe Puro* had its beginnings as a one-room, seven-person outfit in Higashi Ginza district of Tokyo, moving later to Hibiya (a Tokyo site noted in Chapter 3 as meaningful due to its proximity to the cultural overflow from the Allied Occupation's offices and barrack units). Watanabe Susumu and his wife Misa started out with only a few female artists in their group, but in a number of years, this company became synonymous with the entertainment elite in the postwar era. The company motto displays stark ambition in a quirky manner:

> 1: creativity.
> 2: communication.
> There is no 3 or 4!
> 5: Stay ahead of trends (Gobuichi 1995: 20).

Nabe Puro shot to fame in the 1960s with its ingenious mix of talent; as noted in Chapter 3's discussion of "Made-in-Japan" pop, they signed singers, dancers, and comedians and got many of their stars to perform in all these entertainment fields, primarily on television. Take notes that there were three changes in the business that *Nabe Puro* instigated in the 1960s' entertainment world: they changed the way artists were managed; they changed the ranking of the role that management agencies played in the larger scene, and they utilized the media (in this case, television) in new ways (1999: 71–72). Fujie describes *Nabe Puro's* powerful position after the 1950s:

> Watanabe Productions . . . not only had control over the contracts of a stable of singers, composers and musicians, but also held the copyrights of all songs produced by their employees. Having acquired their own sheet music-publishing company, Watanabe Productions also had a monopoly on the publication of the songs in their possession.
>
> The careers of singers were completely at the mercy of these production companies.
>
> (1989: 205–206)

The *Nabe* media strategy also included commercial product marketing, as well as the promotion of its stars, through television programming. This was amply demonstrated in its prime-time musical variety show *Shabondama Horidê* (NTV, 1961–1972). Paired with the sponsoring company "Milky Soap," the show catapulted into fame its regular stars, the Peanuts (a dancing and singing duo of identical twins, Izumi Emi and Yumi) and the Crazy Cats and their leader Ueki Hitoshi (see Chapter 3). Guests, all firmly ensconced in the *Nabe Puro* family, such as Sawada Kenji and the Tigers and Nakao Mie, accompanied these regulars on the weekly show. Other high-profile participants such as miniskirted singer Izumi Jun and *enka* heartthrob Mori Shin'ichi kept the show's content and pace quick and varied. The comedy was slapstick, and it frequently parodied the emerging new middle class of urban salaried workers, with a healthy dose of the contrast between "traditional" and the "new" culture of Japan, in the face of increasingly Westernized values and fashions. The musical numbers were lavishly costumed and choreographed, often featuring prominently the lithe figures of the star group, the Peanuts, in tights and leotards.

Nabe Puro extended its female hit star list in the 1970s and ventured into the beginnings of idol music with the enormously successful girl trio Candies (1973–1978) and male stars such as Go Hiromi. Candies – Itô Ran (a.k.a. "Ran"), Tanaka Yoshiko ("Sû"), and Fujimura Miki ("Miki") – debuted as teenagers in 1973 after training at the Watanabe Productions talent school, "Schoolmates." Two years before their singing debut, they gained media exposure as "mascot girls" for the NHK television show *Uta no Grand Show* (Take 1999: 201), demonstrating the grooming process that was always linked to television exposure. Television experience was crucial to getting an act off the ground not only because of increased public awareness but it also allowed for confidence building and training in front of the camera. In the case of Candies, even before the release of their first album, the performers already had experience in television studio performance, enhancing their ability to succeed in front of the media. This strategy is frequently used by other *jimusho* such as *Hori Puro*[4] and Johnny's Entertainment.

Today *Nabe Puro* is located in Jingumae, a posh but trendy district between Shibuya and Harajuku in central Tokyo. Watanabe Productions' main activities include the planning of radio, television, film, stage, and other kinds of performances; the "nurturing of talent" (2005) and talent management; advertising and commercial musical composition; and the planning and marketing of original recordings. Its official website lists accompanying agencies that specialize in newer financial activities such as copyright: there are 17 separate companies and one financial group associated with Watanabe Productions which encompass the fields of "music, audio visual, culture, leisure, sports, the digital media, artist and international entertainment business" (Watanabe Productions 2005). Watanabe Music Publishing, one offshoot of the larger group, manages the profits of singer-songwriters signed to the agency. Established in 1962, it focuses on profit management: looking after the copyright of composers and the content of music under copyright protection (*kanrionkyoku*); they also work on the publishing and sales of musical scores and the management of composers' careers. Meanwhile, the branch Watanabe Entertainment now performs basic management, in terms of face-to-face relations between managers and stars. Signed stars are divided into four categories: male talent, female talent ("talent" here primarily refers to actors and personalities/variety show celebrities), musicians, and comedy (*owarai*). In 2005, its top act was RAGFAIR, a six-member male vocal group that has had success with its *a-capella* group-influenced melodies and close harmonies.

Nabe Puro's prominence in the field is demonstrated not only by its own financial success but the success of former employees who have branched off and established new businesses. Amuse Inc. was established by Ôsato Yôkichi in the late 1970s. Ôsato was a ten-year veteran manager at *Nabe Puro*, and after the break up of his assignment, Candies, he went independent with his own company. Within its music section, Amuse manages the influential rock band The Southern All Stars, the visual band Siam Shade, actor and singer Fukuyama Masaharu, and the rock band Pornograffiti. Amuse Inc. illustrates jimusho diversification, not only including domestic film and TV – as the others have all done – but also branching out internationally. Amuse has three Asian subsidiaries: Amuse Hong Kong Ltd, Amuse Korea Inc., and a Beijing-based office as well as an American visual media group, Sprite Entertainment. Following the huge *kanryû* boom in television, film, and music, Amuse signed Korean actor Jang Dong Gun in July 2005 to allow his management to negotiate directly with contractors, rather than working as an "outsider," imported into the *geinôkai* from overseas. Over the years, Amuse has grown into large agency located in Shibuya, a youth-centered entertainment district in central Tokyo.[5] Both *Nabe* and its offspring, Amuse, demonstrate the diversification strategies of *jimusho* in providing services to (and managing the control of) a wide range of artists in the twenty-first century.

Johnny's Jimusho

Johnny H. Kitagawa, president and founder of this *jimusho*, began his management career in 1963. An American of Japanese descent, he was born in Los

Angeles in 1931 and migrated to Japan after he served in the Occupation as a US soldier. In Tokyo, he worked a variety of jobs such as interpreting for the American Embassy and playing in bands. His current business is described by industry observer Keith Cahoon as a "talent agency, child star training center, management company, marketing powerhouse and media conglomerate that has been consistently and stupendously successful for nearly 40 years" (2005). Johnny's stars are constructed according to his *jimusho* formula and show how a niche market became a dominant mode of mainstream entertainment (as described in Chapter 3 with regard to SMAP).

Although SMAP is Johnny's probably most successful group, the company has been in the business for decades before SMAP's breakthrough in the mid-1990s. After a few hits in the late 1960s, in the 1980s, Kitagawa's management found nationwide success with solo male idol singers such as Tahara Toshihiko and Kondo Masahiko. Kitagawa worked with groups as well as solo performers: popular groups were *Shônentai*, *Shibugakitai* (including Motoki Masahiro), and *Hikaru Genji* (the famous roller skating singing group that took its name from the Heian period romantic hero). All shared one important attribute: they were (relatively) young and absolutely male. Johnny's did not – and still does not – handle female acts. *Shônentai* celebrated its twentieth anniversary in show business in 2005 and is listed at the top of Johnny's official website, signaling their *senpai* (senior) status in the agency (2005), and suggesting that the social hierarchy that is often associated with corporate Japanese society is still observed in this management company.

Cahoon (2005) calls Johnny's a "factory," with amateur boys signed in their early teens for their looks rather than their talent, for talent is created through a long and intensive process of learning. Much like earning karate belts, boys must move through ranked positions before "making it": first as backup dancers to established acts, giving them the opportunity to acclimatize to the industry before the pressure is put on them to perform in the spotlight. Johnny's owns their "recordings, videos and even names" in return for the costly capital invested in their training. Once their position is recognized, they become "advertising pitchmen" (Cahoon 2005), signing contracts with companies where they become the face of various products.

Nabe Puro and others had been using television to promote their stable of talent in diverse ways (musical comedy rather than straight musicianship, for example) since the 1960s. Johnny's picked up this technique and refined it, marketing his boys on television specifically outside the sphere of music, as all around "*tarento*." This term is loosely translated as entertainment personalities who work as actors in commercials or serialized dramas, and talk show hosts, and in some cases even sporting or cooking figures in specialized variety shows. Television and other pubic appearances often precede bonafide hits – KATTUN, for example, performed a concert tour even before their first single was released, and SMAP members' forays into other public arenas such as radio and nonfiction writing are documented throughout this volume. Johnny's has also been successful in garnering the print media for exposure: *Popolo* (advertised as an "interview magazine for ladies") features beautiful actresses and popular comedians favored by younger audiences, but Johnny's acts dominate its cover and contents.

It is not uncommon for gossip to fuel fires in the *geinôkai*, but Johnny's is remarkable for weathering controversy. Johnny's stands apart from other *jimusho* for many of its distinguishing characteristics: first, its focus on male-only stars; second, its unmatched levels of cross-media success; and finally, its survival of intense press scrutiny. Kitagawa is rumored to be homosexual and to have had inappropriate relationships with some of his younger charges, as recorded in at least three former performers' media statements (Cahoon 2005, Schilling 1997: 237). In 2002–2003, Kitagawa sued the magazine *Bungei Shinju* that had published an allegedly slanderous article in this vein. The courts found in Kitagawa's favor (citing insufficient evidence) and the magazine had to pay him 1.2 million yen, far less than the 1 billion yen they had sued for (Tantei File 2003). The courts investigated the magazine's allegations but found Kitagawa innocent of criminal charges. According to an underground mass media investigation website, however, he was convicted of "sexual misconduct" in a civil case. The website notes that the major media outlets were coerced by the powerful agency not to publish this court case outcome.

Johnny Kitagawa had further troubles in July 2003 when it was announced that the two affiliated groups of Johnny's *Ongaku jimusho* were accused of hiding income over a period of three years to the Tokyo Tax Office; the total amount of "*shinkokumore*" (under-reporting) was over 600 million yen, which included a heavy penalty of about 200 million yen (Ugaya 2005b: 221). Like the sexual misconduct ruling, the general mass media did not widely circulate this news due to alleged pressure from the agency, demonstrating how powerful the *jimusho* has become. In many ways, the jury is still out on just how Johnny's is functioning at the top levels, but for the time being, mass audiences are still interested in the symbolic meanings of hierarchical yet ambiguous masculinity as produced by this organization.

Smaller, artist-focused Jimusho

The above *jimusho* are featured for their ongoing prominence in the field, but as discussed in Chapter 3, starting in the 1970s, there were important changes in the management roles in the music industry. As noted previously, successful artists from that period such as Yoshida Takurô, Inoue Yôsui, and others began their own companies to wrest creative control back from the executives and to keep profits closer to the musician. These early examples of self-managed artists stand in contrast to a widely held image of entertainment executives as "powerful owners exercising an almost omnipotent control over the practices of musicians and choices of consumers" (Negus 1999: 15). Haw notes that the real turnaround – from executives taking commissions in exchange for professional management to self-managed artists – occurred in the mid-to-late 1980s (2005b).

In the latter case, artists work harder to promote themselves and negotiate their own contracts but pay fewer fees and royalties to other parties. When musicians are experienced enough in the business to go solo, it is often in their benefit: they receive individualized attention because they do not share their managers with other artists. On the other hand, even though large entertainment agencies may be managing a hoard of other contracts, they have greater resources for promotional campaigns that could make the difference between a single that achieves modest sales and a massive hit. In each case, the artist chooses between what the agency can offer and what they feel is in their best interests: staying with the large agency or "going independent" (*dokuritsu shita jimusho*).

Why would an artist leave a large-scale *jimusho* for a smaller, artist-focused company? Sometimes the smaller office is a venture of the larger institutions; in other cases, it works in competition with them. Sometimes, the breakdown of personal relationships can trigger the change. Imawano Kiyoshirô, for example, was originally signed as a member of RC Succession with *Hori Puro* in 1971, but the band broke away due to personal differences in 1985. He and his partners created the company Umm (*Umu*) to take over the band's management and Imawano started his own office, Baby's Ltd, in 1991 (Imawano 2005).

As a venture of a larger institution, *jimusho* are connected through personal relationships or the investment of capital. The Alfee's company, Project III, for example, has always been under the wing of large-scale agencies. It is small scale, with an executive level of two or three men who have close relationships with the artists. The artists work closely with the executive; at many times, it is impossible to distinguish between the two levels, as artists make management decisions and management can also work as producers in the recording studio.

Project III's company name reflects the fact that the only act currently signed to the *jimusho* is the Alfee, drawing on the strong imagery of its three male members (in the past, the agency has managed the careers of other artists as well – Kawamura Kaori who debuted in 1988, as well as the idol "unit" SKIRT who debuted in 1996). The main company is Project III, which promotes itself on its website as an artist-focused *jimusho* through its motto in English: "AN ARTISITS [sic] AGENCY." Established in 1985, it is headed by Sekiguchi Noboru, manager of the band from their early days at the large-scale Tanabe Agency. Their split with Tanabe to establish Project III does not represent conflict as much as it does continuity in this particular case, as the other major stockholders are the Tanabe Agency and K-Dash Inc., both well-established *jimusho*. Affiliated companies include a concert tour production company and two music publishing companies.

Jimusho *in the larger business context*

The distinction between large-scale and small-scale *jimusho* reflects the classic divide between medium and small companies versus large corporations that create the "dual economic system" in Japan. Small agencies are often connected to larger ones for start-up money, and individual effort and talent (as well as a bit of luck) are crucial to the success of these small companies; they do not have the large amounts of capital to ride out downswings in the market. Many of these small companies, however, begin when seasoned veterans leave the large agencies seeking artistic and financial independence or, more seriously, disassociation due to personal disagreement or even illegal activity. One of the most newsworthy splits was between Komuro Tetsurô-produced singer Suzuki Ami and her *jimusho* AG Communications. In 2000, Suzuki sued the company over refusing to release her from her contract after the agency president was accused of tax evasion. Yet, after her successful court case in 2001, Suzuki has struggled to stay working, despite showing efforts to start anew by changing the characters of her first name and shifting from Sony to Avex in late 2004.

Generally, only established artists are able to take the risk of "going independent." In these cases, these new *jimusho* are not marketing "high-risk" products; these are market-tested individuals with an already recognized measure of success. In some ways, going "solo" can be seen as a measure of status in the *geinôkai*, and this is only achieved by an elite group of artists. Unknown artists often do not have the capital, or the ability to attract others' capital, to start their own *jimusho* before breaking into the charts. Thus, large-scale *jimusho* are more likely to "discover" musicians, promote them to fame; the question as to whether or not the celebrity stays or moves on depends on the individual's satisfaction with the *jimusho* contract. Overall, the *jimusho* is the site for the enactment of a variety of social relationships, both personal and professional, and often it is difficult to distinguish between the two. Independence is valued in this sphere of business culture, but only when the independence has a reasonable expectation of yielding profitable results.

The preceding argument relies on a pragmatic understanding of business practice in the music management industry. Individuals operate within cultural frameworks, but in ways that best maximize their outcomes. Yet, amongst employees as well as observers of the *jimusho*, there also exists an abstract and romanticized vision of the work done by these management companies. Referring to the classic industry myth of the "magic touch," executives often believe in a "culture of production" where they make "intuitive" decisions about artists (Negus 1999: 21). No matter how we rationally analyze the process, intangible ideas – of intuition, and even destiny or luck – are still important to the perception of success in the music industry. A *Hori Puro* executive is quoted as saying

> If the process is aided by luck, hits are possible. If you aren't lucky, you won't have a hit, but what remains is an interesting [experience] (*omoshirokatta koto*). Well, that's the great failure of this job. But, on the other hand, if you are lucky and get a hit, and your luck multiplies, then it's a miracle.
>
> (Takahashi 2005: 19)

Record companies

Record companies, or *rekôdogaisha* in Japanese, constitute the next important link in the chain that links various parts of the Japanese music industry. This section examines the role of record companies in the Japanese music business, with reference to structure and ownership, the royalty and pricing system, and recent trends in sales. Although the international sheet music industry was long the leader in the industry in the first half of the twentieth century, the record company emerged as a new force because of its association with celebrity (Buxton 1990: 429). Record companies, receptive to the management agency's pitch (or to individuals representing themselves), choose and promote talent locally, nationwide, and internationally. A universal aspect of the relationship between musicians and record companies is the tension between music, or "artistic integrity," and money, or "financial strategies." These two camps tend to be polarized in times of conflict but in reality can overlap in meaning and function, as record executives are "constructing knowledge" about the audience to guide their decisions as a kind of creative reality (Negus 1999: 19). Furthermore, the shape of the record company industry (in terms of internal organization and relationships to other corporations) reflects the market in general, as it has changed to follow both global and domestic trends – to meet demand and to cut losses over the years.

Structure and ownership

The most reliable source of information about the structure of recording industry is the Recording Industry Association of Japan (RIAJ or *Nihon Rekôdo Kyôkai* in Japanese). The Association's previous body was formed in 1942 and took its current name in 1969.[6] In 1990, "twenty-five major recording companies in Japan" were members (Kawabata 1991: 327), but in 2005, the association listed 41 members under various levels of financial commitment (RIAJ 2005a) showing rapid growth in after the 1990s. The association's goals are "enhancing harmony and conciliation across the recording industry, diffusion of high-quality recordings (pre-recorded CDs etc.), protection of record producers' right, and efforts to promote proper use of recordings" (ibid.). Note the current goals take into account the recent issues posed by new music technologies that challenge not only the concept of ownership and copyright but also the idea of "proper use" or consumption customs that respect these ideas.

Broadly speaking, there are two kinds of labels in Japan: major and independent, the former referred to as *mejâ* and the latter as *indîzu*, or "indies" in Japanese. Major labels account for the majority of the 41 members for the RIAJ (see Appendix). But independent labels must not be dismissed as unimportant players in the contemporary Japanese music market. Some independent labels are entirely "independent," while others are subsidiaries of major labels (Warner's Indies Network, for example). As evidence of the rising importance of indies music, the mainstream chart Oricon has begun to include a separate indies single and album ranking along with its major label rankings.

Independent labels release a variety of musical genre. Independent labels are reputed to be artist-focused – some of the early labels were founded by artists after they found little success with the commercial labels. This initial distance from commercialism gives rise to a commonly held notion that indies music is too "alternative" for mainstream audiences, but as noted in Chapter 3, there are indies artists with "mellower" sounds as well. One of the most famous stories of indies success translated into major stardom is the hard rock band, X-JAPAN, who started their own label in order to sell their records, spurred on by an original investment by the drummer's parents. X-JAPAN then went on to achieve nationwide followings in the 1990s. Acts such as GLAY (originally picked up by an X-JAPAN-associated label, but currently with Toshiba–EMI), Kiroro (currently with Victor Entertainment), Judy and Mary (who moved from indie label Chainsaw Records to Epic/Sony in 1993), Love Psychedelico (later signed with Victor), and Orange Range (currently with Sony) all had indies starts before making it in the major scene.

Although the acts listed above made the change to major labels after (or on the brink of) national success, there are many artists contracted to independent labels that are thriving. Many of these record companies were started by musicians (rather than businessmen) (Schaefer 2005), reflecting the further blurring of the lines between artist and management since the 1970s. Art Union is an example of a self-proclaimed independent label working out of Tokyo; Loop Ash and Under Code Production are two other labels that had numerous rankings in the Oricon indies chart in 2005. By the mid-1990s, independent artists and underground music scenes had spilled into the mainstream, thanks to the distribution efforts of foreign-held CD retailers such as HMV and Tower Records who were more willing to promote these bands than their Japanese counterparts (ibid.), probably because as outsiders to the market themselves, they needed to take risks to compete for consumers.

Many major labels in Japan have "parent companies," mainly in home electronics, reflecting prewar markets (record companies were created by phonograph producers) (Kawabata 1991: 333). Compared to their UK and US counterparts, major Japanese label contracts tend to be shorter (the standard contract is three instead of five years) due to the fact that US/UK labels with substantial overseas sales can take advantage of a longer selling period per unit than the primarily domestic Japanese label (Ugaya 2005b: 173–174). Record companies in Japan are internally structured similarly to their Western counterparts, with the A&R (Artists and Repertoire) departments of particular interest to observers of global flows in Japanese popular culture. This department originally served as "intermediaries" between foreign companies and the Japanese public (Kawabata 1991: 339). Today, most Japanese record companies are comprised of three main sections: *seisakubu* (literally, the production department, or A&R), the *sendenbu* (publicity or public relations department), and *eigyôbu* (the management department, which is primarily devoted to communication and relationships with product retailers around the country). The following quite clearly demonstrates the links in the industry chain from the artist's perspective:

> If the music director [of the record company] hears the song once and says "Let's go with this one", the director will tell his colleagues in the record company "This is a good song". If his colleagues in the publicity department (*sendenbuin*) are told "really good", then they should tell those in the sales department (*eigyôbuin*) [the same thing]. Then, the salespeople go to the CD retailers and start the sales talk. Then – depending on the salesperson's nature – his request for a display with impact is unlikely to fail.
>
> (Takamizawa 2004: 129)

Record company royalties

In 1998 there were approximately 12 records that sold more than 1 million copies; considering that the set price for full-length albums is about ¥3000, a million-selling album can net substantial profits for musicians and composers, and for the record companies, depending on how the royalty is settled. How are these royalties determined? Ugaya states that in the case of million-selling albums, the band can net up to 300 million yen in royalties (an informant, however, told me that this was very optimistic, and songwriting and backing musician royalties would have to stay within the band to reach that level of profit). Ugaya does admit that most artists do not receive as much as 10 percent; many artists receive substantially less, however, with rates such as 1–5 percent not uncommon (2005b: 176).

Concomitant with increases in music consumption in the 1970s, there was a rise in royalties due to competition between proliferating labels. Japanese label royalties represent a percentage of sales profits, but at varying levels, depending on whether there were extra costs incurred during production (Kawabata 1991: 339). De Launey notes that major Japanese labels like Sony offer two kinds of contracts for artists, divided by nationality: a foreign artist contracted to Sony pays back the cost of recording out of royalties earned, but in the case of Japanese artists, their recording costs are fronted by the record company (1995: 217). This demonstrates a difference in business practice between the United States and Japan but it also may be as practical as it is cultural (the foreign artist's connection to Japan may not be as long lived; compared to the Japanese artist, he or she may not represent a good long-term investment but rather a short-term venture and thus is funded differently).

How much are the labels paying? According to Hoguchi, a successful pop composer in his own right and head of a popular music training school, even a conservative royalty contract (1–5 percent according to Ugaya), is unrealistic when considering the case of new composers:

> The reality of the situation [for young composers] is, according to contract awarded to the individual composer, the best is about .14 percent and most are

> about .1 percent; what is unforgivable is that the cases of .05 percent [royalty awarded] are increasing. Namely, even if a fan buys a 3000 yen CD with 14 songs in it, the composer earns 1.6 yen per sale.
>
> (2005)

As a composer himself, it is expected for Hoguchi to defend the composer, but his comments also illustrate concepts of musical ownership in the larger economy:

> Apart from the portion of celebrated writers, most authors have been put in a weak position, both social and financially. The copyright law is a law that was formed to take as its goal the protection of the rights of authors. Accordingly, those who should be protected are the authors who create . . . [art, music, plays, and written work]. In spite of this, [the concept of] current copyright is watered down by the business transactions that are blind to copyright law, and the structure by which large profits are earned – "the composer's regulated society" (*ongakukensakuken kanrishakai*) – becomes the status quo.
>
> (ibid.)

Probably the most important context where royalties are calculated in the Japanese pop industry is in the case of karaoke. As we will see later in this chapter, the Japanese hit charts change frequently due to promotion through temporary or short-term tie-ups with television (e.g., a seasonal television ad campaign or a drama series spanning three months). Thus, the sales life of an album or single is relatively short compared to its US or UK counterpart. This is compensated, somewhat, by the extensive network of karaoke establishments which purchase the rights to broadcast music as karaoke; thus they pay royalties on these songs every time they buy anew, or re-new, their repertoire from music publishers. A composer can make more money on karaoke royalties than CDs sales royalties, especially if the song is considered a "classic" and has staying power. Thus, a song's karaoke affability is important when analyzing its overall income potential, underscoring the relationship between hit-making and Japanese musical practice, which includes not only consuming CDs and live music through concerts but also reproducing music through karaoke.

Negotiating record company contracts is one of the more difficult maneuvering positions any artist – Japanese or American, newcomer or veteran – experiences. Furthermore, record companies tend to be socially and financially conservative in their ventures, which can frustrate creative and/or risk-taking artists. Takamizawa writes of the disappointment after his band's record company at that time cancelled the release of a single of a "parody song" that made reference to the notorious 1968 "Three Hundred Million Yen Incident," which was at the time the largest bank robbery in Japanese history; the reason given by management was "social concerns" (*shakaiteki na hairyo*). This concern arose from the single's release date coinciding with the expiration of the statute of limitations in this case (2004: 52–53). We see domestic politics affecting the decisions made by record companies again in the late 1980s with RC Succession (see Chapter 6), yet in this case the cancelled album achieved notoriety and success after a minor label picked it up. Generally, record company executives avoid controversy, but as RC Succession proved, it can still fuel sales profits if it strikes the right chord with the public.

Pricing and sales

Japan's pricing system is said to lack "diversity" because of a "re-sale system" whereby the record companies set a sales price for their products which is observed nationwide (Ugaya 200b: 178). Set contracts determine the cut of the distributor (either wholesale or retail); the vast majority of Japanese-manufactured CDs have its "*teika*" or fixed price (both with and without the consumption tax figured in) printed on its back cover, making it near impossible for retailers to compete by cutting prices. The "recommended resale price contract" between distributors and manufacturers came about due to anti-monopoly laws; records and CDs have, since 1953, been classified in pricing by law in the same category as newspapers, books, and magazines (179). As noted earlier, 3000 yen is an approximate price for Japanese-manufactured CD albums, although competition from overseas manufacturers in the 1990s, imported at a cheaper price, has driven down the cost to a pre-tax range between 2700 and 2800 yen. CD singles run from 980 to 1000 yen.

As nearly all *hôgaku* is produced in Japan, the pricing system for *yôgaku* CDs that are "made in Japan" appear to disadvantage the products of the Japanese record companies. Why would a consumer spend between 500 and 1000 yen more for a U2 compact disc made in Japan when the US version contains the same music? Japanese record companies justify the higher price by "value-adding" critic liner notes, and Japanese translations of the English lyrics. Thus, for Japanese consumers of *yôgaku*, there is diversity in pricing and increased consumer choice, but there are no consumer options for *hôgaku* (Ugaya 2005b: 179).[7]

Since its peak in 1998, sales in the Japanese music industry have been in decline. In 1998, there were 12 different releases which hit the million-seller mark; in 2005, there were just nine albums and singles from Japanese artists that sold more than 1 million copies (RIAJ 2005: 15).[8] The only area where record companies are experiencing sales growth are music videos (video recordings in VHS, DVD, and LD format) (Haw 2005a; RIAJ 2005b: 5).

Sales figures show that Japanese "million-seller" artists sell the majority of their CDs in a short period of time (as opposed to extended periods of steady sales); one of the best-selling albums of all time was released by B'z, who sold 5 million copies of their greatest hits album in one month (Abe 2003: 51). To achieve these quick figures, the record company often undertakes an intensive marketing blitz, including appearances on music television shows, jingle contracts with commercial products, or opening themes for serialized dramas.

Except for uneven performance in the early 1980s, generally, overall sales of music units increased in moderate rates since the 1970s (Ministry of Information [Statistics] 2005). The year 1988 appears to be a crucial year for recent changes in consumption of music, paving the way for "million-seller" artists. Asô Kôtarô writes that 1988 was the year that a "trendy drama" first hit number one in the ratings, that karaoke boxes were widely available, and that the CD single first appeared on the market. This appealed to a new market of consumers who had previously not purchased CDs or records in bulk: women in their twenties and thirties (Asô and Miyadai 1999: 85). Previously, adult men had been the prime audience for popular music. By the mid-1990s, record companies and promoters made the conscious decision to change their target market from general adult/young adult to female high school students (Ugaya 2005b: 188). As examples of this focused marketing, radio stations introduced "high school ranking" charts; teenaged female duo Puffy were frequently seen as spokeswomen on nationally broadcast television commercials; Komuro was readying his female troupe for success through the new record company Avex Trax (188–189). High school girls were explicitly targeted by marketing campaigns; they did have expendable income, due to part-time work or as allowances from affluent families, and they responded to these promotions by making stars out of female artists who resembled their ideal representations of femininity.

To demonstrate the significance of the new consumers, we see an unprecedented jump in the twelve months between 1994 and 1995 of over 50,000 units sold; as illustrated in Table 4.1, this had previously represented five to ten years of sales increases. This was precisely the start of a new era of "girl power" in Japanese pop music. Sleek feminine sophistication was personified by Amuro Namie; Aikawa Nanase was the ultimate rebellious "rock chick"; and Puffy were the down-to-earth girls next door. Although this golden era of CD sales has passed, female artists still hold their own: in 2004 four out of the eight Japanese "million-selling" artists were women (RIAJ 2005b: 15). These sales figures to this specific market echo the investigation of pre-teenage girls and their engagement with pop music in Australia, which showed that "the girls' play with popular music . . . enabled the testing of (symbolic) boundaries and their 'making sense' of music and nuances of identity" (Baker 2004: 90). The ideology and discourse of popular music in Japan plays an important role in the construction and maintenance of femininity from the 1990s to today as well as propping up a faltering market that would not have survived if it had relied on its old audiences.

Hôgaku versus yôgaku

When looking at music production in Japan, how much is domestic (*hôgaku*) versus international (*yôgaku*)? In 1948, when the Occupation first allowed the import of musical recordings, records imported from the West "dominated" sales charts (Mitsui 1997: 169). In the postwar era, Japanese record companies (or Japanese branches of North American or European labels) were first divided

Table 4.1 Record company sales in Japan (domestic and international sales combined)

Year	*Units sold (in thousands)*	*Wholesale revenue (in millions of yen)*	*Comment*
1946[a]	6,420	N/A	"SP disks" only
1955	14,500	3,018	33 and 45 rpm disks (LPs and singles) on the market
1965	90,934	29,393	Popularity of overseas music (The Beatles) expands the market significantly
1970	155,875	65,720	Cassette tape market opens in 1968 and by 1970 is a significant seller against LPs/45rp singles
1975	203,665	184,883	The Japanese rock movement underway; New Music also starting – Japanese music is diversifying and expanding
1985	219,673	281,337	First compact disc sales in 1984; increase steadily after 1985
1990	290,494	387,770	CD sales surpassing album sales in 1987
1995	465,515	574,031	Sales begin dropping in 1998 and have never recovered from the late 1990s high
2005	309,952 (note: if DVDs are added, the total rises to 448,265)	367,237 (with DVD 553,114)	Sales continue to drop year by year. CDs are still the largest unit of music sold but face competition from rental shops and file downloads through the Internet and mobile phones; the value of digital music sales is over 30 billion yen. DVDs or music videos are the only music product sales figures to rise in this era.

Sources: Haw (2005a), Kawabata (1991: 327, 329), RIAJ (2005b, 2006), and *Sômushô (Tôkeikyoku)* (Ministry of Information [Statistics]) 2005.

Note

a The RIAJ did not keep records from 1943 to 1945.

into *hôgaku* and *yôgaku* divisions, with each department specializing in different kinds of artists and audiences; at this time, the product itself was more highly distinguished. In the mid-1960s, however, *hôgaku* began sounding more like its Western counterpart, and the A&R executives from the Western division began working with Japanese artists, furthering the transition of Japanese music to the Western sound (Kawabata 1991: 338).

Mitsui writes that in the late 1960s, purchases of records that were "pressed from imported master tapes" were surpassed by "records originally recorded by Japanese artists," highlighting the fact Japanese record companies began production working with foreign masters – not importing the records themselves (1997: 169), creating an industry infrastructure that could further develop later on. The late 1970s and the early 1980s were a time of fierce rivalry between record companies and the expansion of discount record shops; it was also in the late 1970s that record shops began promoting Japanese music more actively, as most of the profits earned by record companies in the early postwar period came from sales of Western artists' records. This occurred because industry members were concerned as composer royalties were leaving Japan and the record companies could not earn as much from records sold by foreign artists (Ugaya 2005b: 30).

Kawabata also writes of conflict in the 1980s between Japanese labels that managed *yôgaku* music and their executives; this was because their promotional work was rarely reciprocated; for example, before Sony's 1987 purchase, CBS did little to promote Japanese artists in the United States, while Sony promoted and distributed CBS artists as well as their domestic acts (1991: 332) The Japanese arm of Epic/Sony records, formed in 1978, broke ground because it supported the Japanese rock movement, promoting Japanese musicians rather than merely selling carryover contracts from the US parent company (De Launey 1995: 209). In 1989, 73 percent of production was *hôgaku*, with the remainder imported music (Kawabata 1991: 330), while in 2004, 74 percent of total audio recordings produced (including DVD and MD) were considered "domestic" (RIAJ 2005b: 2). These figures demonstrate a relatively steady rate of differentiation between the two products over the past two decades. Overall, *yôgaku* consumption, while in decline in the late 1960s and 1970s, has stabilized in the 1990s; we should be aware, however, that these statistics include other genre (such as classical and jazz music), where consumption of *yôgaku* can be significantly higher than in the pop and rock categories.

As discussed in Chapter 2, Japanese artists have had limited success in overseas markets. The specifics of taste, language, and culture are not the only hurdles that Japanese promoters face when selling *hôgaku* overseas. Ugaya gives the example of Hong Kong artists who conduct successful overseas tours in not only Taiwan and mainland China but also the United States, Canada, and Europe; this is because the Chinese diasporatic audience supports these artists' overseas ventures (2005b: 176). The lack of depth and breadth in international audiences prevents Japanese acts from widespread appeal. Shops catering to Japanese expatriates or Japanese Americans in Hawaii or in Los Angeles might be an exception to this, but in most foreign communities, Japanese audiences are too thinly dispersed to allow *hôgaku* to feature prominently in overseas markets. Therefore, *hôgaku* remains targeted at the Japanese domestic market and is the primary business activity of Japanese record labels. Another difference between *hôgaku* and yôgaku is their focus on format. *Yôgaku* tends to do best with album sales, while *hôgaku* tends to sell as singles; in the latter category, Japanese artists consistently outperform their US or UK counterparts (De Launey 1995: 205–206). This is most likely due to the connection between singles promotion and domestic television, discussed later in this chapter, and the connection between single consumption and karaoke practice, discussed in detail in Chapter 5.

Challenges to the system

One of the earliest challenges to record companies was the introduction of rental record and CD shops in the late 1970s and early 1980s (Kawabata 1991: 340; Kimura 1991: 329). At their conception, it was thought that these shops would boost sales as they allowed consumers to try out a recording before buying it (much like a consumer tries on clothing before a purchase), but many renters made cassette tapes of the originals or later burned their own CDs, and sales increases did not result (Ugaya 2005b: 185). Kawabata notes that many record companies claimed compensation for these losses as part of the Copyright Act (1991: 340). Ever since rental shops appeared, the recording industry has made several civil cases against them, including the 1984 "Tentative Measures (against) Rental Records Law," the 1985 "Revised Copyright Law," and other rights to claim compensation, which have been recognized by Japanese courts (Ugaya 2005b: 184). New laws were instituted from 1991 to 1994 to protect *shinpu*, or newly released CDs, legislating that rental shops had to wait a fixed period of time after the release of the CD before putting it on the rental shelf (ibid.). Arguments over CD rental shops were not merely domestic squabbles between different arms of the music industry, but extended as far international politics. For example, on US side at GATT talks, accusations were made of these shops being in alliance with Japanese recordable tape manufacturers (De Launey 1995: 215). In general, the Japanese record industry has decided to work with these shops rather than against them and uses contracts with the CD shops to promote certain singles on a regular basis, not necessarily raising sales but at least enhancing the artists' profile (215–216). The number of CD rental shops peaked in 1989 at 6213 shops; in 2004, there were 3379 registered (Ugaya 2005b: 185).

To what extent copyright royalties are paid to individuals and to corporations in both the distribution and the consumption of Japanese music today is difficult to quantify, but shifts in this system have brought about changes in the music culture; Chapter 5 addresses the challenge that technological advances have made to notions of musical copyright. A composer in the avant-garde field of electronic music writes:

> Without the need to claim copyrights, one doesn't need to be introduced by a mentor in order to publish. I am entirely free, but paradoxically, this freedom leaves me the entire responsibility for what I produce, a freedom which encompasses the whole production chain, from the production of sonic material all the way to decisions regarding target audience and packaging.
>
> (Shirashi cited in Loubet 2000: 25)

With this in mind, it is possible to consider the eventual emergence of a genre of Japanese music that stands outside the standardized relationships between the *jimusho*, recording studio, record label, and record retailer. For the time being, however, most mainstream Japanese popular music is firmly entrenched in the chain of human relationships between these kinds of companies.

Producers and recording studios

The recording producer – as a facilitator – and the recording studio – as a production site – are the next two links examined.

> The characteristics of the mode of production they have created, from the function of the producer to the recording session, all have one aim: the problematic fusion between the universe of techniques, by which objects are made, and that of images, in which an audience wants to invest.
>
> (Hennion 1990: 202)

The producers are thought to be "representative" of the audience's tastes, in that they have special knowledge of what will be successful in the market, and because this is such a subjective task, "it becomes even more of a social role" (205). In the recording studio, there is "mutual criticism," "subjective listening," and "collective anticipation" between the artist, producer, and studio employees (203), all of which contribute to the fashioning of the final product for sale.

There are generally three types of record producers in Japan. The first kind is the "traditional" professional, an individual who concentrates on producing other artists. They may be employed by a recording studio or have their own companies that are contracted by other artists to make records. In British terms, the traditional professional is personified by a figure like George Martin, famed as a rock and pop producer who focuses on clients rather than his own individual career as a recording musician. For many years, this kind of production role was associated with the behind-the-scenes professional, often a full-time employee of a large-scale production company.

Since the 1970s, artists have taken this role themselves and "self-produce" (an English-inspired Japanese phrase) describes a group of Japanese pop stars who take responsibility for the musical decisions made in the recording studio. This trend was first documented in Chapter 3 and is associated with the shift from industry-"produced" stars to self-made, "authentic" musicians who fulfill the role of "singer/songwriter" rather than functioning as a mouthpiece for big industry executives. Since the 1990s, a further development occurred, adding to the landscape: "self-producers" then turned to work for others, combining the role of celebrity in his/her own right with the traditional role of producing other stars; this shift coincided with the development of small, artist-focused *jimusho*.

Bourdieu's (1994a) concept of fields of production is an important tool for understanding particular industry developments, and for understanding the effects of these shifts in public perception of the popular music industry. "The . . . artistic field is a field of forces but it is also a field of struggles tending to transform or conserve this field of forces" (Bourdieu 1994a: 51). In other words, struggles between the positions held in the field result in both innovation and preservation of artistic tradition, depending on the players' motives and the outcomes of their interactions. By focusing on the power relations between "positions" in the "field," we can avoid fetishizing the musical outcomes of the industry (56) and contextualize the music more appropriately vis-à-vis its consumers as well as producers. This also allows for the diversity in the industry, as individual power struggles result in individual outcomes, not one uniform business culture.

Bourdieu's concept that dominant "bourgeois" art is in constant struggle with "art for art's sake" (60) can be illustrated in the Japanese underground folk movement and many indie releases since the late 1980s, but we can also discern an interesting fusion of "bourgeois" with "art" in mainstream folk to New Music movement in the 1970s. Artists, taking control away from the "professional machine" that had created *wasei* pop in the 1960s, became "mainstream" through similar marketing techniques (e.g., appearing on television), yet they offered for sale a different kind of artistic "reality."

Professional producers were not to disappear entirely from the map. After New Music pioneers set a standard in the 1970s for self-production, artists whose star had faded somewhat could use their production skills to find new life as musicians/producers/celebrities whose magic touch allowed other artists to find fame. Often, these new roles reinvigorated their own careers. de Ferranti refers to these "individual producer–composers" in his discussion of social practices in the popular music field; "Hosono Haruomi, Komuro Tetsuya, Cornelius [a.k.a. Oyamada Keigo, formerly of the early nineties' band Flipper's Guitar] and Oda Tetsuro" are cited as significant players (2002: 204). It is notable that de Ferranti's examples are drawn primarily from the late 1980s to mid-1990s. Hosono, de Ferranti's first example, was a member of Happy End but found global fame in the 1980s with YMO; Komuro made it big in the 1990s after the dissolution of his band TM Network. His success with female vocalists then recharged his own career as member of the trio globe. Cornelius pioneered an independent music movement in the early 1990s called the "Shibuya Sound" but went on to produce Pizzicato Five, which has an international following. Oda Tetsurô enjoyed wide success with his mid-1990s "girl rock" singles. Okuda Tamio, formerly of Unicorn and a solo recording artist in his own right, became a producer after his band broke up in 1993, finding musical and financial security as the producer of the female duo Puffy (who debuted 1996 in Japan and in 2004 in the United States). Tsunku has probably made more money as producer for the ever-changing female idol group Morning *Musume* (who debuted in 1998) than he ever did as lead singer for the Osaka-based band Sharan Q. The musician-as-producer shift is first discerned in the 1970s as a "self-producer," but the phenomenon of musician-*turned*-producer is seen most markedly in the 1990s. Here is a new breed of producers, whose reputation is so strong behind the scenes that the "star maker" roles have achieved celebrity status in itself.

As argued in Chapter 3, the producer is one of the roles that changed significantly in the past fifty years. The swing of power from production team to individual artist (and possibly back again) is nowhere more apparent. Artists who produce themselves are in control of their musical creative process and do not have to pay outsider fees, keeping costs down. This signals a shift away from the external focus of the role of the producer (as some one who "understands" the public and therefore must mediate between the audience's desires and the artist's musical expression [Hennion 1990: 201]) to one that is more internally focused: the musician rather than the businessperson in Japan is more in tune with the needs of the music public. In the case of several of the previously listed "super producers" in the 1990s, notably these are men who entered the industry under a corporate identity (as a member of a group) which over a period of time disintegrated; they took on the role of producer as a "second career," which then engendered a third musical career, catapulting them back into the spotlight as individual, as in the case of Komuro Tetsuya. The *ura/omote* (front and background) roles in music production have thus become blurred, and now Japanese producers can be celebrities in their own right. To some extent, the role of producers has been elevated and mystified in recent years, distancing them from the ideal of the "authentic" singer-songwriter of the 1970s, demonstrating a subtle shift from that "[s]uccess is a gamble by the producer on his identification with the public" (Hennion 1990: 203) to one where the producer is a rarified individual with a "magic touch."

The primary site of producers' work is in recording studios. Record company executives usually make recommendations to new artists on which studios and engineers to choose for their recordings, based on their past experience pairing artists of a certain type with technicians who can enhance their style. One of the first decisions is location: should the artist record at home or overseas? Japanese audio technology in the postwar era was comparatively advanced, so at first recording and/or mixing and mastering overseas was not an attractive option because the level of Japanese studios was equivalent to that in the United States or the United Kingdom. Still, the pull of authenticity gave work done in foreign studios a kind of caché, and as noted in Chapter 2, the exchange rate favored Japanese consumers in the 1980s. But there were practical benefits aside from the status of an overseas recording gig. Independent record producer Matsumoto Yasuo noted that working overseas creates a different working atmosphere, so that musicians and producers are truly able to concentrate on achieving the best sound (Takahashi 2005: 11). In a foreign country, celebrity musicians can travel from hotel to studio relatively unknown and unencumbered, and without the custom of *aisatsu* (making greetings to other artists, especially senior colleagues, who were also using the studio at the same time) which slowed down recording sessions; thus, an artist could produce an album for about the same cost as working in Tokyo, and possibly in shorter time. Finally, the level of individual technological prowess with respect to recording engineers was regarded more highly in the United States and in Britain than in Japan. This is in contrast to the generally held notion that recording studios in Japan had equivalent or superior technology, but the personnel in Japan were deemed not as experienced in bringing out the best of the machinery and the musicians.

London and Los Angeles are frequent destinations for recording artists from Japan. Los Angeles is chosen by many as its proximity to Tokyo is a plus. hide, former guitarist of X-JAPAN, recorded, mixed, and mastered his solo projects in LA, and his posthumously released promotion video shows him soaking up the Californian atmosphere: lounging about a rented LA apartment, shopping in trendy retail district Melrose and in the recording studio with American technicians (hide 1998). Yet, twenty-five years earlier, we have a less than positive account of Happy End's LA recording session in 1973:

> The atmosphere in the studio was often tense and the band were disillusioned by the gap between the America they had imagined . . . and the America they were actually experiencing. One of the main problems concerned communication difficulties between them and the various Los Angeles musicians and studio personnel who assisted them on the recordings. The experience made them understand that Japanese rock was/is quintessentially Japanese despite its American façade.
>
> (Hosokawa 1999b: 120)

Working overseas, thus, is not for every one, and it is not always possible for artists who are trying to fit recording with other work commitments such as regular television, radio, and/or concert appearances; for them, staying close to home is the only option. The Japanese Association of Professional Recording Studios (JAPRS) has 38 "corporate" members, 36 of which are located in metropolitan Tokyo, demonstrating the dominance of the capital in the recording industry. Some of the big studios in Tokyo include Studio Take One, located in Tokyo's Shinjuku area. Established in 1977, a variety of artists such as Candies, Sano Motoharu, Yuming, Imawano Kiyoshirô, and Unicorn (Okuda Tamio) have utilized their three studios. Freedom Studios (since 1976) are also located near Shinjuku and offer Japanese musicians three studios for recording work; much of the Alfee's 1980s and 1990s repertoire was recorded here. Tie-ups in this sector of the industry are also common: influential management company Amuse, Inc., has its own studio in Shibuya (established 1987) and Hitokuchizaka Studio AV (established 1978) in central Tokyo is affiliated with radio station *Nippon Hôsô*, Fuji Broadcasting Corporation and Pony Canyon Records, among others.

Watching music: the industry as seen through television

A survey conducted in Tokyo by the RIAJ in early 2005 found that that "television dominated the list of channels influencing music purchases." About 51.5 percent said they were influenced by music television programs, 39.4 percent by theme songs for dramas, 35.8 percent by television commercial themes, and 33.8 percent by commercials promoting musical products (Haw 2005a). These strong figures illustrate the very close relationship television has with the music industry; this is in contrast with the idea that commercial endorsements can lower or cheapen the image of Western artists. Furthermore, American television reaches approximately one-fifth of the overall audience that buys American music; thus, it is not effective to use television to promote its pop music (Ugaya 2005b: 175).

"Terrestrial television services" were established in early 1953 with NHK's station, and the first commercial network, NTV, began broadcasting six months later (MIC 2004: 45). Black and white televisions were introduced in the mid-1950s, with 4 percent of the households surveyed owning one in 1951 but 54 percent of households did only nine years later (Yoshimi 1999: 155). Color television broadcasts were introduced in 1960 and replaced black and white television as a household item in the late 1960s. Digital broadcasting of television programming was introduced in late 1993 in the metropolitan areas of Tokyo, Nagoya, and Osaka (MIC 2004: 45). Community television stations were established in 1992, with 167 stations operating in 2003 (MIC 2004: 45). One such community station is TVK, a Yokohama-based station that broadcasts Japanese pop music videos on week day afternoons (*Mutoma* Japan, the first term an abbreviation for "Music Tomato") and is well known for its play list that includes Japanese independent artists. Music video shows are much less expensive to broadcast compared to live chat and performance shows, so they have become a speciality of under-funded community television stations.

According to the government's statistical office, Japanese individual viewers watched close to four hours of television a day (Ministry of Internal Affairs and Communications 2004: 45). This is in contrast with others who believe that television plays a more ubiquitous role in the domestic lives of the Japanese, with reports of four hours and eight hours a day (Stevens and Hosokawa 2001: 238–239). The disparity in figures is probably related to differences in defining "watching television," with those reporting four hours as categorizing the activity as exclusive, where the viewer is sitting in front of the set and it is the viewer's main focus. Others define the activity by how many hours the television set is actually turned on, even if no one in the room is sitting in front of the TV watching. Television sets may be turned on during household chores, mealtimes, and other activities such as telephone conversations and domestic hobbies such as sewing, reading, and model building.

Television holds a central place held in the history of consumption and distribution of music in the postwar era: "Television plays such an important role in the development of popular music that it has even been seen to constitute its definition" (Stevens and Hosokawa 2001: 225). After the 1970s, television companies assumed many of the "duties" that had previously been the sphere of production companies, creating a monopoly in the music entertainment business (Fujie 1989: 206). For example, the conglomerate Fuji Sankei owns the domestic label Pony Canyon Records, but it also owns Fuji Television and the *Sankei* Newspaper Company (see Appendix). To outside observers, this could mean that Pony Canyon contracted artists are given favor when competing for tie-up and theme songs contracts with Fuji Television productions.

An increasing trend of visualization has affected the way producers promote their music:

> Records are not made to be listened to, but to create points of intersection between the formation of cultural islands. Audio novelties are no longer presented in sonic form on the radio, but rather in visual form on television, as advertisements.
>
> (Loubet 2000: 19)

In other words, the promotion of a commercial product through a television advertisement has now been conflated with the advertisement of a musical product (the song itself). It is increasingly difficult to discern between promotional motives: even if a commercial appears to be promoting a soft drink, when the vocalists providing the background music are the main actors in the advertisement, the messages become intertwined: "If you like this song, buy the drink" as well as "If you like the drink, check out this CD!"

This close relationship between Japanese television programs and music began in the 1960s and matured in the 1980s. As previously mentioned, *Nabe Puro* established a mutually beneficial relationship with the product Milky Soap as sponsor, and both "products" (people in the shape of *Nabe Puro* performers and objects in the shape of soap) were promoted through the show *Shabondama Horidê*. Arguably, since the 1980s, television has replaced radio as the most far-reaching mediator and conveyor of popular music culture in Japan. The music television program (*ongaku* or *kayôkyoku bangumi*) usually features performances and interviews with popular music groups or solo acts. The length of the performance varies with the show; some shows are all "talk" with little music; yet due to the focus on musical stars as guests, these shows (such as *Utaban* [TBS 1996–present] and *Hey Hey Hey! Music Champ* [Fuji 1994–present], discussed below) continue to be categorized as music shows rather than interview or variety shows.

Radio and television industries in Japan used music for advertising in the early postwar period. The tie-up between corporations and music through commercials began in 1951, marked by the first radio commercial to utilize a jingle (Kimura 1991: 318). This practice was soon taken up by the television advertisement industry, but as the music audience's tastes matured, short and target-made jingles were no longer as effective and the *tai-uppu* ("tie-up"), *imêji songu* ("image song"), or *komuson* ("commercial song") was created. As opposed to a jingle, an image song is not anonymously composed and performed. The image song is performed by an established singer (or singer/songwriter), and this credit appears in the corner of the screen during the commercial. Often the performer appears in the commercials as the main actor, and this high level of integration between the pop music industry and the television industry in Japan is seen nowhere else in the developed world. Ugaya argues that the penetration of television viewing in all regions of Japan contributes to its second place status in global music market size (2005b: 175): simply, the Japanese music market is so large precisely because proportionally more people watch TV there than in other countries.

One can measure a Japanese singer's mainstream success through television exposure: through frequent appearances on music shows and through contracts for drama theme songs and commercial endorsements. Darling-Wolf writes: "sometimes [it is] difficult to assess whether a show is popular because of its song, or a song popular because of the show it is the soundtrack of" (2004: 358). A tie-up song with any kind of popular product – which could range from the tangible (a brand of lipstick, for example) to the abstract (general entertainment in the form of a 12-part drama series) – is a hit formula, and performers and their management companies compete for these contracts. On some occasions, the television station producing the program has commissioned the song: "*Rabu Sutorî wa totsuzen ni*" (Suddenly, Into a Love Story) by Oda Kazumasa (formerly of the New Music group Off Course) and "Say Yes" by Chage and Asuka, two of the top selling singles in 1991, were not only tie-ups for Fuji Television's prime-time drama series but were commissioned for the drama and composed so that the plot was reflected in the lyrics (Ugaya 2005b: 76). The tie-up, however, is thought to contribute to the short life span of hits in Japanese pop music; as the television campaigns are intense and reach saturation point more quickly, chart turnover is also quicker. This in turn affects the length of sales and the length of record contracts (174). Record companies encourage individual artists to take television tie-up contracts because they effectively replace the need for separate promotional television campaigns and/or videos of the songs and cut costs (Kimura 1991: 319). One commercial shown nationally could do the work of several local campaigns. Thus, relatively few music videos are filmed and are made primarily for a smaller, fan-supported DVD market.

Accordingly, tie-up contracts with high-profile products are in demand among competing performers and composers. For example, a product that has historically yielded high earnings for musicians is the Shiseido cosmetic company, and it is probably not a coincidence their products are primarily aimed at young female consumers. Past Shiseido songs that were influential hits include a list of both female and male performers that appears as a "who's who" in Japanese pop music: Horiuchi Takao (of *Arisu*), Minami Kôsetsu (of *Kaguyahime*), Yazawa Eikichi, Imawano Kiyoshirô and Sakamoto Ryûichi, Dreams Come True, Puffy, and SPEED are all members of this club of successful Shiseido performers. If the 1980s constitute the initial period of the record companies' tie-up strategy, then the 1990s data illustrate its mature effects: in 1994, only two of the top 50 songs of the year were not tie-up songs. Ugaya charts the top three singles annually from 1990 to 1998 and notes that only one of these 27 singles was not associated with a drama or television advertisement (2005b: 77). Though commercial songs are firmly rooted in Japanese popular culture, it is important to note that not all tie-ups are Japanese. The choice of the song depends on the desired image the company wishes to project, and sometimes luxury items are marketed through Western classical music; others use "classic" Western rock – possibly to appeal to older buyers who still make the association between quality and authenticity and the West – such as the late 1980s campaigns for Nissan, TDK, and Ozuka (a drug company) which utilized Beatles, Procol Harum and Rolling Stones classics (75).

Kimura attributes the development of the image song in the 1980s to the consumerism borne from Japanese postwar economic boom (1991: 318). When Japanese social and economic postwar life had stabilized to an extent, young people felt it safe and desirable to spend a portion of their disposable income on products which were associated with a higher standard of living: fashion, restaurant meals, and music. After the tumultuous 1960s, including the student movement and the economic adjustments of the mid-1970s, taste in popular music had veered away from "message" songs and toward the individual, personal, and more sophisticated. It was these personal songs that were transformed into image songs (ibid.), through focus on "image" rather than "message." Imagery that was loose enough to allow individualized interpretations of the lyric was attractive to advertisers who wanted to make their product appear "just right" for the consumer. Accordingly, New Music artists who penned songs that were introspective but ambiguous could do exceedingly well here, for their lyrics and sounds could be interpreted in a variety of contexts, with relation to a variety of products, and by a variety of consumers. Audiences found the practice of self-interpretation of these songs fulfilling, and this made it unnecessary for the performer to appear personally in the commercial (such as in the case of Yuming, for example, who frequently performs image songs but very rarely appears on television). The tie-up song allowed the audience to participate in the advertising process, and this veneer of empowerment most likely contributed to the overall success of the campaigns, which are still important today.

Turning away from the tie-up, we now focus on the music variety show as broadcast on television. Ugaya writes that 1978 marked an important turning point in Japanese pop history for it was the debut year "The Best Ten" (TBS, 1978–1989) (2005b: 78–79). "The Best Ten" devised a "best ten" list of songs based on viewer postcard submissions. The show's producers invited the top ten performers to appear on the weekly show; if the performers were unavailable due to commitments to national concert tours, the crew followed them to the corners of the country for relay broadcast spots. This darting around the nation created an immediate and fresh atmosphere outside the confines of the television studio. Due to the overwhelming success of the show and the added pressure of acknowledging public support, performers felt compelled to accept an appearance, demonstrating the delicate power relations between artists, audiences, and mediating studio executives. As noted in Chapter 3, the early 1980s was a time of division, where artists constructed their images through carefully planned exposure or absence on the television airwaves. Despite their rock and New Music roots, Takamizawa's band the Alfee was a 1980s mainstay of this show, and he writes about his experiences with this show in his memoir. Their participation with The Best Ten caught many off guard because programmers for other shows had always assumed the Alfee would refuse to appear, and thus they were rarely invited. But The Best Ten's chart was fan driven, and the Alfee were put on the spot; Takamizawa writes that in the end, they accepted these invitations because he felt it important to give fans a say in what was considered a hit and what was not (2004: 105).

Music shows declined in the late 1980s and early 1990s due to the rise of other of music consumption (increases in concert attendance, concert video sales, and rentals, for example), but music promotion through tie-up contracts with products and with serialized dramas persisted as the preferred venue for mainstream media promotion. In 1998, there were 28 "regular" music shows broadcast per week in prime-time and late night slots, according to the weekly entertainment guide, *TV Pia* (1998: 48–50), but the majority of these shows were late night, low-budget programs or music video shows on local television stations. In 2005, there were 35 regular music programs on seven free-to-air channels (*TV Pia* 2005: 74–103), similarly scheduled into evening time slots.

Prime-time music television shows are more expensively produced and fewer but have greater impact on the media landscape. One of the more enduring contemporary music shows is *Hey Hey Hey! Music Champ* (Fuji, 1994 to present), an hour-long program that focuses on interviews rather than musical performances. The stars of the show are not the guests, but the hosts Matsumoto Hitoshi and Hamada Masatoshi, also known as the Osaka-based comedy duo "Downtown." The two alternatively flatter, harass, and confuse the guests, with Hamada usually playing the straight man to Matsumoto's *tsukomi*, or the gag man, all to create hilarity with the studio audience and for viewers at home. Music shows since the 1990s have carved a new viewer niche, focusing on personal interaction, and not musical performance. Thus, we can surmise that the function of the music television show is not just to distribute and promote music, per se, but to distribute and promote ideas about the music and the celebrity associated with the music. This is because music itself can now be too easily accessed in a variety of other informal formats (an Internet sample download or a rental CD shop, for example). Music television needed to offer something besides music to the consumer.

In the peak period for music television, the 1980s, audience ratings regularly topped 40 percent (Stevens and Hosokawa 2001: 228). During this period, hit charts were introduced as regular segments of the shows, explicitly linking music sales to television programming. This is seen today in many television shows including *Hey Hey Hey! Music Champ* which boasts the "perfect ranking" that is to outdo all other rankings. *Hey Hey Hey! Music Champ* combines *Oricon* rankings of CD single sales, CD rentals, karaoke requests, radio requests, *yûsen* (or pay for play subscription radio), and the newest category, *chakumero* (ring tones for mobile phone use) (Fuji Television, 2005). By averaging all the categories, *Hey Hey Hey! Music Champ* can arrive at the "perfect ranking." The charts broadcast on these shows are supposedly based on objective sales, but these broadcasts can conversely influence sales and it is common knowledge that many rankings are manufactured – merely because rankings from show to show vary. *Oricon*, as Japan's "official" music ranking organization, does factor into many shows' charts, but television producers may have equal power over the charts by picking and choosing guests for their shows and manipulating the statistics to fit their agenda.

Music Station, one of the longest running music show (TV Asahi 1986 to present), does not rate as highly as some of the other talk-focused shows, but it has stayed competitive by recently introducing a hook for viewers from the previous hour. Five minutes before the *honban* (real show) starts, the "*Mini Sute*", or the Mini Station, shows some of the guests backstage, seemingly live (merely unscripted) with the MCs who give the viewers a taste of what is to come in the next hour. This ploy – catching the viewers from the previous program with a bit of informality – is clearly a response to the competition for viewers in the

Friday night prime-time slot, and despite being firmly entrenched in a mutually beneficial relationship with the CD sales business, music shows are not immune to general programming and rating pressures.

Music television shows have come and gone, but one standard in the annual repertoire which has also influence in the maintenance of musical careers is the New Year's Eve special, the *Kôhaku Utagassen*, or the Red and White Song Contest. Since 1951, the state-sponsored station NHK holds this live performance every year, choosing a lineup of performers that reflect both current and classic tastes. *Enka*, pop, and rock performers are divided into teams (the female singers are "red," while the male singers are "white"). They compete before a panel of judges, consisting of celebrities in the fields of music, drama, literature, and even sports. Kitajima Saburô, the elder statesman of *enka*, has appeared on the show a total of 41 times as of 2005. To be asked to participate in the *Kôhaku Utagassen* is an honor for performers, and considered to some extent a measure of success in the industry. In 2004, the show featured for the first time Korean performers on each of the teams (I Jyun Hyun for the red, Ryu for the white team; both singers were associated with the hit Korean drama "*Fuyu no Sonata*"), serving as ample evidence of the mainstream commercial success of *kanryû*, or the "Korean wave" of film, television, and music in Japan.

Anime (animated films, or cartoons) is an important Japanese media that spans both television and film and, as noted in Chapter 2, is also linked to the music industry as *anime* themes constitute the bulk of overseas Japanese pop music sales. Even though most of these overseas sales stem from film-length *anime*, television *anime* themes have also met with enormous domestic success. In 1990, BB Queens performed the theme song for the animated television series, *Chibi Maruko-chan* (Little Maruko; Fuji Television, 1990 to present), a long-selling number one hit. The theme song for an NHK children's show *Dangosan'nin kyôdai* (the Three Rice Dumpling Brothers) was released in early 1999 and made CD sales history, demonstrating the power of the children's music market. *Anime* enthusiasts come from a variety of backgrounds, and thus, their themes draw upon a wide variety of musical genre: indie pop group Pizzicato Five have written for *Lupin III*; rock/visual band L'Arc en Ciel have earned throngs of foreign fans for their work for *Kurouni Kenshin*. The J-rock band Asian Kung-Fu Generation also gained international fame for their work with the *anime* *Naruto* and *Full Metal Alchemist*, and in 2005, the R&B hit duo Chemistry recorded the theme song for the television series *Kidôsenshi Gandamu SEED DESTINY*.

Whether for commercial, drama, or *anime*, television tie-ups are so important to the Japanese popular music industry; it has been suggested that it even influences composition: a song becomes nothing but an overemphasized chorus, repeating the television commercial or drama theme song's sound byte over and over again (de Launey 1995: 210). The television industry provides an arena for artist competition for public airtime that supplements and even replaces conventional promotional campaigns. Just as the practice of karaoke (and the possibility of a sustained royalty income) affects the way Japanese popular music is constructed, television marketing is another related practice that has a hand in determining the shape of mainstream pop music.

Conclusion

As noted in the introduction, there is no one cultural determinant that drives the Japanese music industry. Historical precedents and cultural preferences play a role in the business decisions that any individual makes, but in the end, I find no particularly "Japanese" strategy that dictates this scene. For example, it may have been deemed by critics "un-Japanese" for Suzuki Ami to break contract with her *jimusho* – according to the stereotype of "group" mentality, she should have borne some of the responsibility of the tax evasion case through her association with the *jimusho*. Yet she did not; she sued the company to ensure her break with the group, although struggling, she continues to perform. Similarly RC Succession's troubles with *Hori Puro* are well documented in their album liner notes and website profiles; personal differences in how the band should pursue their career resulted in the band being neglected by their *jimusho*. After a period of inactivity, RC Succession "comes back" with a different sound, a different label and new management. The question remains: if conflict not culturally sanctioned, then what motivates people to respond outside the realm of the expected? Obviously, there exists an ideal to which reality does not always correspond. But the existence of ideal positive working relationships and loyalty may only be marginally more "Japanese" than it is Chinese, or French. Ideal working relationships exist in all business cultures, but for the most part, the reality is that individuals make decisions based not on merely loyalty or harmony but on what outcome best suits their needs.

Antoine Hennion challenged the cultural stereotype of the artist as individual genius in the West; he demonstrated that the end product could not be solely attributed to one individual. The audience may interpret the music as an individual artist's "creation," but this disregards the important role of other producers who give ideas to musicians of an "imagined audience" (Negus 1999: 18) during the early stages of composing and recording. Similarly, this chapter has argued for a collaborative view of the postwar Japanese popular music industry. We see collaboration on the individual and the corporate level: people are linked to management agencies, record companies, and recording studios, and industries (such as management, record companies, advertising companies, and television studies) are linked to each other. In fact, the links between certain industries in some cases have strengthened some and weakened others. The *jimusho* has broadened its sphere of influence, replacing the record label in its premiere corporate position vis-à-vis the artist. This is because the *jimusho*, not the label, has taken charge of scheduling television shows and advertisement recordings, and branching out of *jimusho* into copyright holdings further consolidates their position (Ugaya 2005b: 95). With weakening CD sales, it appears that of all the parts of this industry, the formerly powerful record companies are currently in the most vulnerable position today.

The global contemporary music industry generally operates on the level of "small-scale productions" with "changing niche markets," surviving day-to-day, which runs parallel to the occasional huge hit that subsidizes the rest of the industry (Negus 1999: 17). In fact, very little of its business activity is on the "monster hit" level; success is unevenly distributed and enjoyed. Working in the entertainment business is not "mechanical and factory-like" (ibid.), with everyday's achievement similar to the last. Even luck is considered a major factor in determining success, something that we could say is culturally conceived but completely out of human control.

There are arguments to be made for and against culture. People work in a general environment where they try to maximize the income for their investment. I would say that in this case, individuals are maximizing their outcomes by utilizing cultural ideas that are valued in the wider community (communally determined ideas of independence in the 1970s and 1980s; or utilizing new notions of femininity in the mid-1990s, for example); therefore, culture does have a place, but it is a factor in the process. It does not play a sole determining role. We cannot make assumptions between the meaning of the culture and the structure of ownership and organization (Negus 1999: 24), especially in the case of Japanese popular music because in such a diverse market, there exist many different "cultures" related to different genre. Johnny's *Jimusho* operates differently than Baby's Co. Ltd because the products they offer to the public are different. Negus warns against both the dichotomization and the conflation of artistic creativity and business organization (1999: 29).

Is there an artistic truth reflected in business practice – is quality music successful, or is it just a matter of good spin? Takamizawa writes about his early years as a composer and of how colleagues assured him that certain songs would hit it big (and how they were right). At other times, he was personally stumped when songs he thought were just as good as the hits but did not sell (Takamizawa 2004: 97–99). In the end, he claims that critics are just as influenced by the public perception of success of the song rather than the quality of the song itself:

> Before [our first hit] the critics said, "Alfee's music has no integrity", and "the three of them are disconnected". However, after [our first hit] . . . they changed to comments like the Alfee display "a broad musicality" and "a rich variety". Certainly I, composer for all of the songs, thought "Huh? What's going on here?" but that's what the "magic of hits" means. I finally understood that's why I had to *sell* records.
>
> (2004: 101–102 emphasis added)

In other words, success in the music business is a social process where audiences make their own decisions but, at the same time, are influenced by other positional actors even before forming their own relationship with the artistic product. True, there are audience-driven trends (*The Best Ten*, for example), but these occur within a larger industry that is moving toward the consolidation of its parts.

Ugaya uses the phrase *kyôzon kyôei no bijinesumoderu* (the business model of coexistence and coprosperity) to describe the relationship between the players in this field (2005b: 73). If we see the glass as half full, there is a highly creative collaboration between executives in the management, recording, and television industries that make the Japanese pop music scene one of the largest markets in the world. On the other hand, the close relationships between these spheres can hinder those who fall outside the boundaries of mainstream pop music practice. Hopefully, for some of these people, the emerging category of independent music is allowing some diversity for the future of the Japanese music industry.

5 Technology, consumption, and authenticity

Technology, in this context, can be defined as objects and techniques involved with production of music (guitars, amps, and MIDI recorders, for example) and their recorded manifestations (compact discs, MiniDiscs and digital video discs, and their respective playback machinery). This is, however, a purely functional definition. Technology can be also viewed as devices that create and maintain musical simulacra, or the recording and the play back of a musical performance. Simulacra are the duplications of human performance: "[t]echnologies . . . are our lieutenants. They stand in place of (in lieu of) our own actions" (Wise 1998: 412). Technology replicates human action and interaction on a variety of levels. For the purposes of this argument, the replication in focus here is that of human reproduction of sound in the form of popular music *through* technology. One outcome of simulacra is the dichotomization of humanity and machine/technology; replacing human action means that some of its spiritual essence is also removed in the mechanical duplication. This is the crux of the struggle between technology, consumption, and authenticity in Japanese popular music.

Despite this loss of human warmth, Harumi Befu notes that technology made in Japan is "value added" and enhances the product's desirability (2003: 14–15). This is especially true with respect to information transfer. When facilitated by technology, information enhances the audience's experience. Like Marx's commodified fetishism, information is no longer an abstract "object": it is identified with "bundles of social relationships, transcendentals, with a life of its own" (Bullock *et al.* 1998: 144). While we must always be aware of what values are being "bundled" in the commodification process, technology has enhanced the consumer experience by adding values of perceived immediacy and authenticity to the personal interactions that occur within the context of consuming popular music.

Dramatic shifts in the outcomes of music production have occurred all over the world, but Japan is often thought of as a society at the forefront of this revolution. Advances in music technology mean not only changes in the modes of *production* but also the modes of *consumption*. The material object most closely associated with the consumption of popular music has changed radically from 45 RPM singles to three-inch CD singles, and then to MP3 files. We also see shifts in the way music is circulated: first through the radio, then later through the personal computer and the mobile phone; first from the corner record shop, then to downloading files from the Internet.

Implicit in these developments are artistic conflicts:

> Recent innovations in musical technology thus pose two kinds of problems for musicians: on the one hand, they alter the structure of musical practice and concepts of what music is and can be; and, on the other, they place musicians and musical practice in a new relationship with consumer practices and with consumer society as a whole.
>
> (Théberge 1997: 3)

In other words, technology makes consumers of not only the audience but also the producers. Increasing quality in technology often means increasing complexity: how does the escalating role of technology affect the concept of authenticity, where direct human interaction (often translated as artistic honesty) is highly valued? Authenticity is extremely important to rock musicians around the world and a crucial foundation for Japanese pop music (Hosokawa 1995: 7–8). Advances in technology affect authenticity in another important artistic area: copyright ownership. Is the music being listened to the "real thing" or a dubbed "fake" (and to whom does this matter the most: consumers or producers)? Piracy and illegal access to music are thought to have had a great effect on the music industry worldwide, causing sales to plummet in the wake of copied CDs and pirated MP3s.

This chapter contemplates the role of technology in postwar Japanese popular music, focusing primarily on consumption (rather than instrumental production) and its accompanying quest for authenticity. First, a postwar history of relevant technologies is offered, covering radio, personal stereos (and the variety of software that can be played therein), the personal computer, and the mobile telephony, which are the main front-runners.[1] Next, the concept of simulacra is explored through karaoke performance, a fusion of music and technology. A discussion of the consumption of music technology through live performance and information transfer follows, noting the perceived conflict between authenticity and technology in this realm of pop music, and how nostalgia as an aesthetic value works to remedy this.

This search for a balance between technological advancement and human authenticity is another example of how Bourdieu's concept of the "field of struggles" shapes both artists' and audiences' positions in the field of cultural production. In this struggle, artists, to stay competitive in a quickly changing market, increasingly employ technology to promote their music and their images. From the fans' point of view, increased technology can mean dehumanization, but not all the consumer outcomes of this process have been negative. Technological advances have also gradually decreased the cost of music. Despite the belief that consumers are often manipulated by cultural industries – the masses are "dominated" by the dissemination of preferred meanings attached to products, and resistance is represented by the rejection of these meanings (Lash and Urry

1994: 138) – changes in the cultural industries related to music technology include increases in choice and decreases in cost to Japanese consumer, despite the large profits earned by the producers.

"Techno music" as a genre is not the focus of this chapter. Techno does not necessarily employ technology on a greater level than other genre such as pop or rock music – its definition lies in its reliance on certain instrumentations and arrangement.[2] "Techno music" is characterized by the sampling of sounds, recorded and mixed, and played back by a computer that is operated by an individual. My definition of music technology includes technological interactions between musicians, and between musicians and consumers: the "hardware" and "software" that mediates the social practice of sharing music in everyday Japanese life.

Modes of music technology

Radio

The first Japanese AM radio broadcast was March 22, 1925 at 9:30 a.m., transmitted to Tokyo, Osaka, and Nagoya from the national studio that was to become NHK. The first commercial broadcast was on September 1, 1951 (Take 1999: 68); other commercial radio stations were established soon after (Nakano 2002: 411). One of the most demonstrative moments in the history of radio as simulation was the transmission of Hirohito's voice in 1945, a *gyokuonhôsô* (the broadcast of the Imperial Voice). This term refers to any broadcast of the Emperor or Crown Prince's voice, but most often it refers to the famous August 15 *gyokuonban*, or the recording of the Imperial message of surrender. This broadcast truly heralded the postwar era, both politically and technologically: "At noon on August 15, the Japanese people gathered around their radio speakers and *heard for the first time the high pitched voice* of their emperor" (Bix 2001: 526, emphasis added). The surrender rescript was written and announced by the Emperor in the elite Imperial court language, but immediately a radio announcer read out a version in plain Japanese to ensure comprehension (527). The Imperial Ministry advisors most likely recommended the direct transmission of Hirohito's voice – the very first *gyokuonhôsô* – because they believed that unless the message was delivered directly from the Imperial leader, it would not have immediate and meaningful impact, demonstrating the early power of simulacra in technology. Ivy also begins her account of popular culture in the postwar era with the Hirohito surrender radio rescript (1993: 244) and notes that only simulacra could have allowed the event because the divinity of the Imperial family had separated them from the populace for so many years.

> [H]earing the divine voice of the emperor for the first time could have occurred only through layers of mediation. In retrospect, this mediation seems to portend the later powers of electronic reproduction that have come to pervade postwar Japan.
>
> (1993: 245)

This is one of the earliest examples of technology standing in the place of a person: in this case, dramatically representing divine authority in the form of a human voice, to ensure the maintenance of Japanese political identity in the face of drastic change and social upheaval.

Although radios were used for entertainment, it is important to note that during the wartime years, as well as the early postwar period, radio provided an important information source for the Japanese public. NHK (*Nippon Hôsô Kyôkai* or the Japan Broadcasting Association) was the only operating radio station between 1925 and 1951 and the centralized source for information, first authorized by the Imperial government and then by the Occupation. The American authorities introduced jazz, station identification breaks, and the role of the DJ in this period (Ivy 1993: 245). The Ministry of Post and Telecommunications was the official government instrument in the postwar era to regulate radio; in 2004, the Ministry was renamed the Ministry of Internal Affairs and Communication (MIC).

In the early postwar period, the most popular electronic appliance in the home was musical: 67 percent of homes in 1951 owned a radio (Yoshimi 1999: 154). The radio was an important focal point of family life as it supplied not only music but also other forms of entertainment such as drama, and news and information. Radios symbolized "urban modernism" (157) and were used to promote an "American way of life" (158): one where home electronics filled the home with a clean, breezy air of leisure and family contentment. Tiresome household chores were lightened with the aid of technology, and this meant more time for leisure, most likely spent with other home electronic purchases – the radio and the television.

Radio shows were the most popular form of entertainment in the 1950s as they were relatively inexpensive to produce and consume. The advent of television, however, meant the start of Japanese radio's decline, as reflected in the media history of other industrialized societies. Radio producers responded to the challenge of keeping ratings with call-in programs, taking advantage of radio's "immediacy, mobility, and coverage of fast breaking events" (Kodansha 1993: 1242). FM radio stations began broadcasting in 1969, and these producers capitalized on new superior sound quality to focus on music programming. Ugaya writes that in the current era, the differentiation between consuming music on FM radio to that of purchased CDs is the existence of free "access" to music (2005b: 182); thus radio, as symbolic culture, is a democratic pop cultural medium. Design advances meant that smaller and more affordable radios could move with the listener, taking the act of listening to the radio out of the living room and into the car, and the greater outdoors (Nakano 2002: 411).

In the 1960s, radio reasserted itself in the media entertainment industry by using the strategy of "audience segmentation," targeting specific markets by age and gender; this had worked well in other industries such as magazine and comic publishing. One of the most successful "audience-segmented" programs was the *shin'ya hôsô* (late night broadcasts), beginning in 1960. These shows were aimed at students, especially those studying for competitive university exams, and other shift workers such as taxi and truck drivers. The student slot was usually midnight to 3 a.m., with the truck driver shows following. The programs were distinctive because of their focus on direct interaction between the audience and DJ, via fax or telephone requests, and sometimes this interaction included personal advice. There were (and still are) many female late night DJs, providing an idealized image of feminine companionship to male students and late night workers. Late night slots also allow for flexible margin in determining content standards. Darling Wolf notes that some celebrity radio broadcasts include information not appropriate for television prime time (2004: 360), suggesting that faceless radio allows more freedom of expression.

Shibata Kaoru worked as a radio announcer in the early 1980s, with *Nippon Hôsô* (AM 1242). She was the "assistant personality" to a male DJ for the show "*Kayô Barêdo Nippon*" ("Ballad Japan"). In her book, Shibata tells that gender expectations were embedded in the program audition; she recalls being told by the producer at her audition that he wanted a young woman (*musume*) who was sweet, pretty, innocent, and virginal – in other words, nonthreatening – to appeal to young male listeners, and her opening line to every broadcast was "I'm Kaoru, I'm delicious!" (Shibata 1998: 14–15). Despite following the producers' commands, the next day the listener reaction was negative (18). This was because her audience segment was completely different. "My program was between 13:00 to 16:00 (Monday to Friday). That meant most of our audience were middle-aged people, so we mostly played standard pop (*kayôkyoku*) (not J-pop) and some American sixties and seventies pop music" (Shibata, K., 2005, Personal communication). Housewives, small business owners, daytime taxi and truck drivers comprised her main listener categories, and after her first failure, she was instructed to speak with a "sense of the common people" (*shominkankaku*) (Shibata 1998: 18). Shibata (Personal communication 2005) notes that the radio station managers, rather than the individual broadcasters, were most concerned with age segmentation with the *eigyôbu* (sales department),[3] ensuring that proper sponsors were recruited for time slots with certain audiences.

Audiences responded to the audience segmentation strategy, and by the 1990s, the number of radio stations had expanded. In the early 1990s, 85 stations operated nationwide; in the mid-1990s, there were 36 FM stations in the country, with seven located in Tokyo (De Launey 1995: 214). This increased to 10 major Tokyo-based FM stations broadcasting with six AM stations plus an Internet radio (*Asahi Shimbun* 2005; Ugaya 2005b: 182).[4] Today, Japanese AM and FM radio stations consist mainly of news, music, traffic reports, variety and talk shows, and sports broadcasts. Although audience segmentation still exists to some extent, it appears to have decreased in importance, and radio stations are trying to reach a number of different audiences in one show. Nakano describes most commercial stations as "mixed," with few offering programming in one genre (2002: 412), but in Ugaya's opinion, the 10 major FM stations offer limited formats: "a lot of talk and not much music. Lots of hit chart music. As for content diversity, it will be a long time before it can reach the equivalent of New York's radio scene" (2005b: 182). In agreement is the American publication *Billboard's* take on the Japanese radio scene: "FM plays a key role in introducing foreign music to Japan, but the emphasis is on the mainstream" (cited in De Launey 1995: 214).

Also important to the discussion of Japanese radio and pop music is the influence of FEN, or the Far East Network (currently known as AFN or the Armed Forces Network), on the AM dial. This station was established in 1945, and operating outside of Japanese law, FEN began by broadcasting important information and instructions to US soldiers. Now, most shows are geared toward entertainment: local FEN DJ music shows, syndicated US radio shows, UPI news bulletins on the hour, and American professional sports coverage. Despite FEN's official goal to foster a sense of community around the military bases, other audiences created alternative interpretations of its broadcasts. Japanese audiences did not always understand what the DJs were saying, but it was the fast track to US trends and thus became a hit with a wide variety of listeners. Interviews with musicians who grew up in the early postwar period often cite FEN as an influence: Yoshida Takurô on his official home page profile states that hearing "Blowing in the Wind" in 1962 on FEN had a profound impact on him (2006).

After the advent of FM programming, the poor quality of FEN's AM broadcasts made discriminating consumers turn elsewhere for music, but the lingering influence of FEN can be seen in the proliferation of English (and other foreign languages) in radio programs on Japanese FM stations. For example, one of the most successful Japanese pop radio stations in Tokyo, J-WAVE 81.3 FM, frequently uses foreign DJs or bilingual Japanese to broadcast in both Japanese and, usually, English. The FM station J-WAVE was launched in 1988, in the midst of the CD revolution, and, as noted in Chapter 2, was the first organization to use the initial "J" to refer to this new concept of technologized, mass marketed, mainstream pop culture. Not only was J-WAVE the first to coin the term "J-pop" but was also the first station to include CDs in their record library (Ugaya 2005b: 31), demonstrating its ability and willingness to integrate new technology. Despite the heavy influence of US and UK music on early Japanese pop radio and the disk jockeys' use of English language today, Japanese artists have been more prominent on Japanese radio airwaves since the mid-1990s. In the early 1990s, J-WAVE's airplay consisted of 95 percent foreign music (De Launey 1995: 213), but by the 2000s, the station's Tokio Hot 100[5] featured many if not most Japanese artists in the top six spots, demonstrating the maturity and independence of the Japanese pop industry since the mid-1990s. J-WAVE is primarily a pop rock station, but it does support other genre as evidenced by its July 2005 lineup, which included an hour of jazz programming and a late night hour of "afro beat" music (*Asahi Shimbun* 2005: 6).

J-WAVE is closely associated with central Tokyo geographic sites: J-WAVE's main studios are located in Roppongi, a fashionable and expensive section of the Minato Ward in Tokyo.[6] They also run a studio in a retail outlet of HMV in Shibuya where the audience can see DJs and their guests perform in this crowded central Tokyo location, a clever promotion technique as fans can go and buy the CDs upon hearing the music. J-WAVE's broadcasts cover a large metropolitan area, and since 1998, listeners in regional Japan can tune in to J-WAVE through cable TV subscription; listeners who have access to digital satellite receivers can listen to J-WAVE anywhere for free. Thus, through the J-WAVE's full engagement with technology through radio, satellite radio, Internet, and CD, this Tokyo has penetrated all parts of the nation. The simulacrum at work here is the replication of a central popular culture throughout a varied national landscape. The music, the talk, the "Tokio Hot 100," and the idealized attributes of the Tokyo lifestyle are replicated and consumed across all Japan.

Technology in radio is humanized by the presence of a DJ, or radio personality. Some, like Shibata, are media professionals who are trained as announcers and DJs. Others have already made their name in the music industry and then turn to radio as another facet of their public image, making the celebrity radio personality an important expression of the interpellation of musical fame and technology. Many figures in the music industry use technology to promote their identity as celebrities and radio was one of the first such media used; television and websites on the Internet, of course, followed, but some figures, because of the faithful followings to segmented shows, choose to stay with radio as their main media projections.

According to Shibata, who interviewed musicians as part of her work as a radio personality in the 1980s,

> New Music singers didn't appear on TV, because [they thought] that way they could make themselves more valuable, [through avoiding overexposure and creating an air of exclusivity]; then they could sell more records. Some of them didn't like TV. But now some of them appear on TV, even with "idols".[7]
>
> (Personal communication 2005)

Nakajima Miyuki belongs, generally, to the genre of New Music, though some of her songs have been classified as "new *enka*." Debuting in the early 1970s, her career spans three decades, yet she is rarely seen on television. She does appear frequently as a radio DJ, particularly on her regular shows TOKYO FM, and *Nippon Hôsô*. She is a good example of what Shibata refers to as a New Music performer who avoided television exposure, as did her colleague Matsutôya Yumi. Both women, however, have active radio careers and use this media to avoid the downfalls of commercial overexposure through television but gain the benefits of extra promotion through radio.

On the other hand, musicians who do appear on television do not eschew radio opportunities; rather they constitute a complementary pathway to enhance the overall media exposure of the artist. Sakazaki Kohnosuke, acoustic guitarist for the Alfee, currently has two long-running radio shows; one is broadcast an hour a week in the Tokyo area, and the other is broadcast on an additional 19 regional networks, bringing together audiences across the country. Sakazaki's national show introduces "classic" pop music (both Western and Japanese) to younger listeners through "artist data files," as well as featuring new Japanese music.

His shows often focus on albums rather than singles, underscoring his own and the show's "musicality." His fellow band member Takamizawa hosts one radio show in Tokyo (broadcast on additional seven regional stations) and another on FM Aichi. Takamizawa's national show focuses on Japanese rock, and one of its main objectives is to introduce new rock bands to audiences, such as "break through" indies rock bands such as Asian Kung-fu Generation, Remioromen, and Elle Garden, giving them a foot in the mainstream market. Both Sakazaki's and Takamizawa's radio broadcasts take music from the center (Tokyo) and distribute it to distant areas of Japan, reinforcing Tokyo's position as trend setter and power capital of the Japanese music industry.

Many veteran New Musicians are famed radio personalities – Yuming, Nakajima, and the Alfee as mentioned above, plus Kuwada Keisuke of the Southern All Stars broadcasts from Tokyo FM – but they are not the only celebrities utilizing radio to project their image and music; younger and upcoming artists can be heard on the radio waves in increasing numbers. Hirai Ken, an R&B singer, has a Saturday slot on J-WAVE, while the Johnny's *Jimusho* presence on the airwaves is omnipresent: SMAP's Kimura Takuya on J-WAVE, Arashi on FM Fuji, and TOKIO, KinKi Kids, and Nakai Masahiro (SMAP) on *Nippon Hôsô*. JIRO, the bassist from million-selling band GLAY, has recently begun broadcasting on the Osaka station FM802, stating his motive was to widen his own and the audience's understanding of new music (*Nikkei Entertainment* 2005c: 8). Despite "educational" explanations, it is clear that celebrity radio DJs – old and young – find that radio profiling helps to support both mature and emerging careers.

Radio's role as "introducer" can also be discerned in content. For example, I found that daytime Japanese FM programming, in comparison to the United States and Australia, focused more on DJ talk than music, and it was not uncommon for music to be played in shortened forms rather than a song in its entirety. These radio shows also *introduced* music: the audience could get the "feel" of the song through the DJs' spoken prelude to the snippet, making it unnecessary to play the entire song. Japanese FM radio programs seem to move quite quickly in that sense, from song to song, topic to topic, and idea to idea; those who want to hear the whole song could rent or purchase the CD at their leisure.

Radio's influence can be interpreted as a unifying force through national shows such as J-WAVE, which supports the concept of Tokyo radio as a national distributor of a uniform popular music across Japan, but the flip side of radio's effect on music listening is to further distinguish between the center and the periphery. For example, speaking mainly of urban Japanese society, De Launey rates radio's influence on Japanese music consumption as a distant second to television, because most of this population commutes (using public transport) rather drives (using one's own car). This means the opportunity to listen to the radio, as opposed to recorded music on personal stereos, is limited (1995: 214). De Launey is correct with respect to urban Japanese society, but less so in regional or rural areas where automobiles are much more widely used, and so we can assume that radio plays a different role in the everyday lives of rural audiences. In these different contexts, its interpretation varies from city to country, and its unifying effect can only be understood by acknowledging different consumption modes such as listening in the car versus at home or out of doors via radio in a personal stereo.

The software revolution: from vinyl to minidiscs

Since the start of the consumer era, music has been marketed in a variety of formats; as a framework for understanding the technological developments in Japanese popular music, Ugaya constructs broad categories that span the postwar era: the "audio record," the compact disc, the cassette, the tape (both cassette and cartridge), and the MiniDisc (2005b: 27).[8] This chapter follows Ugaya's categorization of music software but includes the accompanying hardware – a variety of personal stereos and mobile phones, mainly – which rounds out the audience's utilization of technology in Japanese popular music.

Sheet music was the first mass-marketed popular music product in Japan, as elsewhere in the industrialized world. Audio records were, at the time of Japan's defeat, the highest quality musical technology offered to consumers. Vinyl record technology was introduced in Japan in 1903 (Hosokawa and Matsuoka 2004: 152); the local recording industry was established in 1907 (Nakamura 1991: 266). In the prewar era, phonographs were relatively scarce but hits that scored up to 30,000 sales were recorded (269). The Recording Industry Association of Japan began keeping reliable sales records in 1930 (Ugaya 2005b: 27). In the early years, audio disc technology in Japan was associated with high culture and progress, and thus recordings of European classical music were popular with aspiring elites (Hosokawa and Matsuoka 2004: 152–153). Audio discs were still imported from the West after the end of the war, but instead of classical music, most were contemporary recordings. It was at this moment that records were "no longer associated with the preconception of socio-economic level, and contributed to the creation of a homogenous taste in popular society" (Yamazaki cited in Kawabata 1991: 336).

Audio record sales increased dramatically in the 1960s, most extensively due to the influence of foreign music. For example, in 1960, the total of record sales in Japan was close to 9 billion yen (89 *oku en*), but after the Beatles visit in 1966, this figure shot up to almost 32 billion yen (319 *oku en*). Record sales continued to climb until the late 1970s, levelling off slightly before reaching its peak in 1998 (Ugaya 2005b: 28). The rise in the 1970s is attributed to the economy's general growth (*kôdokeizaiseichô*) and the overall increase in the population born after World War II, or Japan's "baby boomers." Another factor in increasing sales is the diversification of music genre. During this period, major strands of Japanese popular music broke away (*enka*, folk, rock, and New Music branching away from *kayôkyoku*, as discussed in Chapters 2 and 3) and with new genre came new pockets of collecting for enthusiasts (29). LP vinyl records' main appeal was the visual aspect of its cover, and cover art was an important aspect of the artists' marketing potential. Even 45 rpm single jackets had the space to promote an artist's physical and artistic image, and record collecting in this era was just as much about sound as it was image.

Today, records are seen to possess an authentic connection to music, through the totality of "visual, graphic, material and audible elements" (Hosokawa and Matsuoka 2004: 156). Digitized audio lacks the "aura" of vinyl, because records represent a certain and specific moment in musical history, contrasted by CDs, which are often reissues of remastered or reengineered versions (157). Though their technology is outdated, vinyl records persist in the market as collectors' items, primarily in the jazz genre and also in other fan cultures. For example, an Alfee fan I knew bemoaned her purchase of a collection of Alfee singles from the mid-1970s to the mid-1980s because of the space demands it made on her small home; yet, she "couldn't let them go." Records are items to have rather than to listen to – a visual rather than an audio possession – as repeated playing damages the records and results in a loss of value. Vinyl records' very transience, however, contributes to their intrinsic value both as musical representations and as objects of consumer prestige as the original performance for which it stands is both exclusive and temporary.

In the 1950s, reel-to-reel tape recorders were the norm in recording technology in both public and private sectors. Tape cartridges were first introduced by RCA in 1958, and many were impressed by the mechanical threading function as this made tape recording and playback much simpler. At the time, Sony was Japan's number one reel-to-reel recorder producer, and thus was in a position to approach the German company Philips in 1963 for a joint project proposal (Philips already had developed a small-size cartridge cassette). Sony introduced cassette tapes and recorders in Japan in 1966 (Sony Global 2005). These products did not have same sound quality as reel-to-reel did but were much smaller and lighter; cassette tapes soon became the main technology used to listen to music in the 1970s in Japan and other consumer societies as well. The popularity of cassette tapes arose from a divergence in its functionality: cassette tapes could be used for recording music as well as listening to music. Consumers could tape audio records (to preserve them, edit them, or for transportation convenience) or buy the music prerecorded on an audio cassette.

The late 1970s to the early 1980s in Japan was a bleaker period in sales of records and tapes (and their accompanying stereo hardware) than the upward early 1970s. This was in part due to the increasing value of the yen against the US dollar, and Japanese stereo exports were down. The compact disc revolution was thus to rescue many Japanese manufacturers. This revolution was, in part, due to the innovative and persistent efforts of one particular Japanese company, Sony. Sony had interest in this area for two reasons: they were a major player in the hardware market, and they had recently acquired CBS and Columbia Records (two major US labels) to form Sony Music Entertainment. Their desire to create new technologies would profit them in the areas of both playback hardware and music software.

Audio discs, predecessors of the compact disc, were introduced in the late 1970s to mid-1980s (Ugaya 2005b: 29). Sony had worked on a prototype of a digital audio disc in 1976, using binary data to record the disc, but early models were found to have significant data error. Meanwhile, in Germany, the audio long-playing (ALP) disc was developed, which was 30 cm in diameter. Sony engineers took the German model and, with modifications, created a disc that was small enough to play on a car stereo but large enough to hold one hour's worth of music. A Sony–Philips team, both competing and cooperating with JVC, presented their 12-cm DAD (digital audio disc) at conferences in the early 1980s (Sony Global 2005). Meanwhile, Sony was also developing CD hardware, holding back the disc's introduction in the general market until the playback machine was ready for release. Sony's first CD player cost 168,000 yen, prohibitive at that time for many music fans except for the classical and jazz enthusiasts at which it was aimed (Ugaya 2005b: 34). Two years later, a much smaller and more reasonably priced model was released at 49,980 yen – about half of its production price. Sony took a loss on its hardware to promote its software, but this strategy succeeded in the long run.

The Japanese CD revolution did not occur without hiccups. There was opposition from critics and promoters as the decrease in size (compared to the LP album) meant that the record companies had a lot less space to promote the artist visually; the record cover had an important marketing function. But once audio makers convinced the record companies of the profits to be made by connecting the sales of software to hardware (Ugaya 2005b: 29), the promotion of this new market began in earnest. In 1982, the first compact disc integrated system was launched by a partnership between Sony, CBS/Sony, Philips, and Polygram (Sony Global 2005). There were over 3000 titles published as compact discs in Japan in 1984, but only about 10 percent of them were recorded in the analog format (Ugaya 2005b: 35); 90 percent utilized digital recording technology, demonstrating that technological advances in the recording studio had come to fruition with the new compact disc technology. Compact disc sales outstripped record sales either in 1986 (30) or in 1987 (Kimura 1991: 329), depending on the interpretation of statistics, but it is thought this occurred concomitantly with the price reductions in stereo playback equipment. It seemed that consumers would not migrate from the analog to the digital side in large numbers if they paid more than 50,000 yen for a CD player (ibid.).

As previously mentioned, analog recording technology was associated with LP records, and digital recording technology became the mark of compact disc music. As cassette tapes were being phased out of the market, Sony engineers wanted to preserve the dual functionality of magnetic tapes and create a digital audio disc with a recordable function; they created the MiniDisc (MD) in 1991. It was smaller than the 12-cm compact disc and recorded sound from another recorded source or live music through a microphone like a tape, but it had the sound quality and the functionality of a CD. Music enthusiasts now had the best of both worlds: convenient size, recordability, and quality reproduction.

Concomitant developments: personalized listening

The 1980s saw one of the most revolutionary advancements in the consumption of popular music – not only in Japan but also throughout the world. Sony's "Walkman" was a personal stereo (cassette player with headphones and sometimes radio) where the experience of listening to music was made personal, private, and individualized. In the past, families had gathered around the radio, record player, or television to listen to music. Now listeners were able to use music to delineate personal space, whether inside the home or in public. This personalization of music echoes the solitary enjoyment of record collecting that Hosokawa and Matsuoka note; "an exclusive and exclusionary relationship between subject and object" (2004: 164) is projected into the everyday practice of enacting the relationship between music and individual. Music fans could always listen to their records or tapes on their living room stereos through headphones, but this was the first time that listening could be taken from the private sphere (the home) to the public sphere (the train, the café, the street, and so on).

The personal stereo began with the "Walkman," produced by Sony. Simply put, it was a smaller version of the cassette recorder minus the recording function and attached to headphones rather than speakers; the prototype was called the "Pressman" (probably due to the fact the listeners pressed buttons to engage the functions). In readying the prototype for the market, one of the more difficult engineering tasks was getting quality headphones at a lighter weight (50 grams, down from 300 to 400 grams). Because of its mobile use, the machine had to be stronger, marking a departure in design priorities – the product had to be light but unbreakable, rather than stationary and stable as were home stereos. The first project was in March 1979 and went on sale in July later that year; the first portable CD stereo Discman was introduced in 1983, followed by the portable MD player in 1992 (all produced by Sony).

The first reactions to the Walkman were negative: in the early days, a tape player that could not record was considered an anomaly. Public demonstrations at first were ridiculed by the press as no one could hear the music playing in the model headphones. The first major buyer market consisted of young people in their mid-twenties. Other companies followed with similar products with different names, but Sony's term "Walkman" became more than a brand associated with a particular corporation but a word synonymous with a product and a lifestyle, listed in major Japanese and English dictionaries in the mid-1980s. Today, considering the proliferation of formats (including CD, MD, and MP3 as well as tapes) and brand makers, the more generic term *keitai ongaku purêyâ* (mobile, or portable, music player) is used to describe any personal stereo in Japanese, but the word "Walkman" persists in the global popular culture history as iconic of music consumption in the 1980s and 1990s.

The differences in the technological formats of music (in terms of both hardware and software) affected the "methods of listening" (Kitagawa 1991: 306) of Japanese consumers. For example, personalized listening through "mixes" became popular with the spread of inexpensive cassette recorders in the 1970s.

Record collectors could tape their favorite portions of their collections and put together their own mix, often based on mood or theme. There was an important overlap between the functionality of producer and consumer: tape recorder allowed consumers to collapse the traditionally separate roles of music interaction (listening/playing/composing) by allowing "re-arranging, re-editing and re-composing" as an ordinary listening habit (310), and thus Kitagawa notes a departure from the traditional notions of musical *production* versus *reproduction*: "Is there any difference between making [an edited, personalized] 'My Tape' and playing in an amateur band (with copied songs) . . . Do they not both represent two aspects of the same re-editing or re-composing process?" (311).

The outside of the cassette tape provided a further canvas for creativity. Perhaps in response to the visual caché lost after albums were phased out, collectors artistically personalized their tape cases as well. Stationary stores sold decorated, but blank, paper cassette labels, with graphic borders and artistic lettering to be inserted in the newly created personalized tape. The personalized tape played in a personal stereo (often a Sony Walkman) created the ultimate statement in privacy and personalized consumption, but the frequent practices of creating these tapes as personal gifts also allowed them to symbolize human connection as well as solitary enjoyment.

Recordable MiniDiscs continued this trend in the 1990s and improved the sound quality of these personal mixes. The much greater storage of the minidisc per gram carried allowed the personal stereo great flexibility; many more songs could be recorded on the disc compared to the now bulky cassette. Haw writes that Walkman sales suffered greatly after the introduction of the iPod in 2001 and in 2005 has only 16.5 percent of market share in personal stereos (2005d); Sony introduced an MP3 player as part of their Walkman range, but their tie-up with mobile phone maker Ericsson has allowed them to expand with some success in the digital music market through mobile phones with MP3 capability.

Computing music

Music and computer use in Japan, and elsewhere in world, is a controversial subject that confronts issues of ownership, intellectual property, and copyright – all facilitated and complicated by the increasing ease and availability of Internet "connectability." While Internet connections in Japan still appear to be less common than other equally developed countries (40 percent of the population owning a PC and 20 percent with an Internet connection in 2001 [Fukukawa 2001: 86]), since Japanese mobile phone users have access to the Internet through "I-mode," these Internet connection rates do not reflect real use. Gottlieb and McLelland note that in early 2000 – not long after their company launch – I-mode, NTT's branch of mobile phone Internet service, was the number one Internet service provider in Japan (2003: 5).

Music on the internet was first accessed in WAV ("wave") or AU files. WAV files were introduced by Microsoft and were used for any kind of audio file – system alerts, video games, and CD quality playback. Real Audio, a different strategy, consists of links to web pages that allowed personal users to connect to a separate server for playback. WAV, AU, and Real Audio usually comprised of snippets of music, and artists placed them on their websites as previews to entice their listeners to buy the entire song on CD. One of the first Japanese artists to set up an official home page in the early 1990s, Sano Motoharu, equipped his site's discography section with short selections of his music via these early music file formats to entice visitors to buy the whole song in CD format.

Consumers wanted better sound quality but a format that took up less storage space; with this accomplished, MP3 has become the most common format for computer audio playback. MP3 files include codec, an algorithm that allows the large size of audio files to be compressed to a manageable size for ordinary computer users.This compression algorithm was developed in Germany in 1985, and in 1997, it became a "standard" form of music distribution (Kretschmer *et al.* 2001: 419). Once these files were widely used, the software for distributing them developed amongst users. P2P refers to file-sharing, an abbreviation of the phrase "peer to peer," and is based on a local network set up between individual users rather than a centralized network (as in the World Wide Web). Computerized music files were made and posted on the local network, allowing limitless copying. This kind of exchange, however, is not one-way: reciprocity is the key as users download files but also allow others access to their files.

Using computer files as its source, MP3 players represent the ultimate in listening variety at a low weight and mass in personal stereos and comprise the cutting edge in all "digital media players" (including PCs and CD and DVD players). Even though the Sony Walkman was the first hardware to "free" the listener from the traditional binds of heavy and stationary stereo enjoyment, digital media players such as iPods and MP3 capable mobile phones have taken music consumption to a higher level of integration into daily life. Because of their light weight and their ability to store masses of music files, their capacity to be included in a larger number of daily activities is unlimited. The iPod is the number one selling MP3 player in Japan (Haw 2005d).

Mobile telephony, as a further step in the development of personalized technology, deserves special mention in the discussion of music consumption in Japan. There are a variety of ways music can be integrated with the mobile phone user: *chakumero* (literally, "call arrival" melody, or ring tone), *merokôru* (ringing back service), and *chakuuta* (music download). The first, the *chakumero*, lends its name to one of Hey!3's latest "perfect" ranking lists; this ring tone alerts the user of an incoming call and can be chosen according to the user's tastes and preferences. Furthermore, to distinguish between phone calls, the ring tone can also be configured to different profiles in the handset's address book. The *chakumero* began as a small file that could manage one to three chords but now can contain up to 64 chords, and its quality is close to that of the original recording (Takeishi and Lee 2004: 5) and can be up to 15 seconds in length (Multimedia Internet *Jiten* 2006). The *merokôru*, or ringing back service, allows the caller to listen to music while waiting for their telephone partner to answer their phone. Music downloads (*chakuuta*) consist of a full version of the song (rather than a snippet of the song as in most *chakumero*) and is only available for more expensive handsets. *Chakumero* are the most popular form of music telephony, and the sales of these music files make up 40–60 percent of the major mobile companies' Internet sales figures (Takeishi and Lee 2004: 6).[9] These functions also tie the hardware producers to the software producers, as the mobile network companies are contracted to record companies to receive the rights to these songs. Music playback on mobile networks is rapidly developing as this manuscript goes to press and the combination of mobile phone and MP3 player is emerging as the newest invention in personal music consumption and most important invention since the Sony Walkman.

Interlude: virtual music communities

Until this point, this section has focused on computer files for audio playback, but one cannot ignore another important function of personal computers with respect to pop music consumption: the diffusion of information about music through Internet websites and the creation of virtual fan communities. Following the introduction of the Internet in Japan for private and commercial use in 1993 (Gottlieb and McLelland 2003: 3), figures in the Japanese popular music industry launched "official" websites to both disseminate information and promote their product to the computer-linked public. Official sites followed, often accompanied by unofficial (fan-based) sites, which were created by IT-literate fans looking to foster virtual communities. "Official sites" (*kôshiki saito*) are distinguished by the artists' participation in the design and content and are copyright protected both with respect to any music files that may be accessed there and the photographic images of the artists posted. Some official sites are hosted privately through a named server (e.g., Imawano Kiyoshirô's site is http://www.kiyoshiro.co.jp) while others are hosted by record company servers (Matsuyôya Yumi's "Yuming's Sound Library" at http://www.toshiba-emi.co.jp/yuming/; SMAP's site is through Victor Records).

Moto's Web Site (the official site of singer-songwriter Sano Motoharu), mentioned earlier in this book, was launched in 1995 and was one of the earliest examples of such a virtual community. Sano did not hire a professional IT group to launch the site; rather, he chose to work with a group of fans ("volunteer staff") in creating the website, calling it a "community-based fan network" (MWS 2006b). By highlighting the grass roots aspect of website authorship, Sano turned the focus of his site away from himself and toward the support of his fan base. So successful was the site that it has now been professionalized, but its fan roots still figure prominently in the site's history. The Alfee's first website was a similarly fan-based project, launched in 1996 by a group of fans who called themselves "Liberty Bell 21"; "volunteer staff" maintained the site until approximately 2004. Shortly before that, the group's management company decided to create their own server (http://www.alfee.com) and privatize the maintenance of the site by hiring IT professionals and utilizing the emerging computer skills within their existing management company. This shift was in part due to the difficulty integrating fan/volunteers who had liminal status into the tight ring of social relations that constituted their *jimusho*. Compared to a large *jimusho* like Johnny's, Project III was not as organizationally complicated, without many hierarchical layers, but there was a marked consciousness of "insider" and "outsider" status; this was partly necessary to protect the privacy of the stars contracted to the office. Liberty Bell 21 members were uncomfortably in between the inside and outside; not full-fledged staff members but not outside fans either, as they provided an important free service to the management company. This tension was only resolved through the clear absorption of the website within the *jimusho*.

Many J-pop artists' sites are available for access by both personal computers and mobile phone-based information access I-mode (which supplies a more text-based and limited view). Official and unofficial sites are important not only for domestic J-pop community but also to allow quick and easy access to music information by foreign audiences: primarily Japanese communities overseas and other international pockets of consumers in East Asia, North America, and Europe. Without the Internet, the global presence of J-pop would not have reached its current level of moderate penetration in general audiences and high penetration in niche audiences (see Chapter 2). The Internet allowed *anime* fans in Europe, North America, and other parts of Asia to receive further information about artists and songs that accompanied successful animated films, and gave soundtracks cultural lives of their own.

J-pop websites are divided between those that conduct "official" activities (as illustrated by links with management companies, record companies, official fan clubs, and other institutions) and those categorized as "unofficial" activities (primarily fan sites). These two kinds of sites generally complement each other but they can also compete for accuracy, legitimacy, and detail in an information-hungry, music consumer market. Information content ranges from dates of album or concert ticket releases to background information about the creative process, as well as exchange of formal or informal reviews of CDs or concert tours. For both the overseas fan and the domestic fan, information via the Internet is knowledge that enhances the consumer process by empowering the fan to read symbols in a particular, preferred fashion. Through the "immediate" Internet connection with the artist, fans can now access the "authentic" creative process to supplement their personal interpretation of the song. The struggle between the two (staff/professional versus fan/amateur) provides the variety and diversity of information available, but result in difficulties when combined, such as those described in the case of Liberty Bell 21, where the fan/volunteers and the management could not resolve differences in role expectations.

Copyright: whose music?

Copyright protection is one of the most controversial issues in music technology around the world, and Japan is no exception. Copyright represents the connective tissue between the performer and the audience: by consuming an "authentically" copyrighted piece of music, one is, hypothetically, supporting the artist directly; through the consumption of non-copyright music, the power to simulate (reproduce) is in the hands of the listener rather than the musician. Once the original recording is made public, the control over its reproduction is thus contested.

In most industrialized societies, copyright is defined as "ownership of an original work of music to the author (i.e., composer and lyricist). Neighboring rights secure ownership of sound recordings to the producing company and the performing artists" (Kretschmer *et al.* 2001: 424). In the postwar era, Japan became signatory to many international treaties concerning these rights, and this action helped to return Japan to the Western economic community. Although Japan first established "bilateral copyright relations" with the United States in 1906, the signing of the 1956 Universal Copyright Convention Treaty in Geneva superceded earlier treaties and set a new standard for trade between Japan and other nations (US Copyright Office 2006). It is likely that Japan's signatory actions in the 1950s had been strongly encouraged by the United States first to protect the rights of foreigners selling products in Japan would be protected (and secondly for the establishment of Japanese rights overseas), as demonstrated by the earlier nomenclature of Law No. 302: "Law Concerning Exceptional Provisions for Copyrights Owned by the Allied Powers and the Allied Nationals," enacted in 1952 (*Chôsaku kenjôhô sentâ* 2005). Until the 1960s, there had been much "Western criticism" in terms of the less than vigorous terms by which Japan persecuted violators of copyright law and pressure to reform in the lines of European and North American standards (Kawabata 1991: 344).

In 1971, a new copyright law was passed in Japan, and this law, with various amendments made over the years, stands as the constitutional standard today. In 1971, this law defined copyright and divided it into two, as described above: authors' copyright and neighboring rights. Copyright belonged to the composers who may, or may not be, the performers. The 1971 law divided the neighboring rights into two parts: the first belonging to the performer (including the backup musicians who performed on the record) and the second was considered a reproduction right, and this belonged to record companies, broadcasting and "wire diffusion" organizations (*Chôsaku kenjôhô sentâ* 2005; Kawabata 1991: 341, 344). "Lending rights" in Japan were established in 1984, in response to the proliferation and the need for control of rental record and CD shops in that period. The length of record protection, since 1990, is thirty years; record copying is permitted for *personal use* in Japan.

There is no specialized labor law that protects composers and musicians from being exploited by powerful corporations. The collecting society JASRAC (the Japanese Society for the Rights of Authors, Composers and Publishers), however, does function to protect copyright holders from exploitation but takes a percentage of the record's sale to provide these services. JASRAC functions as the main "collecting society" (Kretschmer *et al.* 2001: 433) for Japanese authors of popular music. Established in 1940, JASRAC joined the International Confederation of Societies of Authors and Composers (CISAC) in 1960, four years after Japan's ratification of the Geneva UCC.

JASRAC began collecting broadcast royalties on behalf of composers under contract in 1978, and karaoke royalties in 1987 (JASRAC 2005), and was the sole collector of royalties until 2001 (Takeishi and Lee 2004: 8). The year 2001 marked the year that a new copyright law was enacted, Law 131 or the "Law on Management Business of Copyright and Neighboring Rights." This law instigated a registration system for businesses involved in copyright (*Chôsaku kenjôhô sentâ* 2005) and thus made it possible for management business to "break into" the publishing business and start collecting royalties on behalf of their contracted composers and performers; this is reflected in the immense functional diversification of management companies as described in Chapter 4 regarding the *jimusho*, and it is thought that copyright has accounted for the vast increases in their reported income. Despite this new competition, JASRAC is still the dominant collecting society in Japan. In 2003, JASRAC collected approximately 109.47 billion yen (*1094 oku 7000 man en*) on behalf of Japanese composers and lyricists (Ugaya 2005b: 167).[10]

Contemporary technology challenges the way producers and consumers define copyright and observe copyright law in the music industry. Music piracy is defined as counterfeiting, pirate recording (including the "unauthorized duplication and distribution" of music as MP3 files), or bootlegging (Marshall cited in Kretschmer *et al.* 2001: 434). The main damage caused by music piracy is the potential loss in sales to record companies, but Kretschmer *et al.* challenge this notion as it is entirely possible that many who consume pirated music would not necessarily be individuals who would buy at full price, so declining CD sales figures may not be entirely due to illegal copying (2001: 435). Empirical studies support this, providing evidence that downloads do not have discernable effects on sales (Oberholzer and Strumpf cited in Condry 2004a: 349). It is just as possible that the slowing of sales in Japan is due to the deepening recession since 1991, and competition for expendable income from other entertainment sources such as mobile phones and other computer services that divert leisure expenditure to other areas than music consumption. In other words, consumers (especially young people with limited expendable income) can only spend so much on CDs if they also owe significant amounts for mobile phone and internet bills.

Because widely available software (such as Limewire, Grokster, and Streamcast) make file-sharing possible between individual users, software companies became the target for lawsuits, for contributing to the infringement of copyright. These cases recall the famous 1984 case against Sony, which was sued unsuccessfully by movie studios for creating a VCR that allowed consumers to copy movies using Sony VCR technology. In this technology context, however, record companies have filed suit and won. RIAJ successfully sued a Tokyo-based company called MMO that makes P2P software called "Filerogue"; judges ruled that MMO owed 19 record labels approximately 40 million yen (Haw 2005b).

The RIAJ began investigations in early 2005 of other individuals, foreshadowing further lawsuits (ibid.). Despite arguments against the impact of downloading music on CD sales, the widespread success of MP3 files and players presents a strong perceived threat to the record industry; the RIAJ has targeted technology (or, more to the point, its individual consumer use) as a culprit in declining music sales. Again, it is hard to know if file-sharing can be pinpointed as the major cause or if file-sharing is merely the scapegoat of a flailing industry, in decline for a myriad of other economic and social reasons.

To prevent further infringements, the industry is working to reinvent music technology to work in favor of the copyright holders. In the early 2000s, some Japanese artists released audio CDs that could not be played back on computers, preventing easy pirating. It was soon discovered that these versions did not provide top audio quality, and a new technology, CD locks, was next instituted as a way to prevent unauthorized copying but "copy-control CDs are widely used in Japan with uncertain effects" (Condry 2004a: 352). When technology did not remedy the situation, the industry responded with an educational campaign. "Respect our Music" is an example of an artist and recording company-led promotional drive, established in 2002; it represents the six industry organizations' combined efforts to change the way audiences perceive musical copyright. This campaign was endorsed by major figures in the industry, such as the rock/pop star and producer Okuda Tamio, Komuro-produced idol Kahala Tomomi, and others.

Internationally, DRM (digital rights management) "focuses on strengthening the property aspect of music, and making file-sharing less attractive" (Condry 2004a: 344). This involves education and the creation of new technologies to protect music from infringement. SDMI (secure digital musical initiative) is a forum for protecting copyright in digital formats. It includes protection technologies such as encryption, royalty systems, "watermarking" files (limited playbacks) (Kretschmer *et al.* 2001: 427) but its attempt to promote this new technology was expensive and ultimately, a failure (Fisher 2004: 4). Another concept is Alternate Compensation Systems (ACS), which embraces SDMI measures but in a spirit that embraces sharing and helps copyright holders to "offset" losses through unauthorized copying (Condry 2004a: 344). In an ACS system, a centralized registration system would allow composers who wanted to declare copyright to do so and insert a registration code into their work (Fisher 2004: 4–5) allowing a centralized office – presumably, a national copyright office – to monitor the copyrighted piece's activity. Fisher argues that this system would, if implemented effectively, allow the consumer a wider range of low-cost choices while providing the copyright holder with a "reliable source of income" (41). These projects, however, are still in the process of discussion at the time of writing rather than implementation in the United States and in Asia. It appears that only further technological advances can save music technology from the economic perils it has itself created!

Generally speaking, Japanese concern over music piracy is muted compared to similar press in the West. Despite the RIAJ action against the corporation MMO,

Japanese suits against individuals involving illegal duplication numbered merely three, versus hundreds seen in Europe (Condry 2004a: 345–346). One of the reasons file-sharing is not as common in Japan as in the United States is because of users' reliance on mobile phone networks and CD rental shops (351–352), which generally observe copyright law. For example, *chakumero* or ring tones were made available on mobile networks by the telecommunications companies after negotiations with JASRAC, who had been accustomed to collecting royalties in this way in the case of karaoke machines. Copyright on the mobile network was agreed upon in 2000 (Takeishi and Lee 2004: 9), and it is thought that JASRAC's participation in the creation and distribution of *chakumero* ensured quality by policing "improper free services" (ibid.).

Simulacra in music technology

The preceding section recorded the developments in music technology with reference to the concept of simulacra, which is a representation of the "reality" of music encapsulated and delivered through technological means. The radio broadcaster represents music as a voice of authority and information, and his/her status can cross over to celebrity status in the J-pop world. This disembodied human voice circulates aesthetic "taste," both creating and preserving the concept of a central popular culture. Television (as discussed in Chapter 4) later added a visual element, and by replacing musical performance with other kinds of artist representation, it has skilfully combined musical simulacra with other genre (such as comedy and interview) to vary the viewer experience and strengthen their interpretation of the artist's total public image. While the discussion of music television in Chapter 4 focused on industry connections, the music television show encompassing talk and variety is an enrichment of simulacra processes: it reproduces not just the music but also the visual and emotive attributes of musicians (their looks and personality). This process uses a specific formula: musical celebrity = attractive personality + musical skill (or comedic, humorous lack of skill).

The technological products listed above serve to represent and preserve the music of individual artists, but they also act as repetitions – first, of the live experience of hearing a performance and, secondly, of the experience of listening to the recorded version, again and again. Vinyl records linger as representative of an authoritative musical source and are still important to specific fan bases; their material fragility adds to their value. Audio tapes could be endlessly reproduced; they represented the first technology that allowed consumers to have an imprint on the listening experience, through dubbing and arranging tracks to their own interpretations of the music. In the case of the cassette tape and the Walkman, we see a clear connection between the "body and advanced electronic technology" (Yoshimi 1999: 168), and as the body moved, so did music. Music consumption first became mobile with the car radio, but personal stereos allowed listeners to integrate the hardware with their bodies and to personalize and privatize the listening experience through increasingly small and invisible headphones.

Compact discs raised the level of quality of listening and provided consumers with improved storage options; this was important because it made it easier for buyers to justify expanding their collections with less worry of storage space. MiniDiscs combined the creativity of the cassette tape with disc sound quality. One might argue that the latest development in musical technology, the MP3, contains two layers of simulacra: first, it represents a musical performance (which was originally performed live) and, secondly, it represents the standard objectification of that performed music (the CD). It is only as a response to this threat that artists have begun releasing music directly in MP3 format, to avoid the second simulation of unauthorized copies (which cuts into profits). This double simulacra can be stretched to include an unlimited number of individuals. The further the simulacra is stretched, the greater the perceived threat to musical ownership in general.

Karaoke as case study of music and technology

A professional musician once told me that he felt his band's recent falloff in sales was conversely related to their technological skill. In other words, the more mature the musicians became, the more complex their music was. The result was their songs were too difficult for most amateurs to perform in karaoke, and without the sales related to karaoke performance (e.g., CDs purchased for home practice), his band could not compete with others who produced simpler melodies with easy lyrics. "The problem is we're too good," he said, and research proves he was correct: Ogawa states that the increase in million-seller artists in the first half of the 1990s was due to the reinvigorated late 1980s karaoke boom, and that hit songs changed from those " 'good to listen to' to 'good to sing' " (2001: 49).

Karaoke is an apt case study for this chapter because its practice blurs the boundaries between technology and musical performance, combining a live voice with recorded and amplified sound. In the Japanese context, it is closely tied to social and business relations, consumption, and creative processes; in general, karaoke and its practice is widespread, symbolizing globalization theory in action (see Mitsui and Hosokawa 2001).

Karaoke also offers an important illustration of simulacra in music and technology. The recorded background music pours from speakers, representing the backing band; the participant sings into a microphone that is in turn amplified and broadcast simultaneously with the recorded music. Flashing lights and video images often accompany the performance and add atmosphere: musical professionalism and amateurism melt in the moment. One of the most eloquent demonstrations of simulation in karaoke is *monomane*, where the karaoke singer tries to imitate an original performance, as closely as possible, often for humorous effect. Even when delivered deadpan, *monomane* is the human attempt to become not just an imitation of a song but of another singer; the imitator molds him or herself to the original, creating a simulacrum for communal amusement and social interaction.

Background

Karaoke is said to have evolved from a prewar practice, *enkai*, a term that consists of the two characters for "party" and "performance." The mix of alcohol and song had been long part of the Japanese dinner party, but in most cases, the only accompaniment was the handclapping of other guests (Mitsui 2001: 39). As men were usually dominant participants at such gatherings, they were the primary participants and this gave the practice a sense of "male bonding." As is the case with many Japanese social skills, talent was not considered as important as the perceived effort and the level of participation at *enkai* performances.

Karaoke literally means "empty orchestra"; in its simplest terms, it is a music recording minus its vocal track, sometimes referred to as "minus one." To set karaoke into action, however, layers of technology are required – to play back the empty track, to provide a microphone to pick up the voice, and to project the voice over the karaoke recording. In most cases, another layer is added through a video or a laser disc (seen through a television screen), used to display the lyrics. *Musen hôsô* (wireless, satellite transmission, as opposed to *yûsen*, or cable transmission) of video lyrics have replaced video and laser discs in speciality bars, clubs, and even in some homes. Karaoke is not, however, merely concerned with wires and hook ups – without the audience, the performance is nothing. One would have to include the social interaction between participants, between the participants and the purveyors of the karaoke bar or box, as well as the technology, to create the most complete definition of karaoke: the people, the technological components, and the action.

According to Mitsui Tôru, for the action to qualify as karaoke, there are certain technological requirements. There must be a visual source (for the lyrics), a sound source that can simultaneously play back two sound sources (the backing "empty" track and the live vocal performance), a microphone with an echo effect (to give the voice a more professional performance-like sound), and also a "device for the instantaneous selection for a song or else the functioning of the machine would not be practical" (2001: 41). More recently, accessories such as pitch and tempo adjustments are available on certain machines, and these give the singer more control over how the backing track is played, allowing for a more personalized performance. One of the recent accessories that eloquently demonstrate karaoke's capacity for simulacra is the scoring function: when deployed, the machine gives a numerical score for the live performance based on its measurement against the original.

Schilling states that contemporary version of karaoke was born in Osaka, invented by a record store manager who dreamed up the idea to replace live musical performers in local pubs (1997: 87). Live orchestras were replaced with reel-to-reel or cassette tape; in the early days of recorded karaoke, jukeboxes and cable radio were also used. Distribution of karaoke repertoire is an important element; this refers to the way the karaoke set continually renews its number of songs. Acquiring new discs keeps the karaoke set current with charts and allows it to constantly expand its repertoire (later, this would be achieved through *yûsen* or *musen* subscriptions). Most professional karaoke sets contain thousands of entries, generally divided between *enka*, pop, and rock standards ("oldies") and latest hits.

In the early days, the visual source consisted of paper; karaoke singers held printed sheets of lyrics that were supplied with the machines. The introduction of compact and laser discs as lyric sources on screen began in 1983 and the change from bulky paper notebooks to the screen allowed for more songs to be stored and a greater variety of music available to consumers at a single use. The other outcome was the addition of atmospheric scenery projected above the lyrics and featured prominently between verses and at other breaks in the song. This visual feature provides mood and sometimes even hilarity, as it can be embarrassing to choose a song, unwittingly, with risqué background in mixed company. This aspect is accentuated in certain situations, such as karaoke bars that employ hostesses (in most cases, these are female workers catering to male customers although "host clubs" where the gender roles are reversed are proliferating). The karaoke performance in this context adds to the sexual banter in these environments.

Karaoke takes place in a variety of settings, and these can be defined by the technology supplied; they also affect the meaning behind performance. As previously mentioned, parties (both at homes and at rented rooms in hotels, restaurants, and bars) often include karaoke. If the party is at home, the set can be rented or is sometimes purchased by an enthusiast (who can also practice for outside parties in the convenience of one's home). The karaoke box – an individual room for 4–12 participants – provides physical privacy as well as soundproofing. Karaoke boxes were introduced in Japan in 1986; this brought karaoke out of the bars frequented by middle-aged men and into a world of women as well as men, students, and salaried workers. Karaoke's image changed from one associated with cigarette smoke, businessmen and out-of-date *enka* songs to one that was feminine and fashionable. In the idol-dominated 1980s, karaoke allowed a method of personal identification with the star. Fans carefully studied the idol's performance on television shows like *The Best Ten* (TBS, 1978–1989) to learn the minute gestures, expressions and movements that accompanied a performance. I found it common to hear Japanese friends comment on others' choices ("She always sings Kudô Shizuka") as a statement about personal taste. Interpreted in this way, we can see karaoke is a method of communicating aesthetic preferences and values to others. In another context, a couple on a karaoke date could communicate emotional rather than aesthetic messages effectively through song choice and performance; often those who do not have the confidence to express there feelings directly can sing carefully chosen love songs to each other. This is precisely why many love hotels are equipped with karaoke sets; karaoke is not only a friendship-oriented social activity but also one that supports the emotive performance of romantic relationships.

Karaoke has also been viewed as an important socialization process, and Mitsui and Hosokawa's introduction to their book on karaoke lists the social "rules" when participating in a karaoke party:

> Do not sing while you are drunk
> Do not sing too loudly
> Do not abuse the echo effect
> Do not sing songs written for the opposite sex [the exception is as a joke, as defined by the *mochiuta* system]
> Do not sing songs too difficult for you
> Do not be too narcissistic
>
> (Mitsui and Hosokawa 2001: 18)

> Do not sing two songs in succession
> Do not sing the same songs as others. Audience must applaud between verses and at the end of song
> Unless people break these rules, everything goes well
>
> (Ogawa 2001: 46–47)

The socialization outcomes of karaoke are social harmony (through noncompetition), equality, and mutual support (even if hollow, as in applauding out of politeness for the faulty performance of a work senior colleague). Ogawa notes, however, that this socialization is mediated by technology. People sit, looking at the screen with the lyrics or video presentation, rather than looking at each other (48).

Anyone who has attended a karaoke gathering in Japan in recent years will have noticed that some of these social rules are being bent. Colleagues will still occasionally encourage the singer with applause and verbal support, but for the most part, the others are focused on the massive catalog, trying to find the next song that they will personally perform. Often karaoke singers are singing by themselves, in front of bowed heads frantically searching for a specific title, or a specific version of a song. This is not necessarily considered rude, as everyone knows how difficult it can be to find the right song in the every expanding repertoire presented at speciality karaoke shops because *yûsen* and *musen* subscriptions increase the capacity for a karaoke machine to store songs exponentially, making an individual's decision even more difficult. In this sense, it seems as if karaoke has been transformed into a more self-fulfilling act, sung for one's own satisfaction. Others witness the event but are not as involved – karaoke simulacra have transformed into performances where one's most attentive audience is the self; one listens to oneself merging with the ideal "reality" of the song through imitation.

Karaoke is a rich symbolic expression in the interaction of music and technology as it demonstrates the simulated practice of consumers aiming to reproduce sound, feeling, and style through performance. It also communicates the ideals and the reality of relationships between individuals. Similar social rules governing interactions occur in other spheres of Japanese social life but they are crystallized in karaoke, because personal identity and relationships (or lack thereof) are given expression through karaoke.

Consuming technology: a conflict between authenticity and technology?

> Rock was a last romantic attempt to preserve ways of music making – performer as artist, performance as "community" – that had been made obsolete by technology and capital.
>
> (Frith 1994:237)

Frith's statement sets up the classic dichotomy between the concept of authenticity and technology with reference to artistic expression. In rock, perhaps more consciously than pop, the aim of the artist is to establish an authentic and personal connection to the audience; the goal of the audience is to experience this connection. Because of the increasing integration of technology and simulacra in popular music, authenticity is an ongoing concern to musicians and audiences. As evidence, we witnessed the rediscovery of rock during the mid-1980s "band boom" in Chapter 3, demonstrating audience yearning for "real" music, after being jaded by the commercialism of idol music.

What is authenticity in popular music? According to Baudrillard, "authentic reality" no longer exists: everything is a reflected construction, "a simulacrum . . . in an uninterrupted circuit without reference or circumference" (1996: 76–77). Yet, audiences and musicians continue to strive for "authenticity" as the preferred aesthetic experience. In Japanese, we often hear the terms *honmono* ("the real thing") and *genba* ("the real place" or the "scene") to describe authenticity in the music. The "real thing" can refer to the artist himself or herself, as in "live in concert"; it could refer to the music itself in terms of its quality and closeness to the genre's ideals (e.g., the blues or rap). The "scene" could also be a concert or smaller "live house" venue, or a nightclub where recorded music is played and *experienced as part of the total environment*, rather than merely *consumed in isolation*. In both of these cases, authenticity is spontaneously performed, directly perceived, and there is direct human interaction between performer and audience (or, in the case of the nightclub, between DJ and listeners). Authenticity, if it can be defined in words, revolves around the quality of human relations in the production and experience of music.

Authenticity in sound refers to "concert hall sound" quality – in other words, like the "real thing." Increased audio quality gives the listener the feeling that the performer is standing before them, and the music is directly delivered from the artist to the audience. At first, "authentic" Western pop and rock music could be accessed through radio on FEN (an AM station), but during the 1950s–1960s, authenticity was not so much related to audio quality as it was to the close connection to the place of production (America). After the pop music audiences became accustomed to higher audio quality sound technology, the shift from AM radio to FM was inevitable, and stations like J-WAVE (which played music from both Japan and other countries) became the norm. In the 1980s, high-quality CDs became the standard for capturing "authentic" reproductions of music. In this sense, technology aids the reproduction of authenticity with improved audio quality as the sound of the reproduction becomes more "life-like."

In the first section of this chapter, discussions of technology were mainly focused on the objectification of musical performance: the record, the cassette tape, the compact disc, and so on. Now we turn to concert performance as a lens by which we can view the struggle between musical technology and personal authenticity. Live performance represents the simultaneous, and sometimes troubled, consumption of both the authentic and the technical. Fans demand personal interaction with the musician to individualize the consumer experience; meanwhile, the artist uses technology to maximize the live performance's capacity to imitate high-quality studio recordings – a replication of the object "live."

Artists who regularly perform in arena style venues combat the decreased intimacy and lack of authentic connection by using video screens with simultaneous playback of stage action. This is becoming more and more common as live concerts are increasingly offered at large arenas (such as the Tokyo Budôkan which seats 14,201; Yokohama Arena 17,000; Tokyo Dome 50,000) and competition for tickets is high.[11] The simultaneous concert screen technology allows for a double experience: the "real" audio and visual experience from the audience's seats, supplemented by the simulation of the close-up performance, giving the audience artificial access to an "ideal" (as in close-up and intimate) performance.

I attended 40 odd Alfee concert tours, special events, and outdoor stadium concerts from 1992 to 1998, and from the point of view of the spectator, I found that performance imperfection was an extremely important factor in creating a sense of intimacy and authentic human interaction between performer and audience. Technically speaking, the concerts appeared to run smoothly: lights go on and off on cue, special effects do not fail, and so on. In reality, technology occasionally fails, but when it does, the audience is often unaware (I only learned of the failure afterward from backstage staff). Perfection, however, can be boring, and some human element is necessary to add to the freshness of live performance. Humanity is shown in vocal performances; the singers sometimes purposefully change lyrics or the parts between vocalists. Most exciting is when the vocalists forget the words. This is a source of great delight to the fans, who scream joyously when a vocalist sings a new line or stops suddenly, groping for the next line. Human imperfections define the concert as unique to the fans' experience, distinct from a mass-produced performance that delivers the same message to tens of thousands of people via compact disc. The members' mistakes show the band's fallibility; this human quality is immensely appealing and underlines the emotional connection between star and fan, and no level of technological intervention seems to break that bond.

Concertgoers are not the only ones affected by technology; Théberge writes that musicians have become consumers of technology (1997), and in Japan, this kind of consumption is a sign of prestige. High technology has always been associated with elite businesses and other social and economic institutions in Japan, and the music business is no different. Advanced technology is associated with commercial and artistic success, for only the musicians who have "made it" can afford all the trappings that modern music industry offers. Aside from the previously mentioned screening of simultaneous performance, concerts are increasingly judged by entertainment value based on background scenery, lights or laser shows, and atmospheric effects. Pyrotechnics (or fireworks, in the case of an outdoor concert) are common in rock concerts in America as well as in Japan.

Technology's importance is demonstrated both in front of the audience and back stage. Takamizawa's dressing room on the Alfee's concert tours is sign-posted not with his name but the phrase "The Marshall Room" because he carries with him, to all concerts, an old Marshall amplifier, painted hot pink. He holds this piece of outdated technology as precious, and nostalgic, for he felt that the Alfee had really "made it" in the business when they could afford to use Marshall amps on stage (now their AV costs run into the millions of yen). It also reminds him of his roots, and not to let the success of his thirty-plus years in the entertainment industry cloud his artistic values.

Another way musicians demonstrate their technological consumption is through product endorsement, both live on stage and in print through CD releases. Takamizawa has a long-standing contract with ESP guitars, and he designs electric guitars both for his own use and for general sale. His Flying A design (since the 1980s) and the Angel Series (late 1990s to present) are available to the public through ESP outlets and special order. The Shibuya outlet for ESP, The ESP Craft House, launched an internet site "A-Guitars" through the internet "shopping mall" *Rakuten Ichiba* in late 2005 to sell Takamizawa's guitars and instruments endorsed and/or designed by the other two members, Sakazaki and Sakurai, as well as amplifiers and accessories such as straps and picks. Prices, depending on the complexity of design, range from several 100,000s of yen to over 3 million yen for the newest ESP "Prince Angel" design; high technology does not come cheaply in rock and roll. Yet fans are often willing to pay these high prices, as the "authentic" design of their rock and roll idol imparts on them a special connection to the music, as they reproduce it at home.

During live performances, Takamizawa changes guitars frequently and introduces his special, one-off designs at important concerts like their annual summer outdoor event. Endorsements are also advertised in album liner notes. The Alfee normally list four to five instrument endorsements on their CDs (electric guitars, acoustic guitars, and drum makers). Fans may purchase the same, or similar, endorsed instruments which then impart some of the imagined technique of the star on the fan. It is not uncommon to see fans gathering early outside a large concert venue like NHK Hall or the Budôkan, listening to fan "cover bands" that play Alfee songs on Alfee-designed and/or endorsed equipment. Acting as a kind of warm-up band for the main attraction, these fan bands provide simulacritic experiences that are up close and personal (yet "false") which are followed by the distant and idealized performance (which is "real").

In this context, the technology that allows the audience to interact with the music can become as important and valuable as the music itself (e.g., the on-screen concert close-up, the newest iPod with extra functions), which demonstrates Baudrillard's concept that "the map precedes the territory" (1996: 76). Baudrillard argues that in the postmodern era, simulation, opposed to representation, is increasingly masking, distorting, and eventually separating the meaning of the symbol with its sign. "When the real is no longer what it used to be, nostalgia assumes its full meaning" (1995: 77). Not surprisingly, the preconcert fan bands primarily perform older numbers, perhaps in reaction to concerts, where audiences commonly complain that the performance focused on newer songs and not old standards.

The compact disc (and increasingly, the MP3 file) now defines what music *is*, rather than merely serving as an object of representation. This idea of simulacra is also intimately tied to the act of performance and is echoed in Wise's statement that technologies "stand in the place" of selves. I would further the argument by saying the technologies also stand in the place of *others* as well as *selves*, because the technology that presents popular music to audiences tends to *objectify* the performer with visual imagery contained in CD covers, DVD clips, concert videos, and the like. The result is, however, mixed: the technology brings both the audience and the performer together through "as if you were there" sound quality but also separates the music as an act and its representation as an object. In this separation between the music and its representation, longing for the original and the authentic is manifested in the celebration of nostalgia in Japanese pop music.

Nostalgia for format is one of the most visible forms of simulacra in later technological expressions. Hosokawa and Matsuoka's study of vinyl record collectors demonstrates the tenacity jazz aficionados have for the nostalgia of the record (2004). But jazz enthusiasts are not the only fans who value authenticity. Rock music is increasingly being marketed as nostalgic. The Alfee's series of single hits, released to coincide with their twenty-fifth anniversary in 1994, contained printouts of the original single covers inside the boxed set of compact discs. More recently, their single *Juliet* was presented on a compact disc that was labeled as a black 45 rpm (2001). The group consume cutting edge technology, yet their artwork pays homage to the idealized past of rpm records. Even live nostalgia is for sale: the 1993 *Confidence Special Acoustic Live*, where the band played early "pre-hit" Alfee songs plus covers of Bob Dylan, Crosby, Stills, Nash & Young, The Who, and others (the "authentic" West), allowing the audience to peek into their memories of amateur musicianship, ripe with authentic, direct human relations.

Nostalgia for the past is a kind of psychological patch over the rents in the relationship between producer and consumer, and perhaps this is what Appadurai means when he says that the consumer believes that his/her actions have agency ("I choose to experience an authentic relationship with a star over an artificial one") but in reality the producer is merely creating a sense of choice and is the only true agent in this structure (1990: 307). This interpretation is certainly disempowering to the Japanese consumer. I offer in contrast the ideas of anthropologist Harumi Befu (2003) who writes that consumers may follow trends set by marketers but do so in their own particular ways, taking on some of the ideas associated with a product but rejecting others. For example, Sony as a major international conglomerate fits into the roles, envisioned by Appadurai, as a producer creating the illusion of choice to the consumer while in reality cornering the market and limiting choice. Yet consumers still find ways to express their own choices (such as file-sharing). Technology presents a double bind: companies control the spread of technology to consumers, yet they cannot control the way consumers use it. This freedom allows them to create their own meanings, and interpretations of the music according to their individual values.

Conclusion

Throughout this chapter, we have seen technology, and its consumption, as representative of individual identity. This representation must also be seen in the context of a larger collective, where technology constitutes not just individual but also national identity. Before Japan's industrialization, technology was considered foreign, but necessary for Japan to stay afloat in the military and economic expansionism that was developing in East and South East Asia. After Japan's defeat and its subsequent economic recovery, however, associations with national identity and technology began to change:

> The United States with its Pax Americana has undoubtedly been the primary point of origin for its innovations in the techniques of the culture industries . . . , cultural forms . . . , technologies . . . and many oppositional social movements and their idioms. Yet as the global balance of economic power has shifted, so has the role of the United States. Japan is now the leader in production and exportation of electronic "hardware" of global cultural industries: tape recorders, Walkmen, VCRs, CD players, tapes.
>
> (Ivy 1993: 257)

Note that many of the examples listed here involve the reproduction of sound, an area where Japan excelled in design and production. The use of technology is ubiquitous throughout the pop music process, including recording, distribution, and consumption. Production and reproduction aside, musical style is also closely related to the embracing (or eschewing) of technology. As noted in Chapter 3, Japanese pop music over history has responded in part to technological trends in music: the *ereki bûmu* (electric boom) of the late 1960s made electrified music at the forefront of the pop charts; later, folk musicians "unplugged" their music, bringing a down-to-earth image to fans. Later, technology again was in favor as the synthesizer, as showcased by bands such as YMO, took the leading role in defining Japanese pop music in the 1980s. Macro-trends aside, we see individual, artist-level changes as well. The Alfee's "big break" came when they shifted from an acoustic, folk style to an electric rock style in 1981. RC Succession also experienced a style and "tech" overhaul in response to their decrease in sales: after a change in membership and under the influence of the band boom ("a rock renaissance") as well as the impact of punk and new wave overseas, RC became an electrified, rock and roll act (Takahashi 1993: 156). Not only did their music change but their image as well: spiked hair and glam makeup hyped up the band's image and gave them another image to market to further audiences. Technology affects not only music but visual image as well and creates new interest in bands that have saturated their genre. RC's consumption of a new style –in terms of both technology and their visual image that accompanied that switch – reignited interest in the band.

New technology has instigated some of the most dramatic changes in music production and distribution in the postwar era. For example, the digitization of music allowed new recording methods and playback techniques and created a new object that came to represent the music (the compact disc). The Internet has created communities of people across the globe that share information as well as music at speeds never before dreamed of. Musicians must keep up with the technology – through copyright protection or by finding ways to cooperate with file-sharing practices – in order to maintain artistic control over their music, for fear (justified or not) of losing it to the virtual community. This has revolutionized the way that audiences and producers view music: "[n]ew technology . . . lies behind the current reorganization of the music business" (Frith 1994: 239).

Technology has thus become mainstreamed into pop music consumers' daily lives and provides consumers with "added value." Even though "recording technologies, electronic instruments and samples hav[e] increasingly reduced the cost of creating music" (Negus 1999: 22), the image of technology as high cost and associated with a high standard of living adds value. Advanced technology means something to Japanese consumers, and its value lies in the way it enhances not only the auditory experience (through improved quality) but also its interpretation. For example, radio and television broadcasts add value because they include extra information about the artist, primarily through informal "talk." The personal stereo with the consumer programmed "my tape" added value because it allowed the listener to personalize and privatize the music experience at any time or place, batteries permitting. Downloading music with up-to-date information and images facilitates the process of enjoying music, enhancing the consumption experience as a total sensory one. Information about music can be just as important as the music itself, just as the map precedes the territory.

Does culture contribute to this integration of technology with Japanese popular music? Ugaya believes that technology is one of the defining characteristics of J-pop (2005b). In the same vein, Yoshimi writes "Japan is considered to be the most machine loving country in the world" (1999: 151), and this attraction has helped to create a "techno-nationalistic discourse," counterbalanced by an internationally fostered "Techno-Orientalism":

> The emerging "Japan problem" that appears in American and European journalistic commentaries and reports – the growing repugnance toward

> Japan – clearly derives from the fact that Japan is breaking up the borderline between the "modern/West" and "premodern/East."
>
> (1999: 151)

Japan's national identity as competitive with North America and Europe relies on its technological achievements, and Japan is one of the most successful exporters of music technology products to the West – Sony as a case in point.

Advances in music technology – like those accounted here with reference to the compact disc and personal stereo – have affected domestic as well as international perceptions of Japanese national identity. It has also helped to foster a musical community, much like the technoscapes described by Appadurai, allowing information and ideas in this case about music (which can include ideas of identity, gender, and political expression) to flow between peoples (1990: 297). For example, the global success of the Walkman was not due to the fact it was particularly "Japanese"; it was because the product was functionally groundbreaking and appealed to a wide variety of consumers. Its global success cemented the image of postwar Japan as a producer of superior hardware in music technology; products as well as ideas surrounding the product and its point of origin were being circulated and consumed on an international scale. This created a fluid technoscape, where the flow of technology included both objects (data compressors that allowed MD technology) and abstract ideas (Japan = advanced, superior, or at least competitive with the West).

Changes in the social relations of pop music production, empowered by the commercial success of the New Music movement, allowed artists like RC Succession and the Alfee to experiment with their sound and image in order to find, and keep, an audience. Musicians utilize technology to increase the quality of their products but promote the nostalgia of pretechnologized objects and musical styles to maintain a sense of artistic authenticity. This echoes Bourdieu's theory that a shift in the balance of social/power relations will affect how taste is shaped and transformed (1994a: 53), for the acquisition of technology and its integration into the overall musical presentation has proved beneficial to artists in the post-period, and their increased success enhances their position in the field. In many cases, successful individual artists have then gone on to produce other artists in line with their artistic vision, altering the map of the cultural production industry along the lines of their tastes.

The integration of technology and nostalgia allows artists to be both cutting edge and authentic in the Japanese pop scene. The chapter thus closes with a challenge: If language decenters the subject ("[t]he self no longer uses language to express itself; rather the language speaks through the person") (Kvale 1995: 22), does technology decenter musicians? listeners? Or does it empower listeners to have a hand in the construction of their listening experience? Only the furthering of technological advances, occurring at a rate almost too fast to document, will tell.

6 Translations: "internationalizing" language and music

Translate: 1. To render in another language. 2a. To put into simpler terms; explain or interpret. b. To express in different words; paraphrase.

(American Heritage Dictionary)

Japanese popular music is striking, in that its language of expression is far from limited to its native discourse: Japanese is, of course, the communication baseline in this field, but other languages are frequently utilized. What meanings do these "othered" expressions hold? Why does Japanese popular music use foreign languages more often than those of other globalized, industrialized societies? Does this practice help us to understand Japanese attitudes regarding Western cultural hegemony in non-Western pop music traditions? In this discussion of the integration of foreign languages in Japanese popular music, I have tried to use the term "internationalizing," rather than "internationalized" or "international" when appropriate, to stress the idea of an ongoing *process*, which is a Japanese reaction to its own experience of global change.

Foreign languages, used in idiosyncratic ways, can be the source of much mirth from overseas audiences; Japanese writers can be equally critical of this practice (Ugaya and McClure 2001a,b). This chapter seeks not to correct or find fault in this practice but first to understand how language can be a symbolic strategy to create atmosphere in Japanese popular music, one that is not dictated by normative rules of grammar and spelling. Furthermore, foreign lyrics translated into Japanese represents another kind of manipulation. This is not merely paying homage to the "authentic" source but also represents a strategy for mainstreaming subversive messages. This chapter first examines the insertion of English lyrics into Japanese songs and then Japanese translations of English songs, to examine how meanings are manipulated through the act of translation.

Linguists, ethnomusicologists, and anthropologists frequently discuss the use of English in Japanese popular culture (Hogan 2003; Hosokawa 1989, 1999a,b; Kitagawa 1991; Miller 1997; Seaton 2001; Stanlaw 1992, 2004). Their analyses include a focus on aesthetics and sound and use a variety of terms such as "Japlish," *wasei eigo* ("made-in-Japan English"), "Pidgin Japanese," or *giji eigo* (pseudo-English) to describe this phenomenon.[1] Most argue against the common knee-jerk reaction that this kind of expression merely illustrates the poor English linguistic capabilities of Japanese copywriters and songwriters. They promote the idea of an emerging and fluid hybrid language, perfectly comprehensible to in-group interlocutors, and interpreted within a shared symbolic framework.

Of all the foreign languages, English is most frequently used in Japanese popular music, due to its affinity with the genre's place of origin: as Hosokawa states, "the ideology of English . . . [is the] authentic expression for rock music" in Japan (1999a: 101). In the first two decades after the Occupation, foreign music constituted the largest volume of sales in the Japanese record industry; because of the political atmosphere, as discussed in Chapter 3, it was considered "natural to accept a song of a foreign language without any understanding of its meaning" (Nakamura, cited in Kawabata 1991: 335). Yet as the Japanese music industry matured in the late 1960s and early 1970s, *hôgaku* staked its place as the dominant sales market in the Japanese record industry. This developing definition of "Japanese" music – now truly separated from its prewar definition as a classical, elite musical tradition – included the integration of Western modalities, instrumentation, harmonies, rhythms, and language through borrowed lyrics.

As more and more Japanese artists recorded, mixed, and mastered their albums overseas in the 1980s, growing numbers of musicians were in contact with the "authentic" language associated with their craft. And English still seemed to be the key to global acceptance (or at least domestic *caché*). We also see incidences of artists recording two versions of one single – English and Japanese, sometimes with the assistance of a foreign professional or amateur songwriter. This is often more related to profit-seeking than anything else, meaning that language is also a powerful marketing tool. Other performers, benefiting from their personal experience overseas in a society with increasing contact with foreigners, record English original compositions for release in Japan. They are regarded as the "true" interpreters of the "authentic" source. Thus we can conclude that language really is about power: in this context, with respect to both selling potential and artistic prestige.

This chapter is more about lyrics than music, and the cultural and artistic notions embedded within. The main function of lyrics is to help link sound to emotion: the "pop song tells a story and comments on it in order to provoke in listeners the feelings appropriate to that song" (Hennion 1990: 188). Furthermore,

> it is through the selection of words that the appeal must be made; certain key words, in contrast with the obviousness of other words, which are like tiny reservoirs briefly holding the social significations of the moment, function as pure signifiers: mysteriously, they have an autonomy of their own with in the meaning of the text and are selected for the way they ring, for the expressive power which gives them their opacity; they have to engage the imagination of the listener and at the same time effect a sort of disengagement from the everyday words of the text so that the role of dream can be given full play. (1990: 198)

Here, the key words, the "tiny reservoirs" of meaning, are not limited to Japanese, but can be found in English, French, and other expressions, and these various terms create different moods as they "disengage" from "everyday words" in contemporary life in Japan.

English + Japanese = Japlish

Before launching the analysis, some background on the interaction between English and Japanese is useful. "Japlish" is a term used, sometimes tongue in cheek, to describe the phenomenon of integrating English terms into Japanese popular culture, most commonly seen on T-shirts or billboards or heard in Japanese music. Japlish is distinct from loanwords, or *gairaigo*, where the original foreign term is adapted to a Japanese pronunciation and is usually rendered in the script *katakana*. For example, the sentence "*famiri resu de kôhî o nonda*" (I drank coffee at a family-style restaurant) employs two loanwords (*fami-resu* = family restaurant, *kôhî* = coffee), but most speakers would consider this an entirely Japanese utterance considering the level of integration of these words into native vocabulary and the fact that this sentence can be entirely written using native orthography. Foreign terms, either in their entirety or in abbreviated form, are integrated into a grammatical utterance based on their acceptance into the language as loanwords. Acceptance into the language is reinforced through the publishing industry: if loanwords can be found in Japanese (*kokugo*) dictionaries as incorporated vocabulary, or listed in specialist dictionaries that focus on foreign terms and/or "trendy" vocabulary (which are often introduced and popularized by the mass media), they are generally recognized as part of the Japanese language, but there are also levels of general vernacular usage that constitute acceptance. Hogan demonstrates these various levels of language use: "According to recent estimates, vocabulary derived from foreign languages accounts for approximately 10% of the Japanese lexicon, 13% of words in everyday spoken language, and up to 25% of the text in general-interest weekly publications" (2003: 43).

Striking in these statistics is the doubling of the rate of occurrences of foreign words in the mass media as compared to the "lexicon" and the vernacular. The mass media, including those associated with the Japanese popular music industry, promote the use of foreign terms because of their association with "hot trends." As we have seen in Chapter 3, in the early postwar era, most of these trends came from the West – specifically the United States – thus we see an overrepresentation of English words in this category of loanwords. Today, many of Japan's pop culture trends are domestically sourced and driven; yet loanwords are often used to describe them. This is because of prior associations of trends with a dominant American pop cultural context: terms like guitar, rock, and singer (*gitâ, rokku shingâ*) all use English loanwords.

Japlish, however, is more subtle and multilayered in meaning and usage than loanwords. On one level, it is similar to *gairaigo*, in that it is borrowed terminology; yet Japlish is not found in dictionaries and is usually written in romanized letters rather than *katakana*. Thus, it stands separate from the "lexicon" (written in Japanese script) in ways that loanwords do not. This highlights their discrete "foreign-ness" in the utterance. For example, Stanlaw gives a well-known jingle for Coca-cola as classic Japlish:

> *Itsumo machi ni* I FEEL COKE
> *Kanji no mama kono toki yo*
> *Sawayaka, teisteii* I FEEL COKE

Stanlaw translates this as "Always, the town feels I FEEL COKE/Feel what you want, be who you are/Refreshing, tasty I FEEL COKE" (1992: 63) [the capitalized words appear in romanization; the remaining words utilize Chinese characters as well as Japanese *kana* scripts]. Note that in the final line, both *gairaigo* in *katakana* (*teisteii* = tasty) and Japlish in roman letters coexist seamlessly in the same sentence. One might be tempted to argue that the use of Japlish belongs only to the sphere of imported products and ideas (as Coca-cola amply demonstrates), but we see Japlish with reference to overtly Japanese objects and ideas as well: the cover of an academic journal concerned with Japanese intellectual history proclaims itself as "NEW JAPANOLOGY" (Ivy 1995: 62, capitals in the original).

Sound and image

The integration of foreign languages into Japanese pop music demonstrates meaning on a number of levels; this fusion combines aesthetic ideas regarding both sound and image. First, the sound: Japanese lyrics do not have to rhyme, as is common in English (Japanese rap vocals do rhyme, and rappers often complain of this difficulty [Condry 2000: 172]). Verbs in Japanese have some similar sound resonances: all nonpast verbs in the plain form end in a "u" sound (*iru* [to be] *miru* [to see], *kanau* [to fulfill], for example) and all past tense verbs in the plain form end with a "ta" sound. Some sentence endings can be carried from line to line (e.g., "∼*n da*" which implies the preceding information answers a request for information or is speaking emotionally of a topic in common with an interlocutor), creating sound similes, but in general, Japanese popular music does not rhyme.

Despite this freedom, lyric composition can pose problems for the composer. Takamizawa Toshihiko (who has composed many other successful recording artists such as Koizumi Kyôko, Tunnels, Nakamori Akina, and Akashiya Samma) states that composing lyrics is more difficult than music, echoing Hennion's subversion of lyrical to musical composition in order and in importance (1990: 189):

> Lyrics [must] match the melody . . . that's what it means to complete composition. Japanese, however, doesn't match music easily. Even now, I have trouble with it!

> I guess it's the rhythm. English has intonation [Japanese is pronounced, generally, in a flat tone of voice except in certain situations where homonyms are distinguished]. I feel there's already a rhythm to English conversation . . . Generally standard Japanese is flat, with no intonation (accent). Because of this, I think it's easier to write English lyrics into a melody . . . for example, the melody for "I love you" has [just] three sounds . . . But in Japanese "*aishiteiru*" already has to have six sounds.
>
> Of course, pop musicians' roots are in the West. Pushing things linguistically can't be helped. This is why composers such as Yuming and Nakajima Miyuki are [so impressive]. I think that they have reinvigorated the Japanese language and excelled at it.
>
> (Personal Communication 2005)

Lyrics determine the content of the song. "Love" songs are the most common in Japanese popular music, contrasted with what is known as "message" songs that make a personal or political statement outside the sphere of romance.

In the distinction between love and message songs, humor, which can be injected into both kinds of songs, deserves a mention here. Humorous songs in Japanese popular music usually employ puns or nonsense syllables (Mita 1992: 84); this kind of word play can be seen in a variety of contemporary J-pop. An example of humor from the "*wasei* pop" era is "*Sûdarabushi*" (Gliding Melody) by Ueki Hitoshi and the Crazy Cats (1961). Overall, this song presents a double-edged attitude (humor plus scorn), combining protest and fun. Mita comments that this song is memorable for its "feel good onomatopoeia" (93);[2] furthermore, the meaninglessness of the lyrics gave the listeners an evocative sense of floating. Yet it was precisely this floating feeling, felt by many urban salaried workers who had lost touch with their roots, that conveyed a fun but still sharp critique of the rapidly changing postwar society. More recently, lyrics in Japanese rap and hip-hop music rely on puns and word play (both in Japanese and using Japanese combined with English rap expressions) rather than violent imagery to attract audiences. For example, "yo!" is frequently used in American rap; coincidentally, in Japanese, it serves as a sentence-ending particle that punctuates meaning emphatically, so that when Japanese rappers call out "*yo*!" there are two meanings, English and Japanese, at play. Because of the difficulties with accented vocabulary and rhyme in Japanese, language represents an "impossible wall" to many rappers (Condry 2001: 231). One example of overcoming this wall is the mix of languages: meaning is clearly stated in Japanese but the "authentic" additions of English tags or endings to their Japanese lyrics not only gives legitimacy but also allows for some rhyming possibilities.

Whether a love or message song, serious or playful, foreign terms add value to the end product. In an interview with singer/songwriter and New Music icon Yuming (Matsutôya Yumi), we learn that she adds "a little fragrance of Western culture to give the song some elegance" (Stanlaw 1992: 66). Stanlaw believes that her use of English is an "individual artistic statement and relied to a great degree on the sympathetic cooperation of her listeners to accomplish her task" (ibid.).

In other words, the success of the song depended on the fact that the audience shared her interpretation of the terms. Yuming does not limit her utilization to English, nor is it constrained to the single function of "elegance." Her 1998 double album of greatest hits, entitled *Neue Musik* (the German translation of the English *gairaigo* genre that she helped pioneer), certainly brings a level of tongue-in-cheek humor to the overall image of New Music – as well as ironically underscoring the fact that a greatest hits album contains rereleases and very little, in any, "new music." Titling her album in Japanese ("*nyû mujikku*" is too broad a term and "*shinkyoku*," or literally, new releases, is misleading) would have been ineffective, but the German phrase imparts a light, clever, and amusing touch.

Another contemporary singer who uses foreign languages frequently is Shiina Ringo, a female rock vocalist who debuted in 1998. She sings in a variety of languages, each with its own cultural baggage – English, French, German, and Portuguese – as well as Japanese. She sings entirely in correctly constructed but in accented English in the Japanese titled "*Genjitsu o warau*" (Laugh at reality) track in the 2004 album *Kyôiku* (Education) with her new band *Tôkyô Jihen*.[3] Shiina's compositions are noted for their singular approach to human relations – rather than typical male/female love songs, she writes of more complex topics, such as the tensions in "mother/daughter" relationships (Ugaya 2005a: 193), expressing the current sentiment of many young women desirous of a departure from their parents' social and moral codes. Even in Japanese, Shiina's lyrics employ complicated *kanji* compounds that express an adult atmosphere, belying any triviality in an adolescent message. This illustrates that any language in this genre – the singers' native language as well – can be manipulated to create a specific image.

Another way to interpret the use of Japlish is by focusing more explicitly on the *sound* of the lyrics rather than their purported *meaning*. Does the English used merely provide an acoustic gloss and its signified meaning (= international sophistication)? In other words, to what extent is meaning a part of the listening experience? Or, are lyrics a purely aural experience?[4] As a case study in sound and meaning, Japanese ethnomusicologist Kitagawa Junko refers to the band The Southern All Stars (who debuted 1978) and how their music completely changed the way that Japanese young people listened to music.[5]

> Kuwata [the band's songwriter] first composes melodies with nonsense syllables that sound like English words, and finishes up with lyrics in Japanese after completing the melody . . . *The lyrics are not taken as a meaningfully constructed entity, but as part of a sound.* Moreover, many of the Southern All Stars' songs are up-tempo ones, in which the words are hard to follow. Such songs tend to replace personal-oriented listening with "sound-oriented" listening.
>
> (Kitagawa 1991: 306–307, emphasis added)

After Kuwata's vocal style became famous in the late 1970s and early 1980s, he took the concept a step further in the 1990 song entitled "*Tôkyô Sarîchan*" (Miss

Tokyo Sally) which includes not only nonsense words in English and Japanese but his own creative vocabulary based purely on sound.

> ESSE-HËIM õ NO RËAH, 'BOOZ
> DAH WËAH
> Hippy Yappy Taxi Sexy 60's JAPANESE
> *Yume no chôin*[6] NATO-MUSICAL 9

Language is a subjective element of the song that Kuwata controls completely; he manipulates not only sound but also meaning to convey an image empty of any referent known to listeners. His lyric sheets are equally flexible, using a variety of specialized characters in idiosyncratic ways – the German *umlaut* over the capital E, the Spanish *linguistica* over the lower case o, shifting cases mid sentence, and mixing romanized letters with numerals as well as "standard" Japanese script. Rather than losing meaning in this process, further potential for interpretation is given to the listener, as the song is presented to the audience as a kind of blank slate, ready to reflect any meaning desired. It is this "blank slate" quality that Kitagawa is referring to when she suggests that in the 1980s, Japanese audiences became accustomed to "sound-oriented" listening. The sound had more impact on its interpretative *potential* for meaning than did the literal meaning of the lyrics themselves.

Kuwata is not the only Japanese singer/songwriter with idiosyncratic pronunciation. The Japanese lyrics of Sano Motoharu's 1989 single "*Shitei Chairudo*" ("City Child," written in *katakana*) are sung with English intonation. In the chorus, Sano sings the title spelled out using roman letters ("C-I-T-Y C-H-I-L-D"); the next line's Japanese phrase "*eien ni*" (eternally) is sung as if pronounced "A-N-E," creating a subtle Japanese pun on the Anglocized title. This song is part of the album *Naporeon Fisshu to Oyogu Hi* (The Day I Swim with Napoleon Fish), which was recorded entirely in London using local musicians and producers. His first Japanese titled album, Sano's website refers to the work as a "Western music [style] album with an Eastern sensibility" (*tôgaku teki na sensu*) (MWS 2006a). The website does not elaborate on just exactly what this "Eastern sensibility" means, but it is notable that the author of this artist-endorsed site uses "Eastern" rather than "Japanese" to describe Sano's expression of blended music.

Ugaya Hiromichi writes of the Japanese music industry's long-standing "fantasy" to stand "shoulder to shoulder with its foreign [counterparts]"; as evidence of this, he cites common use of Japlish in lyrics as well as the common practice of romanizing artists' names (*geimei*) such as MISIA, Bonnie Pink, and hitomi. This was not necessarily to promote the concept of achieved overseas success but to give the artists an "international" image (2005b: 158). Their music results in a kind of "pseudo-English" which is basically incomprehensible to native listeners. Yet, this "pseudo-English" is important because it represents a personal connection to their listeners (whose English was also lacking in grammatical correctness) and also a revolt against long-held notions of the Japanese "respecting" foreign cultures as superior (ibid.). Characteristics of "pseudo-English" are a reliance on "dictionary terminology" (that is, words lifted from dictionaries out of context, a common result of Japan's exam-based education system); errors in particle use (missing or confusing "a" and "the"); and the use of written language instead of more appropriate colloquial terms (Ugaya and McClure 2001a: 132–133, 2001b: 117). All of these characteristics point toward an evolving use of language within a closed group – operating outside contact with "native speakers" (ibid.).

Japanese vocalists may choose to play with the sounds of their own language through the lens of a foreign language for atmosphere, imagery or the "prestige factor" (Wade 2005: 152), but there can be practical issues as well, as noted by this chapter's earlier discussion of Takamizawa's preference for English in pop music composition. He sees using English as a "short cut" to add more meaning – not just symbolism, but actual information – to a phrase with fewer beats, an economy of syllables as it were. In an earlier quote from this chapter, Takamizawa points to Yuming and Nakajima Miyuki as outstanding composers in Japanese. Why are these composers seen as outstanding in the language? If we compare Takamizawa and Nakajima as composers and look at the way they title their singles (recognizing that a song's title carries an important semiotic meaning that influences the listener's interpretation of the song [Cook 1990: 169]), we see sharp differences. An overview of the titles of Nakajima Miyuki's singles over a twenty-year period (1975–1994) reveals that she used *katakana* loanwords in only 13 percent of titles and used romanized English in 0.05 percent (Nakajima 1994). Compared to the Alfee's repertoire in a similarly dated period (1979–1994), Takamizawa used *katakana* loanwords in 16 percent and romanized English in an astonishing 45 percent of his titles. Their 1986 album *Ages* contains only two tracks with Japanese titles (the rest are not romanized but are in English); from 1991 to 1994, only 6 of their 17 single releases have Japanese words in their titles (The Alfee 1994). While many relied on English as a major semiotic force, others were able to, or chose to, express themselves within the boundaries of Japanese. This consistent use of Japanese is probably underlying Takamizawa's admiration for Nakajima as a composer; she makes the language "work" in the genre without falling back on English for rhythmic or other reasons.

Whatever motives that lie beneath the choice of words – a desire for elegance, humor, or economy – observers of Japanese popular music must look beyond the initial impression that Japlish creates to find the intended (and possibly unintended meanings). Seaton discusses the semiotic outcomes of the use of Japlish in a variety of public contexts from the foreigner's perspective and correctly asserts that

> regardless of how grammatically incorrect or unnatural the English is in the eyes of native speakers, by definition, language is about communication, and Japanized English cannot be called incorrect on pragmatic grounds if Japanese consumers are receiving the intended meaning.
>
> (2001: 235)

Here, the key word is "consumers": language has been commodified, replete with aesthetic tags which accentuate the consumers' social status and identity, for sale on the music market.

Singing in English

The pop music industry in Japan is precisely that – an industry – and, cultural and semiotic nuances aside, English at times is used not so much for its sophistication but for its sales potential. This section looks at a variety of ways English is used in Japanese popular music; it contains an account of a recording session in English and discusses the concept of English as branding for Japanese stars who promote themselves as "internationalized" celebrities.

English is not limited to one genre of Japanese music: we see it with equal frequency in pop, rock, jazz vocals, and hip-hop but less likely in *enka*. Loan-words were used extensively in early postwar hits, but the most common way that English was sung in Japan from the 1950s to the mid-1970s was through the retention of original lyrics in translated cover songs. In the 1980s, we see a full integration of English into original Japanese composition, coinciding with the strong yen and an unprecedented increase in Japanese citizens traveling overseas. Foreign languages had always been considered exotic and powerful, but it was not until the 1980s that overseas travel was within reach of ordinary middle-class Japanese, and English, as the *lingua franca* of the overseas tourist, entered the Japanese mainstream lifestyle.

One of the most prominent 1980s idol singers, Matsuda Seiko, scored a hit with "SWEET MEMORIES" (capitals in the original) in 1983 as a tie-up song with Suntory beer. The lyrics, by Matsumoto Takashi, contain middle verses written in idiomatic English. Matsumoto, a major musician in his own right from his days in Happy End (see Chapter 3), went on to become a hit songwriter for a wide variety of performers ranging from bubblegum idols (like Matsuda) to electro-pop (YMO) and *enka* (Mori Shin'ichi). Matsumoto's membership in Happy End associates him with the "Japanese rock movement," yet he displays mastery in English composition. Rather than relying on English as a concrete referent in rock or pop music history, his lyrics in "SWEET MEMORIES" evoke a more abstract image, one of urbane sophistication (which was symbolized in this case, by Tokyo), accented by jazzy saxophone and piano fills between Matsuda's vocals. Many of the words are sung stressed on the wrong syllable – not that it mattered to the audience, who were attracted to the visualization of a cosmopolitan night club atmosphere where foreign languages were part of the overall atmosphere, regardless of meaning.

Matsuda's hit was a blended presentation of Japanese and English, but we also see the double release of singles: one in Japanese, one in English. For example, the 1994 single "Winter Song," by Dreams Come True, is an English remake and re-release of their 1990 hit single "*Yuki no Kurisumasu*" (Snowy Christmas). The 1990 single was re-recorded as the theme for the Japanese release of the US movie *Sleepless in Seattle*; the songwriter of the group Yoshida Miwa's English vocals both conform to and complement the film's portrayal of Hollywood romance. As her able performance proves, this rerecording allowed her to showcase her ability to sing in English, important to many who still felt English was the universal language of pop/rock and vocalists' mastery of the language demonstrated their mastery of the genre (Hosokawa 1999a: 99). Two of the original three Dreams Come True group members divide their residences between New York and Tokyo (Wade 2005: 153), allowing them to develop "authentic" linguistic abilities to complement their Japanese musical abilities.[7]

New York seems to hold a special cast on the imagination of Japanese performers. In 1983, the previously mentioned rock singer/songwriter Sano Motoharu left Japan for a year and lived in New York, working on his English. He recorded his album *Visitors* there, which debuted at number one the following year. Sano later went on to work with Yoko Ono in New York and Elvis Costello in London, further building his foreign "street cred". Kubota Toshinobu, a Japanese R&B vocalist, also moved to New York to allow him to work with American producers and assist him with his attempts to break the American market. Asada Kaori (a.k.a. Bonnie Pink) also lived in New York for many years, working with American and European producers before finding her own sound that made her successful in Japan; Utada Hikaru, discussed at length later in the chapter, was raised in New York City as a "returnee child" (*kikokushjo*).

"Bokenshatachi *(The Adventure Begins)" and* "Eru Dorado" *("El Dorado"), The Alfee, 1994*

Following is a case study in translation, based on ethnographic experience to illustrate the creative process of integrating English into Japanese popular music. This is a firsthand account of one translation process – from the point of view of a translator working in collaboration with a composer – that illustrates which motives and specific musical practices are involved when singing in English in Japan.

In July 1994, I was commissioned by the Alfee to translate two songs into English. I had done shorter translations for the band, and from my previous work, I knew what the composer's expectations were: the lyrics had to reflect the original meaning, they had to "fit the music," they had to rhyme (to fit in with their expectations of *yôgaku*, I supposed) and, most importantly, be realistically "singable" for a Japanese vocalist. To be performable, we had to avoid the danger zone, which included certain sounds (such as l, r, th) during slow sections (where the singer's limited linguistic ability was most vulnerable), and some of the melodies had to be altered to allow the vocalist to slow down for more difficult words.

It only took two days to record the two English versions over previously recorded instrumental tracks. At that time, the Alfee used Freedom Studio, a small recording studio located on the fringe of the busy Shinjuku district of Tokyo. I knew the Alfee worked there specifically because it was a small studio and thus the band could work uninterrupted. At a large studio, they were enjoined to follow industry etiquette and make *aisatsu* (greetings) to senior artists who might also be recording there at the same time; also, their own sessions might be interrupted by junior artists paying respects. Either way, they found that they got more work done in this small, out of the way studio.

I arrived at 5 p.m. – as requested by their "manager" – on a steamy July evening to find the studio basically deserted except for an instrument technician and a few other staff members. The band members rolled in at different times, accompanied by their managers; a "producer" from the record company was also present. The first evening we laid down the English vocal over the previously recorded instrumental of "*Bokenshatachi*" (literally, the Adventurers). The next evening, the band recorded the Japanese vocals for "El Dorado," the other side of the single. I had heard a short tape recording of the chorus and verse of "El Dorado," a prototype version sent to me months before, but at that time, the final lyrics had not been completed. I attended the Japanese recording session to receive the final version then and there. The final recording session was spent completing the newly translated English lyrics to "El Dorado." Three days in the studio, in both Japanese and English: this was a rare opportunity to witness how language operated in Japanese pop music.

As the music tracks for both singles had been recorded in earlier sessions, so the drum and keyboard support musicians were not present at any of the recordings. The first night I worked with Sakazaki as lead vocalist for the song "The Adventure Begins" (I changed the title on the advice of the Pony Canyon producer, who wanted something more "active"). I had been given the lyrics in their entirety some weeks before and had produced a complete English version before I arrived in Japan. Takamizawa had the three sheets of lyrics photocopied, with rhythmic and intonation notes added by hand (see Figure 6.1), and these were taped together to make one long manuscript.

After the lyrics were settled, I went into the recording studio and was instructed to sing my translated lyrics, resulting in the first rough recording of the song. This began the process: they played my version; Sakazaki would listen to how I sang one line, then repeat it, imitating the accent, rhythm, and intonation of the new lyrics as closely as possible; and his imitation was recorded. I sat in the control booth, listening to his rendition piecemeal, approving each line or having

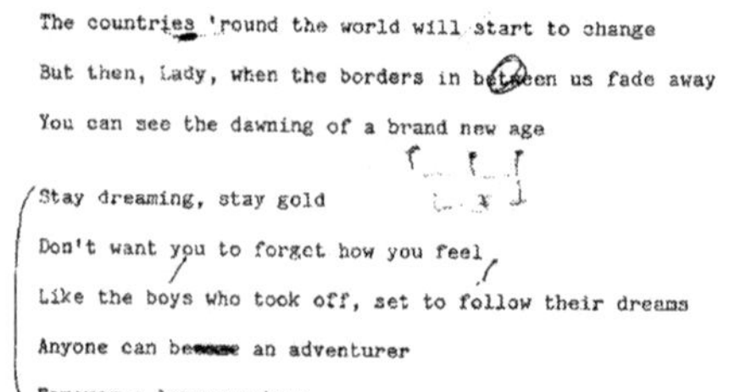
The Adventurers

And then, Lady, if you sigh and look at the world of today

The countries 'round the world will start to change

But then, Lady, when the borders in between us fade away

You can see the dawning of a brand new age

Stay dreaming, stay gold

Don't want you to forget how you feel

Like the boys who took off, set to follow their dreams

Anyone can be[illegible] an adventurer

Forever a lonesome hero

Figure 6.1 Original transcript from the recording session of "The Adventure Begins" with the composer's and translator's handwritten vocal notes.

him redo it when it did not sound right. Adjustments were made to the lyrics to fit Sakazaki's vocal style and ability: for example, we cut words in up-tempo parts (e.g., changing "Anyone can become an adventurer" to "Anyone can be an adventurer" and "calls to me from afar" to "calls me from afar," merely because it was easier for him to get his mouth around fewer syllables). Despite the mouthful of sounds to master, the up-tempo nature of this song meant more flexibility with the rhythm and lyrics (I learned the next evening it was much harder to "fudge" a ballad). The properly imitated "grain of voice" (Hosokawa 1999b: 118) was easier to achieve in faster numbers, probably due to the less precise pronunciation that even native speakers use when singing up-tempo tracks.

Sakazaki performed admirably. I was impressed with his performance, and after that recording session, I realized that this was not thanks to any special linguistic skill but due to his musicianship; he had a finely tuned ear for imitation. Takamizawa, here acting as producer, double tracked all of Sakazaki's vocals (because, he explained later, Sakazaki's voice was "thin" and needed double tracking to "thicken" the final product). We recorded the second section first: "Stay dreaming, stay gold" (see Figure 6.1) was in the original Japanese lyrics, a reference to the Robert Frost poem, "Nothing Gold Can Stay," which spoke of the composer's literary interests. Next, the chorus; the verses were then tracked generally in order, but because of the digital technology, any repeating line only had to be recorded once and was then cut and pasted in the final product as needed. I was vaguely surprised; for some reason I thought they would record the song in order, for no other reason but because that was the natural flow of the ideas and images, but by 1994, digital recording was in full use and the song was put together in seemingly haphazard bits and pieces, according to the producer's direction – the difficult parts of the song that potentially needed more work, for example – these were done while the vocalist was still "fresh."

The following day was the recording of the Japanese version of "*Eru Dorado*." At first, there was some discussion regarding the harmony in the chorus between the three vocalists, but it was recorded relatively quickly. Again, thanks to digital technology, slight variations in the lyrics meant only a few lines were rerecorded to create new versions of the chorus.[8] Background vocals were also quickly recorded and soon the other members were on their way home, or to other work commitments.

The rest of the night's work involved the solo performance of seven Japanese verses. The entire evening, I sat in the control booth with the recording engineers, scribbling English underneath the lyric sheets as they were passed to us from the lyricist/vocalist; while listening and watching Japanese process, I made notes for the following day's English session. The recording studio divides the technician from the performer, with the performer in front of the glass and the producer behind the recording controls. As the main vocalist, Takamizawa could not evaluate his own takes from the perspective of other side of the glassed recording booth. One of the *jimusho* senior employees showed his role flexibility; that night acted he as producer, not just manager. At one point, there seemed to be an impasse over the performance of one verse and the recording halted. Takamizawa left the studio between versions to make a phone call; he returned a short time later with new photocopies for circulation. By the end of the recording session, I had seen three versions.[9] Most of the changes were simplifications of vocabulary, both in sound and in meaning. I do not believe that this simplification occurred because the original was soon to be translated into English; more importantly, the more ambitious and complicated version did not "sound right" in the studio. The composer's lyrics, no matter what the language, have to meet the aesthetic expectations of the record producer to survive the studio cutting stage.

The third night Takamizawa recorded the English version of "El Dorado," which was a translation of the previous evening's streamlined version. Its slow tempo allowed the vocalist the time to enunciate all the lyrics so that the adjustments made to shorten the lines of "The Adventure Begins" were not needed. However, I noticed that the up-tempo numbers "hid" problems with pronunciation more easily than the ballad. It was easier to gloss over "th" sound as "d" in a quick tempo number than it was in a slow ballad; thus there were many takes for "El Dorado." Overall sound quality also was more important in the revealing ballad. Two months later, when I received the final product, I was quite surprised to hear (and see on the back lyric sheet) that the first two verses had been reversed in "El Dorado"; this puzzled me as I felt the verses had a cumulative story to tell and this momentum had been lost in the English version. When I contacted the band to ask why, I was told that in the final mix, problems with the sound quality of the first verse were discovered, and the producers decided to change the order of the two verses to allow the song to start on a strong note . . . .! Again, sound standards overruled the English meaning, which convinced me that use of English was more about image and sound than meaning. It did not matter that the two versions' verses did not match; what mattered was that it sounded "good." At the end of the project, I asked the composer why he had chosen to release these two songs as two singles in such a fashion, and he replied: "two songs, one single, one sale; four songs, two singles, two sales!"

English as branding

The above account illustrates the occasional use of English by Japanese pop and rock artists; this is a strategy to enhance parts of songs or occasional releases. The vast majority of the above-mentioned artists' work is sung in Japanese, even if Japlish is used liberally in lyrics and titles. The next section discusses the more recent phenomenon of some J-pop artists "branding" themselves as those who sing primarily in English, to distinguish themselves both musically and ideologically from other artists in the densely crowded music scene.

At this point, it is necessary to reprise some history; in the early 1970s, Happy End (*Happii Endo*) and other "new rock" bands made an important statement, to sing in Japanese, creating the "new" Japanese rock movement. Previously, the main distinctions between folk and rock were instrumentation (acoustic versus electric guitars) and language (Japanese versus English).

> In the early 1970s several of the emerging rock bands perceived . . . that the international spread of English language rock music offered them a point of access to a global market . . . Rock in Japanese was an odd and parochial concept for them. They shrieked as hard as Led Zeppelin or Grand Funk Railroad so that the words – and their meanings – were mostly unintelligible for audiences. What was important was success in achieving the appropriate "grain of voice"; and the particular style of shouted vocals itself symbolised their anti-establishment . . . orientation.
>
> (Hosokawa 1999b: 117–118)

Happy End, however, was "unique" in its "complex awareness of its own cultural identity" (118): "[b]y singing in Japanese, Matsumoto [of Happy End] aimed to overturn the American hegemony of rock music (which he perceived as simultaneously repressive and gratifying)" (119). (This very same Matsumoto, however, later became a pop songwriting legend, writing "SWEET MEMORIES" for Matsuda Seiko. Clearly, different eras led to different attitudes about language and music.)

The first half of the 1970s was a crucial time for Japanese artists who needed to make a statement about their musical identity: they were independent composers and performers who were creating music for a specific audience and thus needed to connect to this audience in their own language, communicating specific emotions and social and political issues. English (or French or Italian, for that matter) was not an effective medium for communicating these ideas to a discerning Japanese audience. Japanese was the only language that could express these complicated ideas succinctly in the standard three- to five-minute pop song format.

By the 1980s, Japanese cultural identity developed to the point where composers were still conscious of their relationship to the English rock/pop canon, but were more comfortable with their ability to appeal to their own audiences – an aftereffect of Japan's rising social and economic status vis-à-vis the United States and the United Kingdom. Composers had the confidence to "play" with language, sound, and meaning, and audiences were confident in their consumption of these languages. This "playing" with the creation and the consumption of music was then played out on other levels; the technological revolution of the 1970s and 1980s meant that audiences too were playing with music through rerecording and rearranging their choices to suit their needs using cassette tapes (later, this was achieved with MD and computer files as well).

In Chapter 2, I noted a major shift in the number of current Japanese artists who cite Japanese musicians (rather than overseas figures) as major influences. This is, of course, due to the maturation of the Japanese industry and its ability to meet the demands of the audience independently. Yet, at the same time, a recent movement back to the West as the "source" has surfaced in hit acts that claim an "authentic" connection to the United States, which most often takes the form of singing in English (and recording overseas). What is different about this reorientation – or, perhaps more precisely, re-occidentation? Surely, here the connection to the United States is characterized not by surrender or submission but by mastery and competence. This is the main break from the past when considering the late 1990s and early 2000s shift to incorporating English back into Japanese popular music.

"English as branding" means that artists make their ability to sing in English a major part of their image, and this is true for no one more than Utada Hikaru. At the time of printing, she held the record for the top-selling album in Japan – but she is just as famous for her unquestioned "authentic" ability to sing in English, noted as the one outstanding Japanese singer in English (Ugaya 2005b: 159). As a "returnee child" (*kikokushijo*) raised and schooled in New York City, Utada's well-promoted association with the urban culture of R&B's home front gives her brand of J-pop an unmistakable bicultural distinction, even when she does not sing in English. Her official website lists her musical influences widely: from Bartok and Edith Piaf to U2 and Missy Elliot. Yet, in the 13 figures she lists, only one is Japanese: the melodic rocker, the late Ozaki Yutaka (Hikki's Website 2006).

Unlike other artists who slog through minor or independent music work before breaking it big, Utada was a major artist immediately after her debut at the tender age of 15. Three attributes sensationalized her entrance into J-pop fame: she was born in New York City; she had studied at the American School; and she was the daughter of retired *enka* singer Fuji Keiko and music producer Utada Teruzane. Despite J-pop's close relationship to television, she did not appear on television nearly as often as her counterparts. In Utada's case, it may not have been to create an aura of mystery, but because at the time she was also studying at New York's Columbia University. Unlike many other pop divas at the time, Utada was "authentically international."

Despite his praise for her English, Ugaya Hiromichi refers to the Utada phenomena as "a fantasy of self-love" (*jikoai fantajii*) (2005b: 154). The age similarity between the young star and her target audience meant there was close identification with "Hikki" (Utada's nickname) by her fans. "Hikki" and her music represented this generation's values, which privileged youth, attractiveness, and international prestige. More importantly, however, Ugaya states that Utada represents the ability of Japanese pop music to "stand shoulder to shoulder" with the Western original (156), and this idea was the determining factor in her overwhelming and immediate acceptance by the Japanese music industry and a wide sector of its audience. Yet, ultimately, this was a "fantasy"; Utada was not destined for an international career. Her 2002 all-English album *Exodus*, released on a competing label with her Japanese Toshiba–EMI contract, failed to make a mark in US charts, reaching a top rank of 160th for one week before disappearing (157).[10] Thus, she followed the same path that many of her J-pop and idol predecessors took, such as Pink Lady and Matsuda Seiko: a widely publicized US debut to be followed by relative silence. As noted in Chapter 3, to date, the only Japanese artist who has meaningfully penetrated mainstream American pop charts is Sakamoto Kyû with "*Ue o Muite Arukô*": a song that uses no English in its lyrics, even in its adopted American title "Sukiyaki." Unlike her predecessors,

Utada's failure was unexpected because as a New York City semi-native, she was above the usual ridicule of foreign critics; Japanese critics were convinced her brand of J-pop, through her authentic connection to the "source," would gain international fame. This further underscores the idea that internationalism (as represented by English in Japanese popular music) is interpreted and valued as part of shared but bounded community that cannot be easily communicated to others; she is "internationalized" but not truly "international."

Utada's interpretation of R&B is not the only Japanese pop genre utilizing English competence as a branding mechanism. Other Japanese musicians have attempted to "brand" themselves in a similar fashion, singing entirely in English, but success eluded them until they switched to a Japanese repertoire. For example, Asian Kung-fu Generation found local followings for its early independent English language releases but only scored national attention after their first Japanese single in 2002. One exception is Love Psychedelico (often referred to as "*Deriko*" by their Japanese fans), a pop/rock duo that still looks to the West for inspiration, with frequent references to the Beatles, Bob Dylan, and the Kinks. Their use of English, however, is quite different from the Japlish of composers a generation ago. Their official website describes their style explicitly in terms of language: we read of "Japanese-English naturally blended lyrics and [an] unconventional vocal style" (Love Psychedelico 2005); and that their "unconventional but smooth blend of Japanese-English lyrics have had a tremendous impact on the Japanese music scene" (2006). Debuting in 2000, they met with early success: their first single "Lady Madonna~*yûutsu naru supaidâ*" was contracted as an "image song" for an Eastern Japan-based casual clothing outlet franchise; their second single was "tied up" with Seiko watches. This second single, "Your Song," is sung in both Japanese and English, and – perhaps consciously? – the vocalist sings in English-accented Japanese. But instead of playing with the sound of Japanese lyrics, as Kuwata Keisuke and Sano Motoharu did, Love Psychedelico's vocalist meshes the two languages' pronunciation into one seamless sound: English to Japanese to English again.

Love Psychedelico's lead vocalist, Kumi, was born in Tokyo but spent time as a child in San Francisco; this accounts for her natural intonation, and possibly explains her 1960s musical influences, especially heard in the percussion of many of their album tracks. The band toured America in 2001, six months after the release of the first full-length album, adding to their internationalized profile at home. Such was the impact of their music in the field, Love Psychedelico was invited to collaborate by the industry giant Kuwata Keisuke on one track of his third solo album, *Rock and Roll Hero* (2002). Their first "best" album debuted on the *Oricon* album charts at number one in 2004, demonstrating their English brand of pop had successfully established itself in the *hôgaku* market. "Mind Across the Universe" from the album *Love Psychedelico III* suggests the group's debt to the Beatles in its title, but its vocal style and arrangement is more reminiscent of Alanis Morrissette than John Lennon. "Everybody Needs Somebody" is more derivative classic American rock, featuring typically 1960s–1970s style percussion (tambourine and maracas accenting a crisp drum line), and Kumi's vocals sound a bit like the ghost of Grace Slick floating above the tambourine.

Yet, Ugaya, in his discussion of English in J-pop, does not categorize Love Psychedelico in the "native" category (as he does Utada) but labels them "pseudo" (2005b: 159). Perhaps Ugaya's criticism is colored by his perspective. Younger audiences regard their 1960s/1970s sound as fresh and original, probably because the current Japanese *hôgaku* market is saturated with the soft hip-hop, R&B and dance music styles of Hamazaki Ayumi, Chemistry, and even Utada. To critics in their forties like Ugaya, "Delico's" sound seems gimmicky, but to teenagers, it is completely new. Even though its "authentic" foreignness is in contrast to their own "Japanese-ness," it is undeniably "their" music, unlike anything they have heard before, and it appeals to their longings for internationalizing within comfortable limits. Japanese youth are in touch with international current events and travel the world as part of their studies or as leisure, but their listening habits, as demonstrated by sales figures, are firmly rooted in Japanese pop and rock.

Cover songs

Although this chapter has focused up until this point on Japanese to English translations, now we turn to another kind of translation, the transformation from the "original" English to "new" Japanese. Hosokawa writes: "Foreign languages exist not as communicative (semantic) tools but as symbolic sets of phonetic sounds. To some, they represent cultural distinction. To others, they epitomise cultural imperialism" (1999a: 101).

Covers, or songs that were hits elsewhere translated and sung in Japanese, represent the latter – cultural imperialism – and this was especially true in the early days of Western-inspired Japanese popular music (1950s and early 1960s). Mitsui concurs, "The 1950s can be labelled as an adoration and imitation period for those were involved in performing cover versions, both on TV and on records, of imported music" (1997: 167–168).

The Occupation generated a strong American influence on all aspects of pop culture; the earliest pop covers were sung in English to appeal to both domestic and military audiences. Kusano Shô, who died in 2005, was one of the earliest successful "covers" lyricists (McClure 2005). His publishing company was subcontracted to distribute US pop music in Japan, and in addition, they reissued hits under Japanese titles and with Japanese stars. It is through these covers that *yôgaku* was first popularized in the early postwar era, and Western style pop music was first introduced to Japan.

After sovereignty was returned in 1952, Japanese artists began to record American pop numbers in Japanese and "translated" hits from Elvis Presley, Paul Anka, and Connie Francis into songs such as "*Tsumetaku shinai de*" ("Don't be Cruel"), "*Daiana*" ("Diana"), and "*Kawaii beibî*" ("Pretty Little Baby") (Takahashi 1993: 14, 22); even Sakamoto Kyû recorded a cover of the Beach Boys hit "Good Timing" ("*Suteki na Taimingu*") (McClure 2005b). Often the English chorus or hook was preserved in the original language (Hosokawa 1999a:

98), with the rest of the verses in Japanese. Mitsui notes that in the postwar era, original Japanese verses were "sandwiched" in between translated original lyrics, a shift from pure translation (1997: 168). Examples of this are Eri Chiemi's version of "Tennessee Waltz" (1952) and Yukimura Izumi's version of "Blue Canary" (*Aoi Kanariya*) (1954). As songwriting and performance talent in the Japanese pop industry gained experience, however, covers of Japanese versions became less common but remained as novelty, or one-off, songs. The following section argues for a new interpretation of cover songs; not merely an outcome of cultural imperialism, the contemporary Japanese cover song uses familiar musical and lyrical motifs combined with an underlying sense of humor, playfulness, and at times, self-satire. I argue that cover songs in the more mature era of Japanese pop and rock are distinguished from the "cultural imperialist" period by new sensibilities and new meanings created by the Japanese artist/translator.

Cover songs as runaway hits

The year 1967 marked the point when sales of domestically produced music surpassed imported music (Mitsui 1997: 169), but this would include domestic productions of Western covers as these songs were recorded, produced, and distributed in Japan. Probably the most icongraphical Japanese cover song in this new era is the 1979 single *Young Man* (also known as Y.M.C.A.).[11] Its vocalist, Saijô Hideki, performed this cover of the Village People hit many times on television with borrowed choreography (which mimicked the title's letters' shapes), and background dancers dressed as American style cheerleaders. In the late 1990s, one of Saijô's contemporaries, Go Hiromi, capitalized on this formula again and released a Japanese version of Ricky Martin's hit "The Vida Loca" as the ending theme of the TBS show *Wonderful*, revitalizing his flagging career. The single, released in July 1999 under the title GOLDFINGER 99,[12] was so successful it went to a 12-inch remix three months later and a single cover reprinting (Go Hiromi Official Homepage, 2005) and stayed in the top 10 for seven months (Jordan 2005).

Novelty cover songs reemerge from time to time, providing comic relief in the fast-paced Japanese pop market. Both Saijô and Go, who enjoy lucrative decade-spanning careers, had other hits but are often associated with the above-mentioned cover songs due to their runaway success. Saijô and Go belong to the 1970s professional "army" (*gun*, Take 1999: 163) of pop singers which included Pink Lady, Yamaguchi Momoe, Sakurada Junko, Sawada Kenji, and Noguchi Goro. These artists developed their careers primarily through television and radio, a lightweight pop genre parallel to what many critics felt was more serious music (folk and rock), and a precursor to what was to become Japanese idol "bubble gum" pop of the 1980s. This "light and thin" (Hosokawa 1995) music was easily combined with any cliché or awkwardness forced by the translation and was consumed just as effortlessly by the public.

RC Succession's COVERS

Not all cover songs are about light and thin interpretations of Western pop standards. Although the inclusion of foreign lyrics carries symbolic meaning (adding sophistication or exoticism) to the Japanese listener, because of the "sound-oriented" (see Kitagawa 1991) listening habits of Japanese audiences as discussed above, the song is not "married" to the original lyrics and thus can be more easily separated and manipulated by the re-recording artist. This flexibility allows the Japanese artist to "play" with the song and mold it into a new form, retaining desirable attributes and adding new layers of meaning through the translation. In this sense, a cover is truly a transformation.

Although "cover" is used in Japanese (*kabâ*, written in *katakana*) to indicate a Japanese version of a song in another language, there are other Japanese terms that are used in a variety of overlapping contexts that are worth discussing here. *Kaeuta* is a Japanese term used to describe the changing of lyrics for comedic purposes, but this can also refer to the transformation of lyrics in Japanese to different Japanese, and is translated into English as "a parody of a song." In the following case study, the Japanese lyricist has integrated the "cover" with the parodic sense of the *kaeuta* to create a politically pertinent message. It is the combination of political statement, comedy and cover that makes the song featured in this section so interesting.

Imawano Kiyoshirô is the leader of the long-running but now disbanded rock group RC Succession. He was born in 1951 in central Tokyo and was influenced as a teenager by the "electric boom." His first band, The Clovers, was formed in 1966 and performed Ventures covers; after this band broke up, he named the new group "The Remainder of the Clovers." After a new member joined, the name morphed into the awkward "The Remainder of the Clovers Succession," resulting in the abbreviated RC Succession. Debuting on television in 1969, the young musicians released their first single in 1970 and, as mentioned in Chapter 4, were signed by the powerful *Hori Puro* management agency a year later. In 1972, their single "*Boku no Suki na Sensei*" (The Teacher I Like) made them a household name. The mid-to-late 1970s was quiet in terms of sales and media exposure due to problems between the group and its management. In 1976, they recorded "Slow Ballad"; later on, this single became one of the group's most memorable songs. Because of the band's difficulties with their management and record label, this song was not promoted and achieved little success after its initial release; it only became a hit years later when it was used in a feature film soundtrack. After a change in the band's lineup, RC Succession made a commercial comeback in 1980 with the hit single "*Ameagari no Yozora ni*" (The Evening Sky After the Rain). In 1982, Imawano recorded an "image song" for the dominant Japanese cosmetic company Shiseido with the leader of YMO, Sakamoto Ryûichi, entitled "*Ikenai* Rouge Magic" (translated roughly, "Naughty Rouge Magic") which hit number one on the charts and boosted his band's image in the mainstream media. In 1984, the band transferred its contract from Polydor to Toshiba–EMI and followed with a plethora of single, album and live album releases. RC Succession disbanded in 1991, but Imawano has been successful in solo and other "unit" (temporary bands) projects, including many commercially viable television advertisement themes, plus television drama and film soundtracks, which demonstrates the power of the partnering of the two media industries (see Chapter 4).[13]

From RC Succession's wide repertoire, I focus here on one release that demonstrates the power of translation/transformation in language and music. Imawano Kiyoshirô and his band planned to release the album *COVERS* on August 8, 1988 – the anniversary of Hiroshima Bombing. It consisted entirely of covers of US and UK pop and rock standards reworked in Japanese, with lyrics by Imawano. Imawano's official website profile openly states the album was "anti-war" and "anti-nuclear" in message (2005). Two days before its release from Toshiba EMI records, *Asahi* and *Mainichi* newspapers printed notice that the album's release had been postponed; reportedly, Imawano received notice of this decision by telephone only two weeks prior to the release. The record company responded to public inquiry regarding the sudden cancellation with a curt "no comment" but soon it was known that it was due to Toshiba–EMI's objection to the cover of "*Rabu Mî Tendâ*," backed with "*Samâ Taimu Burûsu*." Both songs spoke in opposition to the development and maintenance of nuclear power reactors in Japan. Toshiba, along with Mitsubishi, was a major manufacturer of these reactors and to them this represented a conflict of interest and loss of face (Shinozaki 1988: 61–63; Take 1999: 268–269). The album was released a week later on the Kitty Records label, and probably because of the controversy, debuted at *Oricon*'s number one position.

COVERS took an old formula and gave it a new twist, resulting in controversial content. Many of the songs on this album have "alternative" (considering mainstream Japanese values at the time) social and political messages: John Lennon's "Imagine," Bob Dylan's "Blowing in the Wind" and the Stones' "Paint it Black" are somewhat more faithfully rendered in Japanese. "Love Me Tender" retains one original chorus sung in English, but the rest is a complete turnaround from the Presley original: the lines "Love me Tender/Love me true/never let me go" are sung in Japanese, but instead of sticking to the original lyrics, the next lines can be translated as: "What the hell are ya sayin'? It's no joke/We don't need nuclear power." The song's reliance on the original romantic arrangement and vocal reproduction, combined with the new protest statement, creates an amusing mismatch of sentiment.

Imawano's version of "Summer Time Blues", originally recorded by Eddie Cochran and also by the Who, provides the case study for this section.

Summer Time Blues[14]
The hot summer is just about here
Everyone's goin' to the beach
I found a quiet spot to swim
But when I looked up . . .
There was a nuclear reactor!

[this line is sung in unison with woman's voice, in "proper Japanese" compared to Imawano's more casual pronunciation]
I got no idea, man . . . . what's it for?
Boxed in Japan with the SUMMERTIME BLUES *[with female voice]*

The volcano is just about to pop its top
And the Tôkai[15] earthquake's just around the bend
In spite of that they keep increasing
They keep on building nuclear reactors *[as in verse 1]*
I got no idea, man . . . who's it for?
Boxed in Japan with the SUMMERTIME BLUES *[as above]*

The cold winter is just around the corner
You've also been losing some hair lately (sorry, what?!)
But the TV still says
"Japanese nuclear power is safe" *[spoken, a different man and woman's voice in unison]*
I got no idea, man . . . . they got no proof
This'll be our last SUMMERTIME BLUES *[the title is shouted]*

[a male announcer speaks, as in a radio or television broadcaster, over a background of guitar feedback]

Let's stop to re-examine the phrase "nuclear power"
It's such a bad habit of the Japanese to abbreviate everything
Wouldn't it be better to say Atomic Energy Power Station?
Atomic Energy Power Stations are no cause for concern

We slave away at work and they tax us
Even if once in awhile we get to go on holiday in the country
There are thirty-seven [stations] standing
The "Atomic Energy Power Stations" are proliferating! *[spoken as in verse 3]*
While we didn't notice, they were leaking
I'm disgusted – SUMMERTIME BLUES

We've got excess electricity, we don't need it, we don't need it anymore – no way!
We've got excess electricity, we don't need it, we don't want it anymore – no way!
We don't need nuclear power, it's dangerous and we don't need it – no way!
[each line followed by semi-audible enunciations along the lines of: "we don't need it, we told you already, that's enough!"]

Comedy has long been a part of selling music, from the 1960s groups such as the Crazy Cats to the current variety show performances of SMAP. Radical artists, such as those from the visual genre, have successfully used humor to mainstream or commercialize their work, but no matter how it is packaged, it is exceedingly difficult to make politics "funny" in a conservative Japanese business environment. Humor – through the choice of an up-tempo rock/pop classic, interspersed with unexpected contrast between the vocalist's views and the nuclear establishment – mainstreamed the politics without diluting the message.

Imawano specifically chose these well-known Western standard hits to familiarize and thus facilitate his political message to listeners. I have written elsewhere about J-pop's general failure to deliver strong political and social messages (Stevens 1999), but *COVERS* operates in compromise mode. "Summertime Blues" works because of the ordinariness of the song, well known in Japan as a performance choice for amateur cover bands. Imawano takes a middle class, mainstream image of "summer," transposing the image of a leisurely day at the beach with the imposing and intimidating symbol of the nuclear power plant with lighthearted prose. The juxtaposition of the protagonist versus the authority in the different vocals creates the "mismatch," or gap, that amuses because of the distance between the stiffness of the officials and the casual language of the singer. It is also probably no coincidence that this "cover" utilizes a Western pop standard. Though primarily aimed at the Japanese government that supports the industry, this song also targets the West's role in introducing nuclear power to the world – and to Japan – in the form of nuclear warfare. By using Western "covers," Imawano is highlighting the hypocritical stance of the Japanese government, which allows the US military to store nuclear warheads at its Japanese military bases, while forfeiting its right to commit military aggression in its Constitution.

Thus viewed, covers can be useful on a variety of levels. Because of their foreign origin, the music is more easily separated from their original lyrics because the lyrics, as noted above, merely represent a phonetic quality (and, at best, an atmosphere) rather than specific meaning to Japanese listeners. These meanings can be then molded and shaped to new meanings that are familiar, yet new; Imawano understands the potential of his songs to transform ideas and sounds. In February 2005, to celebrate his thirty-fifth anniversary as a recording artist, he released a "self-cover" of his RC Succession hit, entitled *"Ameagari no yosora ni 35"* (The Evening Sky After the Rain [at] 35). This version features the Japanese rap trio Rhymester in a hip-hop version of the original, replete with original verses sung by Imawano sandwiched between new rap verses penned and rapped by members of Rhymester, creating a new song not only with respect to genre and sound but also with new meaning. Language plays a major role in the re-creation process: the original chorus, which ends with the phrase *"buttobasô ze* [kick it into gear!]," is reorientated to rap with the insertion of English rap tag, resulting in "Say what? *buttobasô ze!"* and, between the lines of Imawano's original chorus, Rhymester inserts a friendly sounding "Goddamn!" in English. The song is clearly a tribute to Imawano: Rhymester's MC calls to him in English, "Hey, *yo*, Boss! Get on the microphone!" and then mixes languages, referring to Imawano "*sugê taffu*" ("damn tough"). Imawano earns this praise for surviving thirty-five years in a fast-changing, hypercompetitive industry, but Imawano's own participation is modest and self-effacing. The original song is a young man's anthem to the frustration of physical and social immobility, but the new song becomes a joyful self-parody of his own middle-aged identity set against the lively and rigorous rappers of the next generation.

Conclusion

Language in Japanese popular music speaks volumes about the performer (and, through the song's commercial success, much about the listener). Whether the liberal sprinkling of English in J-pop choruses or the transformation of an American standard into a Japanese hit through translation, language remains a powerful tool for communicating ideas; words create and refine the atmosphere, or in Yuming's words, the "fragrance," of Japanese pop music. Although the examples given in this chapter all differ with respect to their genre, grammatical "correctness," and intended/received meanings, one common thread unites these songs in this analysis: language is fluid and instrumental in achieving artistic and commercial ends. Composers consciously employ language to communicate their ideas so that audiences will respond to these performances with the intended message. Foreign languages may create a sense of elite "internationalization," serve for mere convenience, or elicit humorous effects: for whatever purpose, language is altered and performed in a myriad of ways in Japanese popular music. We think of language as a *normative* system in many ways; yet in popular music, as in many colloquial contexts, linguistic rules are sometimes adhered to, sometimes not. Pop music's priorities overrule normative systems.

The discussion of Japanese versus English reprises the tension observed between Japanese and mainly Western pop music: what is "authentic"? Whose music represents an indisputable claim to the genre? And how do real audiences interpret these claims? As we have seen in Chapter 4, Japanese artists regularly outsell foreign artists in the Japanese market and have done so for about two decades. De Launey interviewed record company executives in the early 1990s who claimed that Western musicians are not appealing to Japanese listeners because they could not understand the lyrics and believed that by missing out on the words, much of the message of the song was lost on them (1995: 221). This, of course, refers to songs that are fully performed in idiomatic English by native speakers. Japanese audiences are not, however, intimidated by Japanese songs that utilize English, in both meaningful and not-so-meaningful ways. According to De Launey, the majority of Japanese audiences appear to agree that English lyrics are more suited to pop/rock music than Japanese (222).

The use of English in Japanese popular music is no longer limited to an expression of cultural imperialism.

> The use of English is a reflection of a positive attitude; in short, it is seen as "cool" to use English. Equally, it also reflects indifference, in that the Japanese exploit English for their own purposes.
>
> (Seaton 2001: 245)

Using English to meet one's own needs expresses an independence from the former early postwar period. Still, some are unconvinced of the benefits of "independence". Overall, Ugaya, who has written frequently on this topic, is quite critical of the popularity of Japlish in J-pop, because he believes it represents a "consumption of narcissism": that Japanese listeners feel that their social status in enhanced through the mere ownership of a CD sung in English, or that in the karaoke setting, their English is good enough to duplicate the professional singers' skill (both in Japanese and in English) (2005b: 159). One's social standings are not determined by a concrete set of skills (being able to understand, speak, and sing English), but by an abstract attitude of "internationalization." This explains why the grammatical aspects of the Japlish are unimportant to the Japanese listener (160). Ugaya believes this is another aspect of the commodification of Japanese popular music, both of the singer (Utada as a "cool" returnee student, for example) and of the music (which becomes symbolic of the consumer's social standing).

In line with Ugaya's idea of consumption, Hosokawa concludes that singing in English can be "understood as a form of phonetic consumption of others' tongues without commitment to semantics or syntax" (1999b: 118). Lyrics, thus, can be considered just as much of a consumer product, functioning in the same way to promote a song or an artist as the CD cover design would. Language, transformed from one tradition (foreign as "authentic") to another (foreign as "sophisticated") to yet another (English to Japanese, and back again, as fun and playful, but with a serious message). The use of language has developed in the postwar era to reflect the way Japanese composers and audiences view their lives against a global backdrop of these cultural industries. In this way, translations provide both evidence and counterevidence for the maintenance of a US/UK hegemony in Japanese popular music. Language reveals much about Japan's identity in the global pool of pop music culture. If the pen is mightier than the sword, then language here is a double-edged sword, elevating the West, yet at other times deflating its hegemonic status.

Appendix: Major record labels in Japan

Label	*Parent and/or associated companies*	*Comment*
Avex (est. 1988) Avex Trax (est. 1990)	Avex Group Holdings	Avex also offers artist management; signed artists include Komuro Tetsurô, Hamazaki Ayumi, EXILE, and BoA.
BMG Japan (est. 1987) BMG Fun House Polydor/Grammophone	Formed by BMG and Victor; Victor sells its shares in 1996. Merges with Japanese label Fun House in 1999. Venture with Sony in 2004.	This label has a large overseas catalogue through BMG; Japanese artists include Misia, Oda Kazumasa (formerly of Off Course) and Sukima Switch.
For Life Music Entertainment (est. 1975)		For Life was founded by musicians Yoshida Takurô, Inoue Yôsui, Komuro Hitoshi, and Izumiya Shigeru; signed artists include Hamabuchi Tsuyoshi and Bennie K.
Pony Canyon (Pony est. 1966; merged with Canyon Records in 1970)	JOLF and *Fuji Sankei* – includes Fuji Television and *Sankei* Publications	Focused on Japanese artists, Pony Canyon's repertoire includes *enka* as well as mainstream Japanese pop stars such as aiko, w-inds, Kudô Shizuka, and others. Pony Canyon has branches in Malaysia, Hong Kong, and Korea.
Sony (est. 1968); renamed Sony Music Entertainment in 1991.[a] Associated labels launched in 2001: Ki/oon, Defstar, Epic Records Japan, Sony Music Associated Records, Sony Music Records (Japanese artists)	Sony; also associated labels gained through purchase of CBS and Columbia.	Sony holds the largest share of any of Japanese label because of its international repertoire. Its CD sales strategy is closely tied to own hardware production (Walkman, CD and MiniDisc) as well as recording technology; 2005 sees many battles with artists over release of singles in MP3 format in competition with Apple's iPod.

Sony Music Japan International (SME's *yôgaku* artists)		Sony-affiliated artists include SME's Orange Range, Okuda Tamio, Hamada Shôgo, Kubota Toshinobu, High and Mighty Color, and Pornograffiti; Ki/oon's L'Arc~en~ciel, Puffy, Asian Kung-Fu Generation and Rhymester; Defstar's Chemistry, the brilliant green and Hirai Ken.
Toshiba EMI (est. 1960) includes Capital Music and Virgin Music	Toshiba	Toshiba EMI holds the Beatles' catalogue; like Sony, the company is tied to Toshiba's manufacturing arm. Japanese artists include The Alfee, GLAY, Matsutôya Yumi, Makihara Noriyuki, and Utada Hikaru.
Universal Music Japan (est. 1990 as Polygram; renamed Universal in 1999)	MCA breaks from Victor and merges with Polygram and Universal in 1997.	This label promotes international artists such as U2 through Universal International. Japanese acts include TOKIO, Dreams Come True, Luna Sea, and actor/singer Fukuyama MasatoshiJ
Victor (est. 1927) renamed Victor Entertainment (est 1972–1973)	Matsushita JVC; MCA take over in 1990.	Repertoire features Southern All Stars, SMAP, and Hamada Mari; has subsidiary offices in Seoul and Hong Kong.
Warner Music Japan (est. 1970)[b]	Part of the American Warner Music Group; formed by Warner Bros, Pioneer and Watanabe Productions	Artists include Cornelius (Oyamada Keigo), Yamashita Tatsurô, Sakamoto Ryûichi, Rip Slyme, and Bonnie Pink. Warner Music also sells many popular *yôgaku* artists in Japan such as Eric Clapton and Madonna.
Yamaha Music Communications (est. 2000 by Yamaha with Aardvark, formerly of Pony Canyon)	Yamaha Music Foundation	This label's predecessor released CDs of the winners of the Yamaha's Popular Song Contest, 1969–1986, including Nakajima Miyuki, Nagabuchi Tsuyoshi, Chage and Asuka, and others. Current artists include Nakajima Miyuki, Yano Akiko, and Chage and Asuka; they hold the catalogues for Arisu and Off Course.

Sources: Azami (2003), de Launey (1995), Kawabata (1991), and Takahashi 2005; the labels' official websites.

Notes

a Sony bought CBS in 1987 and Columbia in 1989.

b This company name reflects a Japanese capital takeover of Warner Group in 1989.

Glossary

Japanese terms

aidoru アイドル	The Japanese pronunciation of "idol," came into use in the 1970s and 1980s. Refers to a "produced" singer with a high level of commercial exposure.
chakumero 着メロ	Literally "arriving melody," refers to the downloading of various shortened versions of pop tunes to use as a ring tone notification. This allows the user to personalize the phone.
chakuuta 着歌	Music download through a mobile phone service for playback through the mobile phone.
chanson シャンソン	From the French for song, this term refers to a genre of Japanese popular music since the 1970s. It primarily consists of Japanese covers of French popular music.
dentô ongaku 伝統音楽	"Traditional music"; refers to music that utilizes indigenous instruments and is generally characteristic of music from the pre-Meiji period.
eigyôbu 営業部	"Sales department" in a radio or television station. This section is responsible for recruiting sponsors for the station's income.
enka 演歌	A genre of popular music in postwar Japan that has come to represent a national culture based on regionalism and sentimentality (Yano 2002); it combines elements of prewar Japanese musical technique and Western instrumentation.
enkai 宴会	A drinking party where participants entertain one another singing *a capella*. A predecessor of karaoke, linking singing and alcohol consumption.
enkashi 演歌師	"Political street singers" those who sold printed songs on the streets in the late nineteenth century. Lyrics at this time of political change concerned the new government and social order. Gradually, these street singers moved to become professional entertainers.
FEN	Former acronym for the Far East Network; the radio station serving the US military in Japan. An AM station, it is currently known as AFN (Armed Forces Network).
furusato ふるさと、 also 故郷	Homeland; image used most frequently in *enka* or other folk songs.

geinôkai 芸能界	Literally, the world of entertainment; the entertainment industry.
hayariuta 流行歌	The Japanese reading for the characters meaning "songs that are popular" (see *ryûkôka*).
hôgaku 邦楽	(1) "Traditional" music of Japan, utilizing instruments such as the shakuhachi and koto and (2) Japanese popular music that is composed, produced, performed, and marketed for Japanese listeners (cf *yôgaku*).
iemoto 家元	Head of a school (of music, dance), head family of a school. Also refers to the personal, hierarchical connections that form the music and entertainment industry.
in 陰	Dark, or shadowy.
jazzu kissa ジャズ喫茶	Literally, "jazz café"; a café that specializes in playing jazz music and caters to aficionados. Record albums often adorn the walls.
jigoe 地声	Literally, ground voice; also translated as "basic" or "natural" voice.
jimusho 事務所	Literally, "office" in Japanese, but in the music industry, this refers to an artist management agency.
jo-ha-kyû 序破急	A term which describes different sections in classical Japanese music: consisting of the characters for "slow," "breaking," and "hurrying," it means preface, development, and climax/deceleration.
J-pop J-ポップ	Coined by the FM radio station J-WAVE in 1988, this term refers to Japanese popular music that is made and consumed digitially (see Ugaya 2005b).
kabâ カバー	Loan word for "cover"; a Japanese version of a song in another language, most often an English song. Popular in Japanese music scene, especially in the 1950s and 1960s.
kaeuta 替え歌	Literally, "changed song" or "substitution song" (Nakamura 1991: 271); also translated as "variation." It often carries the connotation of parody, with humorous or ironic overtones.
kanryû *(hanryû)* 韓流	Literally, a "Korean wave" of pop culture into first China, then Japan. Kanryû is best symbolized by the wild popularity of *Fuyu no Sonata*, a KBS drama imported by NHK in 2003. *Hanryû* is sometimes used, referring to the Korean pronunciation of the character 韓.
karaoke カラオケ	Literally, "empty orchestra." Refers to social and public, yet amateur, vocal performances accompanied by recorded backing music.
kashu 歌手	Generic term in Japanese for singer.
kikokushijo 帰国子女	"Returnee children"; people who have spent part or most of the formative years of their youth overseas. With respect to Japanese popular music, returnee children's bicultural image is a draw in the domestic market, but they have yet to find success in US or UK markets (e.g., Utada Hikaru).

kobushi 小節	A voice trembling technique heard in *enka* and other traditional Japanese musical forms.
Kôhaku Utagassen 紅白歌合戦	The Red and White Singing contest, performed on New Year's Eve each year, broadcast live from NHK studios in Shibuya Tokyo.
komuson コムソン	"Commercial song," also image song, tie-up.
ma 間	"Space" or emptiness, which serves to accentuate the contrast between silence and sound, or image and empty space.
merodeikôru or *merokôru* メロディコール or メロコール	"Ringing back service" for mobile phones; users can listen to music while waiting for their conversational partners to pick up their phones. Established in 2003 by DoCoMo, Inc.
minyô 民謡	=*volksleid* in German, translated often as folk.
miyakobushi onkai 京節音階	A traditional Japanese scale, associated with tunes from Kyoto (the former capital [*miyako*]).
mochiuta 持ち歌	Literally, "holding a song" refers to the idea that songs belong to the singer that make them famous. Represents the shift of focus away from the composers and to the stars as the main representation of music talent and celebrity.
monomane 物真似	A category of karaoke where the singer imitates the original performer to humorous effect.
musen hôsô 無線放送	A wireless broadcast; refers to satellite transmission of music or karaoke services to a home set (see *yûsen hôsô*).
nihon no ongaku 日本の音楽	"Japanese music," used to distinguish the traditional music of Japan from that of the West.
nihonjinron 日本人論	"Theories of Japanese-ness," a body of literature by Japanese authors professing cultural essentialist theories about Japanese culture, language, and biology.
Nippon Hôsô Kyôkai or NHK 日本放送協会	Japan Broadcasting Network; the first broadcaster of both radio and television in Japan. A semi-national network.
nyû myujikku ニューミュジック	"New Music" here means the proliferation of folk-pop-rock-influenced singer-songwriters who, in the 1970s, broke away from the set social relationships involved with pop music production. These three distinct roles were composer/lyricist, producer, and finally performer. Artists such as Yoshida Takuro, Inoue Yosui, Off Course, Nakajima Miyuki, Matsutoya (nee Arai) Yumi, Yamashita Tatsuro, Sano Motoharu, and the Alfee are all representative of this movement from the 1970s to the 1980s, which was marked more by a collapse of production roles and empowerment of the performer than by one particular musical style.

omote 表	The front or foreground. What the audience sees in terms of production and performance.
ongaku (kayôkyoku) bangumi 音楽（歌謡曲）番組	Music television show; usually broadcast weekly, and since the 1990s, conversation with musicians is just as important as musical performances.
ongaku hyôronka 音楽評論家	A music critic; usually an author for the popular press who writes articles for magazines and newspapers, and nonfiction books.
onkai 音階	A scale, or modality.
Oricon	The Japanese music industry's hit chart(s), similar to the US' *Billboard*; active since the late 1960s. The name is a contraction of the English phrase "Original Confidence," and currently includes separate charts for *kayôkyoku, enka, yôgaku*, DVDs, computer game software, and TV commercials ratings; the most recent addition includes independent label releases.
ritsu onkai 律音階	A Japanese scale based on Chinese court musical traditions.
Roppongi 六本木	Located in Tokyo's central Minato ward, an area of the city that was formerly occupied by Allied soldiers. Its association with the foreign has continued and it is renown for its entertainment and high-classes establishments. In recent years, it has gained a seedier image as Japanese- and foreign-organized crime organizations have expanded south from Shinjuku.
ryûkôka 流行唄 (pre-war); 流行歌 (postwar)	Prewar popular music term refers to popular songs with the structure and lyrics in a Western style but with Japanese tonality. Musically and lyrically, the predecessor of *enka*.
ryûkyû onkai 琉球音階	A scale commonly heard in folk music originating from the Ryûkyû region, including Okinawa.
samisen or *shamisen* 三味線	A three-stringed lute based on an instrument from the Ryûkyû region called the *sanshin*.
senpai kôhai kankei 先輩・後輩関係	Senior/junior (hierarchical) relationships commonly seen in Japanese organizations where the senior colleague is treated with deference but must provide guidance to the junior colleague. Common in schools and in business settings.
shakuhachi 尺八	A bamboo flute with five finger holes, end-blown.
Shibuya 渋谷	A ward in southeast Tokyo that is known for youth culture, including associations with the music industry.

shimauta 島唄	(1) A vocal *minyô* tradition of the Amami Island chain which forms the northern part of the Ryûkyû islands, and more widely of Okinawan Prefecture. It is characterized by the use of the *sanshin*, an Okinawan three-stringed instrument that preceded the shamisen. It also has come to refer to any music of the Ryûkyû region. (2) The title of a song released by mainland pop band The Boom in 1992, popularizing the *shimuta* style in the mainstream charts.
shin'ya hôsô 深夜放送	Late night broadcasts; part of the audience segmentation phenomenon in both television and radio programming.
shinpu 新譜	A newly released record (CD). In the case of Japanese artists, newly released CDs are protected from rental use by law for three weeks after their release date.
sôran bushi そうらん節	Translated by Nakamura as "work songs" (1991: 275), refers to the variety of folk songs sung by fishermen in Northern Japan, and one term used to describe traditional Japanese folk music.
taishû ongaku 大衆音楽	Literally, "music of the masses," used to describe an urban, twentieth-century, generally commercialized tradition of Japan.
tarento タレント	Literally, talent; means entertainment personality. Crossovers with the music and television industry mean that many singers become *tarento*.
teika 定価	Fixed price; a system of nationally fixed pricing for Japanese-produced CDs which limits the ability of distributors to vary their pricing and discourages competition between retailers.
tsukomi ツコミ	The "gag man," part of a team in *manzai* comedy. Contrasts with the "straight guy."
ura 裏	The back; behind the scenes. Refers to those who work outside of the spotlight to make an artist successful (e.g., producers).
uragoe 裏声	Falsetto vocalization style.
wasei 和製	"Made in Japan"; used to describe popular music (or culture in general) that followed the American style but was not a mere translation or imitation. *Wasei poppusu* (made in Japan pops) was a 1960s genre that demonstrated Japanese asthetics in the Western popular style.
yô 陽	Positive, or light.
yôgaku 洋楽	(1) "Western" music; can refer to the European classics or any music that is structured along those modalities and/or instrumentation; (2) Western pop music sold in Japan; can also include Japanese cover songs of Western standards in the 1950s, 1960s and 1970s.

yonanuki よな抜き	A pentatonic scale in Japanese music, missing the fourth and seventh tone.
yûsen hôsô 有線放送	Literally "a broadcast with wires"; the wires refer to a subscriber cable transmission of music or karaoke services to a home or shop set (see *musen hôsô*).
zokuyô 俗謡	Urban music of the Edo period, in contrast with *minyô,* which originates from regional areas.

Technical terms

AU	A kind of early computer audio file used for Internet distribution
Codec	The algorithm that allows MP3 data to be compressed into small size that makes it so convenient for use in digital media playback machines.
MD	An abbreviation for MiniDisc, a 7.2-cm recordable audio disc first sold by Sony in 1992. The laser disc is encased in a plastic cartridge; it offers the same high-quality sound and quick search functions of a CD but with the option to record. MDs can be purchased both blank and pre-recorded.
MIDI (musical instrument digital interface)	A "code for communications between synthesizers, computers, and related equipment, together with an associated hardware standard." (Cook 1990: 124 n.2). In other words, the pitch and the length of the note held are programmed into a computer; these messages are sent to the synthesizer and, when run, produces "music" as programmed.
MP3 format	MP3 stands for "MPEG-1 Audio Layer 3" and is an encoding format for audio computer files that combines low storage space with high-quality sound.
WAV (or WAVE)	A kind of early computer audio file used for Internet distribution.

Notes

1 Introduction

1 Mitsui Tôru of Kanazawa University was JASPM's inaugural president. Other prominent figures in JASPM are the late Koizumi Fumio, Hosokawa Shûhei (formerly of Tokyo Institute of Technology; currently of Nichibunken in Kyoto), Kitagawa Junko (Osaka Educational University), the sociologist Ogawa Hiroshi (Kansai University), and Satô Yoshiaki (University of Tokyo).

2 Yukawa Reiko (born 1939) is one of the more famous *hyôronka*, who worked both as a critic and has penned many hits for idol and pop singers. Ugawa Hiromichi, after graduating from Kyoto University, became a journalist with *Asahi Newspaper*; in 2003, he went "freelance" and writes frequently on Japanese pop music from a refreshingly critical stance.

3 *Rockin' On* first began as a monthly publication introducing Western music to Japanese audiences and branched out to include a separate publication on Japanese music, *Rockin' On Japan* (later shortened to *Japan*), in 1985.

4 See Stevens and Hosokawa (2001) for the results of this collaboration.

2 Definitions

1 This chapter deals with traditions of Japanese popular music, but excludes currently elite expressions such as *gagaku* (court music) and theatrical musical traditions such as *nô*, kabuki, and *bunraku* (puppet theater). Although an argument can be made that kabuki music could be considered "popular" in the past, this chapter focuses on music that has not crossed over into the "elite" tradition.

2 Most scholars writing in English describe Japanese musical traditions using emic terms, reflecting the difficulty of translating their nuances into English. Unfortunately, this can be alienating to the reader who is not used to reading Japanese words sprinkled liberally in the text. See this volume's glossary for definitions.

3 Nakamura calls these variations *kaeuta*; we revisit this term in Chapter 7 where its meaning of "theme and variation" is further translated as "parody."

4 Post-Meiji Japan ushered in an era of the fastest growth in gross national product and took place during a time of hyper-industrialization and cultural and social change.

5 "Guilds" are Wade's translation (2005: 167).

6 A search of the National Diet Library's holdings in Tokyo reveals that the earliest publication with the term "*taishû*" in its title was published in 1927.

7 *Hayariuta* is written 流行歌 while in the Meiji Period *ryûkôka* was written 流行唄; in the postwar period, 流行歌 was again used. The 歌 is more simply translated as "song" while the character 唄 is associated shamisen music.

8 Mclure writes that one J-pop strategy is "having some overseas exposure" first, and then being sold to Japanese audiences as artists who have achieved international "success." The pace of the J-pop market and its short attention span are drawn from liberal quotes throughout Cahoon, Haw, and Mclure's site *Nippop* (http://nippop.com).
9 Western classical scales are constructed of eight notes (heptatonic) drawn from an octave that is divided into 12 tones; these 12 tones include half steps, or tones.
10 There is an entirely different vocabulary for describing tones in Japan; for example, the Western *do re mi fa sol la ti do* is replaced by the indigenous syllabary *hi fu mi yo i mu na* (Mita 1992: 55). The Japanese notation system is also completely different than the Western classical one, but as the Japanese notation system is rarely used in postwar popular music. In my experience with recording, notation was not used at all – lyric sheets with chords written out over the lines were used for recording. Many musicians can read [or have learned] Western notation but recording is done by ear.
11 The minor mode is similar to the *miyakobushi* or the *in* scale (Mita 1992: 55).
12 The Arabic script serves a purely decorative function; although the characters are legible, most of the text is meaningless or merely repeated lines referring to the "new film" of Kurosawa Akira.
13 Wade's text identifies the musician as Hirose (*sic*) Chitose, and as we will see later, Hajime is from Amami Island, which is part of the Ryûkyû region but not part of Okinawa Prefecture.
14 The *sanshin* is Ryûkyûan instrument that resembles a stringed lute and is the predecessor of the more widely known *shamisen*. The *shamisen* gained popularity among the urban common classes in the Tokugawa period and is associated with traditional Japanese music, as well as the musical geisha tradition (Harich-Schneider 1973: 515–516).
15 The geographical term Ryûkyû refers to a region that was politically independent and culturally distinct from mainland Japan until the early seventeenth century. Today, part of it belongs to Okinawa Prefecture and part of it belongs to Kagoshima Prefecture.
16 The Boom's presentation of Ryûkyûan cultural styles and the "island" imagery in their break through hit represents an interesting internal borrowing of cultural style as the band's members are from the landlocked, mountainous Yamanashi Prefecture.
17 For more on the concept of Okinawan music as a tourist product, see Joyce (2005).
18 Katakana is a script used for a variety of purposes; one of these is the expression of foreign terms. Normally, the word samurai in the Japanese context would be written in *hiragana* or *kanji* (Chinese characters).
19 *Jipangu* is the Japanese pronunciation of Zipangu, allegedly used by Marco Polo to describe the archipelago, from which the English term "Japan" stems.
20 Ugaya records the number one foreign broadcaster of Japanese popular music is France; second is England, and third is Hong Kong (2005b: 168), but it is important to note that his figures are based on royalties *paid* and does not represent all the on-the-ground activity of music played overseas outside the national JASRAC (Japanese Society for the Rights of Authors, Composers and Publishers) royalty system.
21 Wade's text identifies the composer as Hisaichi Yuzuru (*sic*).
22 Kawabata notes that in Japanese record stores, East Asian artists are classified as *hôgaku* rather than *yôgaku* (1991: 335).

3 The particulars of history

1 At first, the Japanese public had no vocabulary to describe this kind of music: Hosokawa writes that Eri Chiemi's version of "Tennessee Waltz" was first described as "*jazzu*" (1997: 2).
2 A more recent example of the lingering impact of rockabilly style can be seen in the 1970s band *Kyaroru* (Carol), and there was also a 1980s rockabilly revival. Followers of this trend were called the "*R & R zoku*" (rock and roll tribe) and gathered weekly at

a central Tokyo park to dance and posture in retro fashions to rockabilly music. Their source of information and goods was the shop, Cream Soda, located in the teenage Mecca of Tokyo's Harajuku.

3 Although America was the primary source of cultural influence in the 1950s and 1960s, this period also saw the French *chanson* style of vocals become popular, giving rise to a small but active group of singers who performed in city nightclubs and bars. *Chanson* singers and fans currently form a minor genre in the contemporary music scene but they claim a major social accomplishment: one of Japan's first publicly accepted male cross-dressers, Miwa Akihiro, is an icon for *chanson*.

4 Nakamura, Ei, and Sakamoto were soon known as the "six – eight – nine trio" (a pun on their names Hachi (eight), Roku (six), and Kyû (nine).

5 See Stevens and Hosokawa (2001) for more on the content of the 1960s' musical variety shows.

6 The original Japanese reads: "*Sore made 'kiku' dake de atta ongaku ga fôku bûmu ni yotte, jibun tachi de 'yaru' mo no e to shinka shita koto de aru [kore wa, sonogo no Nihon no ogaku shiin ni kettei teki na eikyô wo ataeru koto ni naru].*" (1993: 56)

7 The Japanese student movement was at its height in 1968–1969, mirroring other movements in North America and Europe. Its breakdown in the early 1970s can be attributed to the radical activities of the Red Army in the early 1970s; other less radical activists broke away in order to disassociate themselves with terrorism and other marginalized ideals.

8 *honkakuha*; can also be translated as "classical school."

9 Although most of the figures in New Music listed here are solo artists, there are also groups within the genre. *Anzen Chitai*, Off Course, the Alfee, Chage and Asuka, the Southern All Stars, and Dreams Come True have been associated with this genre.

10 One of the members of this club, Kudô Shizuka, went on to solo idol stardom and has resurrected her career as the wife of SMAP star Kimura Takuya.

11 Mori Katsuyuki was an original member of SMAP who quit the group in 1996 to pursue a career in motor racing. By that time, the group had achieved such fame that he was not replaced, and SMAP has since gone forward as a five-man unit.

12 The English term "*famirî*" was often used to describe the acts associated with Komuro, which reflected the phrase *Komuro-kei* [lineage] which was also commonly used to promote these acts.

13 One of the original five Morning *Musume* members, Ishiguro Aya, retired after marrying Shinya, the drummer of LUNA SEA, and they have three children.

14 In July 2005, Orange Range's drummer quit the band; he has since worked with GLAY as a support musician.

4 The business side: connections, culture, and contexts

1 Japan is the second largest music market; yet if the sales are examined on a per capita basis (balancing the value of the sales and the total population), Japan's sales slip from second place to fourth overall. In other words, Japanese music fans do not spend much more than their European counterparts; it is just that its dense population artificially inflates its place in the overall sales market (Ugaya 2005b: 166).

2 In the Alfee's small *jimusho* where I observed these roles in action, the different jobs were clearly recognizable but utilized different terminology. In this particular company, the artist manager was termed an "executive" or a "chief manager" while the "road manager" was listed as an "artist manager": clearly, he was beneath the "executive manager" in rank.

3 This original company was disbanded in 1959 and relaunched as a publicly held company as it is today (Take 1999: 71).

4 Hori Productions is an equivalent counterpart and competitor to *Nabe Puro*. Hori *Puro* was founded in 1960 and is named after its founder Hori Takeo. Employing 241 personnel in 2005, its offices are located in Meguro Ward in central Tokyo and manages influential artists like Wada Akiko (singer and talk show personality who debuted in 1968) and a wide range of other types of performers, such as successful radio personalities and concert pianists.

5 Shibuya Ward in Tokyo seems to be host to many other *jimusho* besides Amuse, Inc.; Baby's Limited is in Shibuya Ward's Daisanchô; Project III is in Shibuya Ward's Yoyogi, just north of Shibuya and Harajuku Station.

6 *Nihon Rekôdo Kyôkai* has also been translated as the Japan Phonograph Record Association by other scholars writing in English, but I use RIAJ as per the organization's website.

7 In 2003, "pirated" copies of Taiwanese and PRC-manufactured CDs of artists such as Hamazaki Ayumi being sold in Japan for 1980 yen forced the RIAJ to appeal against these companies for infringing copyright (Ugaya 2005b: 180).

8 The other two were albums from Canadian singer Avril Lavigne and the British rock band Queen.

5 Technology, consumption, and authenticity

1 Because television is treated extensively in Chapter 4, it is omitted here to allow a tighter focus on radio, but television remains an important technology in communicating music and imagery to the public.

2 This chapter does not focus on techno-music as a genre, but rather the role that technology plays both shaping and responding to the demands of music production and consumption in Japan. Japan does host a number of innovative composers and performers in genres such as techno, noise, and electronic music. Musicians in this genre are identified using variety of terms outside the traditional categories of "musician" or "artist," including "live laptop performers [and] audio CD designers," for example (Loubet 2000: 19). On the cutting edge, these musicians use computers and software such as Max (a code used in music and animation) combined with MIDI (musical instrument digital interface) to create new sounds and methods of producing and reproducing these sounds. Because of this technology, the traditional roles of producer, artist, editor, packager, and promoter are collapsed: the musician can control all aspects of the process (Loubet 2000: 24). Needless to say, this group of artists are truly consumers of the newest technology, as Theberge notes.

3 Other departments in the station included *henseibu* (programming department), the *seisakubu* (production department), and the *jigyôbu* (the operations department).

4 This is not a large number compared to 70 FM stations operating out of Manhattan (Ugaya 2005b: 182).

5 "Tokio" is the phonetic English pronunciation of Tokyo, and is wordplay on a foreigner's accent.

6 Yoshimi notes that Roppongi was formerly an area held by SCAP for housing and offices (2003: 439), and the influence of the foreign occupation lingers as many foreigners working in elite large-scale businesses still live there.

7 Shibata is probably referring to Yoshida Takurô's work with the KinKi Kids (see chapter three).

8 Ugaya excludes the DVD, despite the fact that the DVD is the only area reporting increases in sales of audio-related products (RIAJ 2005b: 4–5).

9 This includes the providers NTT, KDDI, and J-Phone.

10 Of that sum, only 0.5 percent was collected from overseas, compared to 32 percent overseas royalties collected by the UK's PRS-MCPS Alliance and 21.9 percent by Broadcast Music Inc. in the United States (Ugaya 2005b: 169). Most of this music is not "J-Pop" but rather "*anime* theme songs, incidental music and [film] background

music"; the most lucrative royalties paid from an overseas source to a Japanese composer in the period 2002–2004 was for the background music to the children's anime *Pokemon* (168).

11 Fan clubs are the best (and sometimes the only way) for consumers to purchase concert tickets for very popular groups in exclusive settings. Tickets to SMAP concerts, for example, are circulated first to fan club members before becoming available to the general public (*Nikkei Entertainment* 2005a: 57). In the case of artists without registered clubs (as in those with smaller followings), concert tickets are best reserved through promoters hired by the band to sell tickets; these are usually posted on official websites. Fans can also become members of promoters' clubs, which allows them to buy tickets without paying the promoters' processing fee.

6 Translations: "internationalizing" language and music

1 In the same way that Japlish is comical to native English speakers, the reverse – "Bamboo English," or the attempts at communication between "non-Japanese-speaking foreigners and the extensive world of their local lady friends" (Hosokawa 1999b: 127) – is also heard in early postwar pop music releases, and its existence "perpetuates US (neo-)colonial contact with Japan" (128).

2 The chorus begins with a mostly nonsense sequence of syllables: "*Sui sui suuraraatta sura-sura sui sui*". *Surasura* means "smoothly".

3 Steve McClure, a Canadian-born critic and writer on Asian pop music, notes that Shiina's grammatically correct English lyrics lack naturalism, and thus have little impact (Ugaya and McClure 2001a: 133), but considering her main target audience is Japanese, his judgement on her lyrics is debatable.

4 Scholars differ in their interpretation of the semiotic significance "Japlish" to the ordinary listener. To date, there has been no quantifiable research on this specifically, but linguists looking at *gairaigo* have found that transfer of meaning is occurring. Brown claims "These words clearly constitute a 'latent' English vocabulary base" (1995).

5 The Southern All Stars are also given as an example in the definition of "Pidgin Japanese" as termed by Hosokawa (1989).

6 The italicized phrase is presented in Japanese characters and means "signature of a dream." The rest is presented in romanized letters, with its punctuation and case in the original.

7 Dreams Come True released an English album in 1997 but unfortunately were unable to enter the US market successfully.

8 It is very common for Alfee songs to have one word or one phrase different in each chorus, so for a two-line chorus, they would need to record only three lines to get the four completed.

9 I'd actually seen five versions: a proto version, in April (which included only the first verse and chorus), and the three recording versions, and the final released version, with one word change, was printed on the CD jacket in October.

10 Kuraki Mai, who debuted in 1999, has released music in both English and Japanese; yet like Utada, she has found more success in Japan than in the United States with both her English and Japanese releases.

11 Released February 21, 1979: original lyrics and music by J. Morali, V. Willis, and H. Belolo; *yakushi* by Amagai Ryûji (Hideki Saijô Official Home Page 2005).

12 Original lyrics and music by R. Rosa and D. Child; Japanese lyrics by Kang Zhen Hua. This version's lyrics were not closely related to the original, but the chorus included a hook of a repeating line ending of "*[da]rô ka*", reminiscent of the original "loca" in Ricky Martin's version (HMBo 2005).

13 Furthering his cross-media participation, Imawano has also appeared in the film *Katakurike no Kôfuku* (2002) in a significant supporting role with fellow pop idol Sawada Kenji.
14 Translated by the author and Caroline Norma. I gratefully acknowledge Imawano's and permission to reproduce lyrics in this volume.
15 Tôkai refers to the area of eastern Japan bordering the Pacific, which includes the densely populated cities of Tokyo, Kawasaki, and Yokohama.

References

Abe, K. (2003) "*Popyurâ ongaku to gendoshôhi shakai: ongaku ga shôhi sareru shakai*" [Popular Music and Contemporary Consumer Society: A Society Where Music is Consumed] in M. Tôya (ed.) *Popyurâ ongaku e no manazashi* [*A Look at Popular Music*], Tokyo: Keisô shobô, 28–57.

The Alfee. (1994) *Countdown '94 Dreams Spring Season* (concert tour pamphlet), Tokyo: Eight Days.

Anderson, M. (2002) "Matsutoya Yumi," "Nakajima Miyuki," "New Music," "Yoshida Takuro" in S. Buckley (ed.) *Encyclopedia of Contemporary Japanese Culture*, London: Routledge, 305–306, 340, 349–350, 580–581.

Aoyagi, H. (2005) *Islands of Eight Million Smiles: Idol Performance and Symbolic Production in Contemporary Japan*, Cambridge, MA: Harvard University Press.

Appadurai, A. (1990) "Disjuncture and Difference in the Global Cultural Economy," *Theory, Culture and Society*, 7:295–310.

Asahi Shimbun. (2005) "*Bunka· Geinô*" [Culture and Entertainment]. 23 July Evening Edition, Kantô.

Asô, K. and S. Miyadai. (1999) "*Megahitto poppusu* [Megahit pops]" in S. Miyadai and K. Matsuzawa (eds) *Poppu Karuchâ* [*Pop Culture*], Tokyo: Mainichi Shimbunsha, 84–89.

Atkins, E. T. (2001) *Blue Nippon: Authenticating Jazz in Japan*, Durham, NC: Duke University Press.

Azami, T. (2003) "*Mejâ rêbaru no tôgô ga imi suru mono*" [The Meaning of the Consolidation of Major Record Labels] in M. Tôya (ed.) *Popyurâ ongaku e no manazashi* [*A Look at Popular Music*], Tokyo: Keisô shobô, 58–79.

Baker, S. L. (2004) "Pop in(to) the Bedroom: Popular Music in Pre-teen Girls' Bedroom Culture," *European Journal of Cultural Studies*, 7(1):75–93.

Baudrillard, J. (1996) "The Map Precedes the Territory" in W. T. Anderson (ed.) *The Fontana Postmodern Reader*, London: Fontana Press, 75–77.

Befu, H. (2003) "Globalization Theory from the Bottom Up: Japan's Contribution," *Japanese Studies*, 23(1):3–22.

Bix, H. P. (2001) *Hirohito and the Making of Modern Japan*, New York: Perennial.

Bourdieu, P. (1994a) "The Field of Cultural Production" in *The Polity Reader in Cultural Theory*, Cambridge: Polity Press, 50–65.

——. (1994b) "Structures, *Habitus* and Practices" in *The Polity Reader in Cultural Theory*, Cambridge: Polity Press, 95–110.

Brown, J. B. (1995) "Is Gairaigo English?" *The Internet TESL Journal*, 1(2), December. Online. Available at http://iteslj.org/Articles/Brown–Gairaigo/ (accessed June 7, 2005).

Bullock *et al.* (eds). (1998) *The Fontana Dictionary of Modern Thought*, London: Fontana.

Buxton, D. (1990) "Rock Music, the Star System and the Rise of Consumerism" in S. Frith and A. Goodwin (eds) *On Record: Rock, Pop and the Written Word*, New York: Pantheon Books, 427–440.

Cahoon, K. (1993) "Popular Music in Japan" in *Japan: An Illustrated Encyclopedia*, Tokyo: Kodansha, 1284–1285.

——. (2005) "The Boys in the Band: The Legendary Johnny's Jimusho,"*Nippop*. Online. Available at http://nippop.com/features/feature_id-33/ (accessed August 23, 2005).

Caspary, C. and W. Manzenreiter. (2003) "From Subculture to Cybersubculture? The Japanese Noise Alliance and the Internet" in N. Gottlieb and M. Mclelland (eds) *Japanese Cybercultures*, London: Routledge, 60–74.

Chôsaku kenjôhô sentâ (Copyright Research and Information Center). (2005) "Outline of the Copyright Law." Online. Available at http://www.cric.or.jp/cric_e/clj/ocl.html (accessed March 30, 2006).

Clewley, J. (1994) "Japan" in S. Broughton and M. Ellingham (eds) *The Rough Guide: World Music*, vol. 2, London: Rough Guides, 143–159.

Condry, I. (2000) "The Social Production of Difference: Imitation and Authenticity in Japanese Rap Music" in H. Fehrenbach and U. G. Polger (eds) *Transactions, Transgressions and Transformations*, New York: Berghan Books, 166–184.

——. (2001) "A History of Japanese Hip Hop: Street Dance, Club Scene, Pop Market" in T. Mitchell (ed.) *Global Noise: Rap and Hip-Hop Outside the USA*, Middletown, CT: Wesleyan University Press, 222–247.

——. (2004a) "Cultures of Music Piracy: An Ethnographic Comparison of the US and Japan," *International Journal of Cultural Studies*, 3(7): 343–363.

——. (2004b) "B-Boys and B-Girls: Rap Fandom and Consumer Culture in Japan" in W. W. Kelly (ed.) *Fanning the Flames: Fandom & Consumer Culture in Contemporary Japan*, Albany: State University of New York Press, 17–39.

——. (2006) *Hip-Hop Japan: Rap and the Paths of Cultural Globalization*, Durham, NC: Duke University Press.

Cook, N. (1990) *Music, Imagination and Culture*, Oxford: Oxford University Press.

Darling-Wolf, F. (2004) "SMAP, Sex and Masculinity: Constructing the Perfect Female Fantasy in Japanese Popular Music," *Popular Music and Society*, 27(3):358–370.

de Ferranti, H. (2000) *Japanese Musical Instruments*, Oxford: Oxford University Press.

——. (2002) " 'Japanese Music' can be Popular," *Popular Music*, 21(2):195–208.

De Launey, G. (1995) "Not-So-Big in Japan: Western Pop Music in the Japanese Market," *Popular Music*, 14(2):203–225.

Edgington, D. W. (2003) "Joining the Past and the Present in Japan," in D. Edgington (ed.) *Japan at the Millennium: Joining Past and Future*, Vancouver: University of British Columbia Press, 3–18.

Fisher III, W. W. (2004) "An Alternative Compensation System" from *Promises to Keep: Technology, Law, and the Future of Entertainment*, Stanford: Stanford University Press. Portions available online. Available at http://cyber.law.harvard.edu/people/tfisher/PTKChapter6.pdf (accessed April 6, 2006).

Frith, S. (1994) "Music for Pleasure" in *The Polity Reader in Cultural Theory*, Cambridge: Polity Press, 236–241.

Fujie, L. (1989) "Popular Music" in R. G. Powers and H. Kato (eds) *Handbook of Japanese Popular Culture*, Westport, CT: Greenwood Press, 197–220.

——. (1992) "East Asia/Japan" in J. T. Titon (ed.) *Worlds of Music: An Introduction to the Music of the World's Peoples*, New York: Schirmer Books, 318–375.

Fujioka, C. Y. (1993) "Consuming and Saving" in A. Gordon (ed.) *Post-War Japan as History*, Berkeley: University of California Press, 259–292.

Fukukawa, S. (2001) "The IT Revolution in Japan: Past, Present and Future," *Asia-Pacific Review*, (8)1:86–98.

Gobuichi, I. (1995) *Shabondama Horidê: Sutâdasuto wo, mo ichido* [*Soap Bubble Holiday: Stardust, One More Time*], Tokyo: Nihon Terebi.

Gordon, A. (1993) "Introduction" in A. Gordon (ed.) *Post-War Japan as History*, Berkeley: University of California Press, ix–xii.

Gottlieb, N. and M. McLelland. (2003) "The Internet in Japan" in N. Gottlieb and M. Mclelland (eds) *Japanese Cybercultures*, London: Routledge, 1–16.

Harich-Schneider, E. (1973) *A History of Japanese Music*, London: Oxford University Press.

Haw, B. (2005a) "Retail Channels and Media Formats Increase Amidst Declining Sales," *Nippop*. Online. Available at http://nippop.com/features/feature_id-22/ (accessed August 23, 2005).

——. (2005b) "If You Wanna Play, You Gotta Pay – P2P Networks and Individual Users Targeted for File Sharing," *Nippop*. Online. Available at http://nippop.com/features/feature_id-21/ (accessed August 23, 2005).

——. (2005c) "Artist Management Companies – A Brief Primer," *Nippop*. Online. Available at http://nippop.com/features/feature_id-34/ (accessed August 23, 2005).

——. (2005d) "Run, Don't Walk – Sony Offers New Walkman Amid Nano Hype," *Nippop*. Online. Available at http://nippop.com/features/feature_id-40/ (accessed July 28, 2006).

Hennion, A. (1990) "The Production of Success: An Antimusicology of the Pop Song" in S. Frith and A. Goodwin (eds) *On Record: Rock, Pop and the Written Word*, New York: Pantheon Books, 185–206.

hide. (1998) *hIS iNVINCIBLE dELUGE eVIDENCE*. VHS Video Recording. Pony Canyon PCVE-50792.

Hideki Saijô Official Home Page. "Hideki Single Grafiti [sic] 1972–2003." Online. Available at http://www.earth-corp.co.jp/HIDEKI/MUSIC/1979.html (accessed February 15, 2005).

Hikki's Website. (2006) "Profile." Online. Available at http://www.toshiba-emi.co.jp/hikki/profile/index_j.htm (accessed January 13, 2006).

Hiraga, T. (2005) "*Hajime Chitose: Kataritsugu koto*" [Hajime Chitose: What we Hand Down]. Online interview. Available at http://www.hotexpress.co.jp/interview/hajimechitose_051214/ (accessed February 17, 2006).

Hiromi–Go.Net. "Hiromi–Go Net Profile." Online. Available at http://www.hiromi–go.net/ (accessed February 15, 2005).

Hmbo. (2005) "GOLDFINGER '99" Online. Available at http://www.pp.iij4u.or.jp/~wszhts/HMBo/song/song41.htm (accessed February 15, 2005).

HMV Japan. (2003) "HMV Japan News – Top 100 Japanese pops artists." Online. Available at http://www.hmv.co.jp/news/newsDetail.asp?newsnum=311040091 (accessed July 30, 2004).

Hogan, J. (2003) "The Social Significance of English Usage in Japan," *Japanese Studies*, 23(1):43–58.

Hoguchi, Y. (2005) "*Terebi ga dokusen suru ongaku chôsaku kenrieki no jittai*" (1) [The real situation of composer royalties that television monopolises (1)]. Online. Available at http://www.amvox.co.jp/entrance/vision/ (accessed August 12, 2005).

Hosokawa, S. (1989) "On Tokyo-go: Pidgin Japanese" in *Against Nature: Japanese Art in the Eighties*, New York: Grey Art Gallery and Study Centre, 35–38.
——. (1995) "Performing Arts in Japan Now: Japanese Popular Music of the Past Twenty Years – Its Mainstream and Underground," Tokyo: Japan Foundation.
——. (1997) Lecture notes for the subject *Ongakubunkaron* (Cultural Theories of Music). April–July, Tokyo Institute of Technology (12 lectures, 12 pp.).
——. (1999a) "Rock and National Language: The Japanese Case" in T. Mitchell and P. Doyle (eds) *Changing Sounds: New Directions and Configurations in Popular Music*, The International Association for the Study of Popular Music, Sydney: University of Technology, Sydney, 98–101.
——. (1999b) "Soy Sauce Music: Haruomi Hosono and Japanese Self-Orientalism" in P. Haywood (ed.) *Widening the Horizon: Exoticism in Post-War Popular Music*, Sydney: Lohn Libbey and Company, 114–145.
Hosokawa, S. and H. Matsuoka. (2004) "Vinyl Record Collecting as Material Practice: The Japanese Case" in W. W. Kelly (ed.) *Fanning the Flames: Fans and Consumer Culture in Contemporary Japan*, Albany: State University of New York Press, 151–167.
Hutnyk, J. and S. Sharma. (2002) "Music and Politics: An Introduction," *Theory, Culture and Society*, 17(3):55–63.
Imawano Kiyoshirô Official Home Page. (2005) "Jimihen – History Online." Available at http://www.kiyoshiro.co.jp/history/index.html (accessed June 24, 2005).
Ivy, M. (1993) "Formations of Mass Culture" in A. Gordon (ed.) *Post-War Japan as History*, Berkeley: University of California Press, 239–259.
——. (1995) *Discourses of the Vanishing: Modernity, Phantasm, Japan*, Chicago, IL: University of Chicago Press.
Iwabuchi, K. (1998) "Marketing 'Japan': Japanese Cultural Presence Under a Global Gaze," *Japanese Studies*, 18(2):165–180.
Japan Association for Professional Recording Studios (JAPRS). (2006) "*Nihonongakusutajiokyôkai hôjinseikaiin risto*" (List of Corporate Members of JAPRS). Online. Available at http://database.japrs.or.jp/japrs/display/display_all.jsp (accessed March 24, 2006).
Japanese Association for the Study of Popular Music. (2001) "JASPM – Chronicle." Online. Available at http://www.jaspm.org/chronicle.html (accessed January 9, 2006).
Japanese Society for the Rights of Authors, Composers and Publishers. (2005) "History of JASRAC." Online. Available at http://www.jasrac.or.jp/ejhp/about/history.html (accessed June 20, 2005).
Johnny and Associates. (2005) "Johnny's Net: JFC Info Artist Profile." Online. Available at http://www.johnnys-net.jp/jfc/profile/index.html (accessed August 30, 2005).
Jordan, A. (2005) "Big in Japan: Hiromi Go." Online. Available at http://metropolis.japantoday.com/biginjapan/376/biginjapaninc.htm (accessed February 22, 2005).
Joyce, M. (2005) *Images of Okinawa: The Role of Music in Shifting Mainland Japanese Perceptions of Okinawan Identity*, Unpublished Honours Thesis, Asia Institute, University of Melbourne.
Kawabata, S. (1991) "The Japanese Record Industry," *Popular Music*, 10(3):327–345.
Kimura, A. (1991) "Japanese Corporations and Popular Music," *Popular Music*, 10(3): 317–326.
Kitagawa, J. (1991) "Some Aspects of Japanese Popular Music," *Popular Music*, 10(3):305–315.
——. (1993) *Oto no uchi soto* [*Inside and Outside Sound*], Tokyo: Keiso Shobô.
Kodansha (eds). (1993) *Japan: An Illustrated Encyclopedia*, Tokyo: Kodansha.

Koizumi, F. (1977) "Musical Scales in Japanese Music" in F. Koizumi, Y. Tokumaru, and O. Yamaguchi (eds) *Asian Musics in an Asian Perspective*, Tokyo: Heibonsha, 73–79.

Komai, H. (trans. by J. Wilkinson). (1995) *Migrant Workers in Japan*, London and New York: Kegan Paul International.

Kretschmer, M., G. Klimis, and R. Wallis. (2001) "Music in Electronic Markets: An Empirical Study," *New Media and Society*, 3(4):417–441.

Kvale, S. (1995) "Themes of Postmodernity" in W. T. Anderson (ed.) *The Fontana Postmodern Reader*, London: Fontana Press, 22.

Lash, S. and J. Urry. (1994) *Economies of Signs and Space*, London: Sage.

Loubet, E. (2000) "Laptop Performers, Compact Disc Designers and No-Beat Techno Artists in Japan: Music from Nowhere," *Computer Music Journal*, 24(4):19–32.

Love Psychedelico Official Web Site. (2005) "Profile." Online. Available at http://www.lovepsychedelico.net/english/pro/index.html (accessed November 29, 2005).

——. (2006) "Profile." Online. Available at http://www.lovepsychedelico.net/english/pro/index.html (accessed January 11, 2006).

McClure, S. (2005) "End of an Era: Industry Loses Two Legends," *Nippop*. Online. Available at http://nippop.com/features/feature_id-32/ (accessed August 30, 2005).

Malm, W. P. (1996) *Music Cultures of the Pacific, the Near East and Asia*, Third Edition, Upper Saddle River, NJ: Prentice-Hall.

Mathews, G. (2003) "A Collision of Discourses: Japanese and Hong Kong Chinese During the Diaoyu/Senkaku Islands Crisis" in H. Befu and S. Guichard-Anguis (eds) *Globalizing Japan: Ethnography of the Japanese Presences in Asia, Europe and America*, London: Routledge, 153–175.

——. (2004) "Fence, Flavor, and Phantasm: Japanese Musicians and the Meanings of 'Japaneseness,' " *Japanese Studies*, 24(3):335–350.

Miller, L. (1997) "Wasei eigo: English 'Loanwords' Coined in Japan" in J. H. Hill, P. J. Mistry, and L. Campbell (eds) *The Life of Language: Papers in Linguistics in Honor of William Bright*, The Hague: Mouton de Gruyter, 123–139.

Ministry of Internal Affairs and Communication. (2004) *Information and Communications in Japan* (White Paper). PDF online, 5–68. Available at http://www.soumu.go.jp/joho_tsusin/eng/whitepaper.html (accessed June 6, 2005).

——. (2005) "Production of Disks and Tapes in Quantity and in Monetary Sum." Excel file online. Available at http://www.stat.go. jp/data/chouki/zuhyou/26-05-a.xls (accessed September 5, 2005).

——. (2006) "Foreigners, by Nationality (186 Groups) and Sex – Japan, Prefectures and 13 Major Cities/Total." Excel file online. Available at http://www.stat.go.jp/data/kokusei/2000/gaikoku/00/zuhyou/a001-1.xls (accessed February 17, 2006).

Mita, M. (trans. by S. Suloway). (1992) *Social Psychology of Modern Japan*, London: Kegan Paul.

Mitsui, T. (1997) "Interactions of Imported and Indigenous Musics in Japan: A Historical Overview of the Industry" in A. Ewbank and F. T. Papageorgiou (eds) *Whose Master's Voice: The Development of Popular Music in Thirteen Countries*, Westport, CT: Greenwood Press, 152–174.

——. (2001) "The Genesis of Karaoke: How the Combination of Technology and Music Evolved" in T. Mitsui and S. Hosokawa (eds) *Karaoke Around the World: Global Technology, Local Singing*, London: Routledge, 31–44.

Mitsui, T. and S. Hosokawa. (2001) "Introduction" in T. Mitsui and S. Hosokawa (eds) *Karaoke Around the World: Global Technology, Local Singing,* London: Routledge, 1–30.

Multimedia Internet *Jiten* [Dictionary]. (2006) Online. Available at http://www.jiten.com/dicmi/.

MWS [Moto's Web Server]. (2006a) "Napoleon Fish Day" (Motoharu Sano Official Web Site). Online. Available at http://www.moto.co.jp/works/album/ESCB1326.html (accessed January 3, 2006).

——. (2006b) "*MWS ni tsuite*" [About MWS (Motoharu Sano Official Web Site)]. Online. Available at http://www.moto.co.jp/cover/MWS/about.html (accessed April 13, 2006).

Nakajima, M. (1994) "Liner Notes" for the album *Singles II*. Pony Canyon PCCA-00559.

Nakamura, T. (1991) "Early Pop Song Writers and Their Backgrounds," *Popular Music*, 10(3):263–282.

Nakano, Y. (2002) "Radio Broadcasting" in S. Buckley (ed.) *Encyclopedia of Contemporary Japanese Culture*, London: Routledge, 411–412.

Negus, K. (1992) *Producing Pop: Culture and Conflict in the Popular Music Industry*, London: Edward Arnold.

——. (1999) *Music Genres and Corporate Cultures*, London: Routledge.

Nikkei Entertainment. (2003) "Monthly Digest: *Ongaku* [Music]." October issue, 9.

——. (2005a) "Monthly Digest: *Ongaku* [Music]." August issue, 9.

——. (2005b) "*Ninkisha kenkyû Orange Range Mitsu Senryaku de yobikonda bûmu wa honmono ka*?" [Research on Popular Artists Orange Range: The Trend That Calls in Three Strategies: Is It for Real?] and "*Purachina chiketto* [The Platinum Ticket]," 40–43, 56–64.

——. (2005c) "Funky Music Station on Fresh: GLAY *no* JIRO *ga arata na ongakusei o tsuikyû*" [GLAY's Jiro investigates a new musicality]. September issue, 8.

Ogawa, H. (2001) The Effects of Karaoke on Music" in T. Mitsui and S. Hosokawa (eds) *Karaoke Around the World: Global Technology, Local Singing*, London: Routledge, 45–54.

Ogawa, M. (2004) "Japanese Popular Music in Hong Kong: What Does TK Present?" in A. Chun, N. Rossiter, and B. Shoesmith (eds) *Refashioning Pop Music in Asia: Cosmopolitan Flows, Political Tempos and Aesthetic Industries*, London: RoutledgeCurzon, 144–156.

Ogura, T. (2003) "Military Base Culture and Okinawan Rock'n'Roll," *Inter-Asia Cultural Studies*, 4(3):466–470.

Ohkoshi, T. (2005) "Asian Sounds," *Asia Pacific Perspectives Japan+*, 2(12):24–25.

Okada, M. (1991) "Musical Characteristics of *Enka*," *Popular Music*, 10(3):283–303.

Recording Industry Association of Japan. (2005a) "About RIJA." Online. Available at http://www.riaj.or.jp/e/about/index.html (accessed August 1, 2005).

——. (2005b) *RIAJ Yearbook 2005*. PDF online. Available at http://www.riaj.or.jp/e/issue/pdf/RIAJ2005E.pdf, 1–25 (accessed August 1, 2005).

——. (2006) *RIAJ Yearbook 2006*. PDF online. Available at http://www.riaj.or.jp/e/issue/pdf/RIAJ2006E.pdf, 1–25 (accessed November 28, 2006).

Roberson, J. E. (2001) "Uchinaa Pop: Place and Identity in Contemporary Okinawan Popular Music," *Critical Asian Studies*, 33(2):211–242.

——. (2006) "Loochoo Beat(s): Music in and out of 'Okinawa' " in M. Allen and R. Sakamoto (eds) *Popular Culture, Globalization and Japan*, London: Routledge, 202–220.

Schaefer, O. (2005) "Music from the Masses: Japanese Indies Make Some Noise," *Weekender Online*. Online. Available at http://www.weekender.co.jp/new/040716/music.html (accessed November 22, 2005).

Schilling, M. (1997) *The Encyclopedia of Japanese Pop Culture*, New York: Weatherhill.

Seaton, P. (2001) "Shampoo for Extra Damage: Making Sense of Japanized English," *Japan Forum*, 13(2):233–247.

Seidensticker, E. (1991) *Tokyo Rising: The City Since the Great Earthquake*, Cambridge, MA: Harvard University Press.

Shepard, J. (1994) "The Analysis of Popular Music" in *The Polity Reader in Cultural Theory*, Cambridge: Polity Press, 231–236.

Shibata, K. (1998) *Onna 30 ni shite tatsu* [*Women Stand up at Thirty*], Tokyo: Mainichi Komyunikeshon.

Shinozaki, H. (1988) "*Dokyumento RCjiken Rokku ga chokumensita fukimi na tabû*" [Documenting the RC Incident: Rock Confronted an Ominous Taboo], *Myûjikku Magajin*, September, 60–65.

Sony Global. (2005) "Sony Global – Sony History." Online. Available at http://www.sony.net/Fun/SH/ (accessed June 27, 2005).

Stanlaw, J. (1992) "For Beautiful Human Life: The Use of English in Japan" in J. Tobin (ed.) *Re-made in Japan, Everyday Life and Consumer Taste in a Changing Society*, New Haven, CT: Yale University Press, 58–75.

——. (2004) *Japanese English: Language and Culture Contact*, Hong Kong: Hong Kong University Press.

Stevens, C. S. (1999) "Rocking the Bomb: A Case Study in the Politicization of Popular Culture," *Japanese Studies*, 19(1):49–67.

Stevens, C. S. and S. Hosokawa. (2001) "So Close and Yet So Far: Humanizing Celebrity in Japanese Music Television, 1960s–1990s" in B. Moeran (ed.) *Asian Media Productions*, Surrey: Curzon Press, 233–246.

Takahashi, K. (ed.) (2005) *Ongaku no Zenshigoto* 2006 [The Complete Music Employment (Guide), 2006], Tokyo: Piakabushikgaisha.

Takahashi, Y. (ed.) (1993) *Nihon no ROCK 50s–90s* [Japanese Rock, 1950s–1990s], Tokyo: Heibonsha.

Takamizawa, T. (2004) *Akiramenai Yume wa Owarenai – Endless Dream* [*Dreams Which Are not Abandoned Never End – Endless Dream*], Tokyo: Gentôsha.

Take H. (1999) *Yomu J-Pop 1945–1999 shiteki zenshi* [Reading J-Pop: 1945–1999, a personal history], Tokyo: Tokuma Shoten.

Takeishi, A. and K.-J. Lee. (2004) "Mobile Music Business in Japan and Korea: Copyright Management Institutions as a Reverse Salient." Unpublished conference paper (Austin Mobility Roundtable).

Takemitsu, T. (1989) "Sound in the East, Sound in the West: The Way to 'November Steps.' " The 1989 Soshitsu Sen XV Distinguished Lecture on Japanese Culture, November 14, Columbia University, New York.

Tansman, A. M. 1996. "Mournful Tears and Sake: The Post-War Myth of Misora Hibari" in J. W. Treat (ed.) *Contemporary Japan and Popular Culture*, Surrey: Curzon Press, 103–136.

Tantei File. (2003) "*Janiisan ni sekuhara hanketsu aki ni wa taihô?* [A judgement of sexual harassment for Johnny: Will he be arrested in the autumn?" Online. Available at http://www.tanteifile.com/geinou/scoop_2003/07/25_01/ (accessed January 7, 2005).

Théberge, P. (1997) *Any Sound You Can Imagine: Making Music/Consuming Technology*, Hanover and London: Wesleyan University Press.

TV Pia (Kantôhan). (1998) January 24–February 6, Tokyo: Pia Kabushikigaisha.

——. (2005) July 16–31, Tokyo: Pia Kabushikigaisha.

Ugaya, H. (2005a) *J-Poppu no Shinshô Fûkei* [J-Pop's Impressioscape], Tokyo: Bungei Shinju.

——. (2005b) *J-Poppu to wa nani ka* [*What is J-Pop?*], Tokyo: Iwanami Shoten.

Ugaya, H. and S. McClure. (2001a) "*JPoppu no eigoshi mettaori hyôhan*" [A "Scathing" Critique of J-Pop's English Lyrics], *CNN English Express* (part one), May, 132–133.

——. (2001b) "*JPoppu no eigoshi mettaori hyôhan*" [A "Scathing" Critique of J-Pop's English Lyrics], *CNN English Express* (part two), June, 116–117.

US Copyright Office. (2006) "Circular 38a: International Copyright Relations of the United States." Online. Available at http://www.copyright.gov/circs/circ38a.html#8 (accessed March 30, 2006).

Wade, B. C. (2005) *Music in Japan: Experiencing Music, Expressing Culture*, Oxford: Oxford University Press.

Watanabe Group. (2005) *Official site*. Online. Available at http://www.watanabe-group.com (accessed August 15, 2005).

Wise, J. M. (1998) "Intelligent Agency," *Cultural Studies*, 12(3):410–428.

Witzleben, J. L. (1997) "Whose Ethnomusicology? Western Ethnomusicology and the Study of Asian Music," *Ethnomusicology*, 41(2):220–242.

Yamada, H. (2003) "Popyurâ ongaku no fukuzatusei [The Complexity of Popular Music]" in M. Tôya (ed.) *Popyurâ ongaku e no manazashi* [*A Look at Popular Music*], Tokyo: Keisô shobô, 3–28.

Yano, C. R. (1998) "Defining the Modern Nation in Japanese Popular Song" in S. Minichiello (ed.) *Japan's Competing Modernities*, Manoa: University of Hawaii Press, 247–264.

——. (2002) *Tears of Longing: Nostalgia and the Nation in Japanese Popular Song*, Cambridge, MA: Harvard University Asia Centre.

——. (2004) "Raising the Ante of Desire: Foreign Female Singers in a Japanese Pop Music World" in A. Chun, N. Rossiter, and B. Shoesmith (eds) *Refashioning Pop Music in Asia: Cosmopolitan Flows, Political Tempos and Aesthetic Industries*, Surrey: Curzon, 159–172.

Yoshimi, S. (1999) " 'Made in Japan': The Cultural Politics of 'Home Electrification' in Postwar Japan," *Media, Culture & Society*, 21(2):149–171.

——. (trans. by D. Buist). (2003) " 'America' as Desire and Violence: Americanization in Postwar Japan and Asia During the Cold War," *Inter-Asia Cultural Studies*, 4(3): 432–450.

Recommended websites and other sources

Cahoon, K., B. Haw, and S. McClure (eds) *Nippop*. Online. Available at http://nippop.com.

J-WAVE. Online. Available at http://www.j-wave.co.jp/, includes radio streaming, playlists, and the Tokio Hot 100.

Musicman–Net. Online. Available at http://www.musicman–net.com/.

Oricon, Inc. *Oricon Style*. Online. Available at http://www.oricon.co.jp/.

Takarajimasha Henshûbu. (1997a) *1960nen Daihyakka* [The 1960s Encyclopedia], Tokyo: Takarajimasha.

——. (1997b) *1970nen Daihyakka* [The 1970s Encyclopedia], Tokyo: Takarajimasha.

——. (1997c) *1980nen Daihyakka* [The 1980s Encyclopedia], Tokyo: Takarajimasha.

——. (2000) *1990nen Daihyakka* [The 1990s Encyclopedia], Tokyo: Takarajimasha.

Wikipedia (Japanese version). *Wikipedia Furii hyakkajiten*. Online. Available at http://ja.wikipedia.org/wiki/.

Discography/videography

Multidisc collections

Columbia Music Entertainment. (2004) *Seishun kanenban 50nendai* [Song Yearbook of our Youth: The Fifties]. COCA-70356. Tracks include Namiki Michiko's *Ringo no Uta*; Kasagi Shizuka "*Tôkyô Bugiugi*"; Misora Hibari "*Ringo no Oiwake*"; Eri Chiemi's "Tennesee Waltz"; Frank Nagai and Matsuo Kazuko's "*Tôkyô* Night Club."

Crazy Cats. (1991) *Crazy Singles/Crazy Cats.* Toshiba TOCT-6030-31.

Pony Canyon. (2004) *Seishun kanenban 70nendai* [Song Yearbook of our Youth: The Seventies]. PCCA-02094. Tracks include *Kagyahime*'s "*Kandagawa,*" Horiuchi Takeo's "*Kimi no Hitomi wa 10000boruto,*" Pink Lady's "UFO," and Saijô Hideki's "YOUNG MAN."

RC Succession. (1994) *The Complete Box Polydor and Kitty Edition.* KTCR-1274/8 (contains the album *Rhapsody* with the track *Ameagari no Yozora ni* and the album *COVERS* with the tracks "Love me Tender" and "Summertime Blues").

Toshiba EMI. (2004) *Seishun kanenban 60nendai* [Song Yearbook of our Youth: The Sixties]. TOCT-10970-1. Tracks include Sakamoto Kyû's "*Ue o Muite Arukô,*" Mike Maki's "*Bara ga Saita*"; and the Tempters' "*Emerarudo no Densetsu.*"

Individual releases

The Alfee. (1990) *Arcadia.* Pony Canyon Records PCCA-00117 (contains the tracks "Arcadia," "Masquerade Love," and "Countdown 1999").

——. (1995) *The Alfee Single History IV.* Pony Canyon Records PCCA-00636 (this set contains the A and B sides to both 1994 English and Japanese versions of "*Boken-shatachi*" and "*Eru Dorado*"/"The Adventure Begins" and "El Dorado").

Amuro Namie. (1996) "A Walk in the Park" b/w "Straight Run." Avex Trax AVDD-20161.

The Blue Hearts. (1987) *The Blue Hearts.* Meldac MED20 (contains "*Shônen no Shi*" [A Poem for Youth]).

Dreams Come True. (1994) "Winter Song" b/w "Sweet Dream." Epic/Sony ESCA 5909.

GLAY. (1998a) "*Yûwaku*" (Temptation) b/w "Little Love Birds." Platinum Records/Polydor KK PODH-7020.

——. (1998b) "SOUL LOVE" b/w "*Ai*" [Love]. Platinum Records/Polydor KK PODH-7021.

Happy End. (1970) *Happii Endo* (contains the track "*Haru yo koi*" [Come, Spring]) URC IOCD-40051.

hide. (1996) *PSYENCE.* MCA Victor MVCD-39 (contains the track "Misery [remix version]").

Love Psychedelico. (2004) *Love Psychedelico III.* Victor Entertainment VICL-61290 (contains the tracks "Mind Across the Universe" and "Everybody Needs Somebody").

Matsuda Seiko. (1983) "*Garasu no ringo*" b/w "SWEET MEMORIES" Sony Music Japan 10EH 3204.

Matsutôya Yumi. (1998) *Neue Musik.* Toshiba-EMI TOCT-24001-24002 (contains the track "*Ano Hi ni Kaeritai*" [I Want to Return to the Past]).

Nakajima Miyuki. (1986) *The Best.* Canyon Record D32A0155 (contains the track "*Konbanwa*" [Good Evening]).

——. (1996) *Daiginjô* (Premium Brewed Sake). Pony Canyon Records YCCW-00034 (contains the track "*Tabibito no Uta*" [Traveller's Song]).

NHK Videography. (1991) *Yume de Aimashô* [*Let's Meet in a Dream*]. Tokyo: Take Shobô.

Orange Range. (2003) *1st Contact*. Sony Music Entertainment SRCL5650 (contains the tracks "Shanghai Honey" "Samurai Mania," "Japanese People").

——. (2004) *musiQ*. Sony Music Entertainment SRCL5850 (contains the tracks "*Xièxie*" and "*Jipangu2Jipangu*").

Sakamoto Kyû. (1995) *Shichiji ni Aima-Show* [Let's Meet at Seven o'clock]. TBS. Toshiba EMI TOVF–1229.

Sakamoto Ryûichi. (1996) For Life FLCG-3020 (Japanese release); Milan Records (international) (contains new arrangements of his 1980s film soundtrack themes such as Merry Christmas Mr. Lawrence and The Last Emperor).

Sano, M. (1989) *Naporeon Fisshu to Oyogu Hi* [The Day I Swim with Napoleon Fish] Epic Records ESCB 1326 (contains the track "*Shitei Chairudo*" [City Child]).

SMAP. (2003) "*Sekai ni Hitotsu dake no hana*" [Only One Flower in the World] b/w "*Boku wa Kimi o Tsureteyuku*" [I'll go with you] plus two *karaoke* tracks. Victor Entertainment VICL-35477.

The Southern All Stars. (1990) *Imamura Jane*. Victor Entertainment VICL-60221 (contains the track "*Tôkyô Sarii-chan*" [Miss Tokyo Sally]).

Tôkyô Jihen. (2004) *Kyôiku* [Education]. Toshiba EMI TOCT-25452 (contains the track "*Genjitsu o warau*" [Laugh at Reality]).

Yamashita Tatsurô. (1995) *Treasures*. Warner Music Japan WPCV-10028 (contains the track "*Kurisumasu Ebu*" [Christmas Eve]).

Yellow Magic Orchestra. (2005) *Solid State Survivor*. Sony/Epic B0000DEL9V. Produced by H. Hosono (contains the track "Rydeen") (originally released in 1979 on Columbia Japan).

Yoshida Takurô. (1996) *LIFE*. For Life FLCF-3632. Produced by T. Yoshida.

——. (2006). "Profile". Online. Available at http://www.teichiku.co.jp/artist/takuro/profile/profile.html (accessed April 30, 2007).

Index

Page numbers followed by n are from notes.

Lightning Source UK Ltd.
Milton Keynes UK
UKOW030846140212

187244UK00004B/129/P

9 780415 492218